Raised on Songs and Stories
A Memoir of Place in the Blue Ridge

Jean Thomas Schaeffer

Harvestwood Press
Floyd, Virginia

Raised on Songs and Stories: A Memoir of Place in the Blue Ridge

Written by Jean Thomas Schaeffer

Published by
Harvestwood Press, Floyd, Virginia

First Edition 2014

Library of Congress Control Number: 2013921845

ISBN 978-0-9703758-3-4

Editing by Janet Thomas Coiner

Text Design by Gavin Faulkner

Cover Design by Wordsprint

Printing by Wordsprint

Manufactured in the United States of America

10 9 8 7 6 5 4 3 2 1

This book is dedicated
to the memory of
my father and mother
Max and Clara Turner Thomas

It is also dedicated
to my sister, Janet Thomas Coiner,
who shares my heritage,
and to my husband, Richard Schaeffer,
who has been a faithful steward of this land

Table of Contents

Preface

In 1999, my husband and I moved back to the family farm where I grew up on the Floyd–Franklin County line, near the Blue Ridge Parkway. For over thirty years, we had been living in Northern Virginia, where we raised our two daughters, and looked forward to these beautiful mountains and solitude when we retired. As we planned for our move, my mind was full of memories from growing up in an Appalachian setting with most of my relatives living nearby.

I soon realized that the land and solitude were the same, but almost everything else was different. My re-entry was difficult. My mother had recently died and my father died two years after we returned. I grieved for my loved ones and I also grieved for a way of life that no longer existed.

From feelings of loss and love for a way of life, I began writing. I wrote for my own comfort, but I also wrote for my family, for others who share my heritage, and for the general public. I wanted to preserve on paper, as accurately and beautifully as I could, the history and a way of life that used to be. I didn't want the story to be lost.

I was well equipped to write about these things, for I had grown up in the oral tradition of Appalachia with songs and stories in my memory. I grew up listening to my parents, grandparents, and other older people talk about life in the old days. I also have pages and pages of writing that my parents left behind, as well as hundreds of photographs my mother took or collected over the years. And, too, I have genealogy charts that my parents laboriously researched and prepared.

I was interested in my own family history, but I also wanted, in some small way, to help preserve Floyd County's history. I like research, so I began looking for answers. My parents' friends became my friends, and I asked them to share their memories while I took notes. I also spent hours in libraries and other research places, reviewing old documents and looking at early newspapers on microfiche.

Besides that, I started working with the Floyd County Historical Society. That led to our setting up a Floyd County archives with valuable documents preserved and cataloged, hundreds of historic photographs preserved and scanned, and artifacts stored according to museum best practices.

During that time, I kept researching and writing, and I took some of my pieces to Wanda Combs at the *Floyd Press*. She seemed glad to get them, and I thought the *Floyd Press* was the perfect place to preserve information for posterity.

I researched and wrote about whatever I was interested in at the time, and a quick review of this book's table of contents will show the eclectic assortment of topics. The last chapters focus on local school history. Most of the members of my family were teachers, and I am especially interested in preserving that school information.

Perhaps my most challenging topic involved researching Native American history of this area. Hardly anything had been written locally about it, so I set about trying to find out what I could, going to state and university archaeologists and to primary research—what there is of it. The piece I ended up writing has over 4,000 words and was published as a three-part series in the *Floyd Press*.

Over the years, I kept writing, but I hadn't originally set out to write a book. I just wanted to get words on paper—striving for accuracy, authenticity, and good writing.

After a while, some readers of my *Floyd Press* pieces started asking me when I was going to publish a collection of my articles, so I started thinking about publishing a book. As a result, I have ended up with a collection of 38 pieces (now chapters)—some old and some new writing. I have also included some poems, an appendix section, and over 130 photographs.

So, dear readers, this is the book you requested—in loving memory of a special place and way of life.

~ Jean Thomas Schaeffer

Acknowledgments

As I look back on this fifteen-year writing project, I am thankful to have had the time and opportunity to write about a place and way of life that mean so much to me. That would never have been possible without the love and support of my husband, Richard Schaeffer, and our family.

My sister, Janet Thomas Coiner, shares my heritage, and we've had so much fun working on this book together. Her fine editing skills and ear for language have enhanced it greatly, and her encouragement has kept me going and helped me to believe in my work. Her husband, John Coiner, helped me, too—especially with photographs and in thinking through the book's layout.

Wanda Combs, editor of the *Floyd Press*, has welcomed articles I have submitted and encouraged me to write more. I appreciate her and the feedback and support from *Floyd Press* readers over the years.

I also thank Dr. Grace Toney-Edwards for talking with me early on when I visited her at the Appalachian Studies office at Radford University. She helped me to see that what I was writing was a memoir of place.

And finally, in loving memory and appreciation, I thank my parents Max and Clara Thomas for their love and support and for the legacy of songs and stories they, and my ancestors, passed down to me.

So many people have helped me along the way with research and photographs and in other ways. Some of them were Doug Belcher, Judy Blackwell, Sue Boothe, Effie Brown, Ricky Cox, Phyllis Diane Campbell Cunningham, Kathleen Ingoldsby, Gladys Conner King, Tom Klatka, Bill Moran, Becky Musko, Mary Poff, Henry B. and Maude Shelor, Maurice Slusher, Margaret Smith, Rhonda Smith, Barbara Thomas Spangler, Genevieve Starkey, Daisy DeWitt Thomas, Marguerite Tise, Dorothy Vest, Susie Albert Vest, Rebecca Weeks, Robert Weeks, and Gino Williams. It would take pages to list everyone, but you know who you are and I thank you.

When all was said and done with my manuscript, I still needed help in turning it into a book. Clay Quesenberry, Josh Wimmer, and Gavin Faulkner had helped me with a previous book, and I knew they would make this book just right, too. Clay and Josh work at Wordsprint in Christiansburg, and Gavin is owner of a company in Blacksburg called Rowan Mountain, Inc. Gavin did the text design for this book, and Clay and Josh, and others at Wordsprint, did everything else that was needed in the printing process, including the cover design. Their fine work speaks for itself.

Unless otherwise indicated, photos in this book are from the Thomas–Schaeffer family archives.

This book's title, *Raised on Songs and Stories*, is used with permission and is from the lyrics of a beautiful Irish ballad "Dublin in the Rare Old Times" written by Pete St. John.

On this book's cover is a picture of the house where Jean and Janet Thomas grew up. Their father Max Thomas helped build the house in 1939. Some years later, electricity and indoor plumbing were added. The house, originally owned by Max and Clara Thomas, is part of the family's mountain farm (Chestnut Ridge Farm), which straddles the Floyd–Franklin County line in Virginia.

Introduction

Almost half a century has passed since I first wrote for the *Floyd Press*. I was a young schoolgirl where Schoolhouse Fabrics now stands, writing a report about my fifth grade 4-H club. Pete Hallman ran the *Floyd Press* and, like now, people looked to the *Floyd Press* for news of the county.

Commerce was less centralized than today and each small community had its own stores. Instead of the thirteen miles I now travel for gas or a candy bar, shopping was more convenient then. Beulah Nichols' store was one mile from home and my grandpa's store not much farther.

Besides our country stores, the town of Floyd had most other items—necessary things that would have mattered to my parents and other adults. But the town's offerings satisfied my childhood interests, too—a movie theater, Christmas toys at Mr. Ayers' dry goods store, bicycles at Western Auto, and five-cent ice cream cones at Woolwine and Rutrough's drug store. I used to save up nickels from my school ice cream money and make wonderful purchases. For the rest of our shopping, we depended on the Sears and Roebuck catalog or occasional trips to Roanoke.

Some people went to Christiansburg for shopping, but it was not much bigger than Floyd back then. And the New River Valley—well, it was interesting because of its geology. "Oldest in the world, save the Nile Valley," said my geology professor. I was more interested in our own rivers, and the day trout season opened each year found many of us waiting on the banks of Little River and its tributaries, ready to drop in our lines at high noon.

Thomas Wolfe said "you can't go home again," but I am trying to do just that—living once more on the family farm where I grew up. My perspective is that of a native, but also that of a newcomer. With older eyes, I try to understand a special place and what it has meant to me and those who came before. As I drive through the county, I see what I remember and I see what is new. When I stroll through town, it is like that, too.

In the pages that follow, I hope this double-vision view will become focused as I write about my re-entry—and provide insights into a journey we all must make, in one way or another.

Based on Jean's article published in the Floyd Press *on March 9, 2000*

Chapter 1

Growing Up Near Walnut Knob

I was born in the winter of 1943 and was raised on the same high ridge where my father, grandparents, and great grandparents had lived.

Ours was a remote mountain farm where Walnut Knob is located, and we lived on the Floyd–Franklin County line, near the Blue Ridge Parkway. We paid taxes in both counties. My father had helped Eli Board build our house in 1939. I went to school in Floyd County, first attending Harmony (a two-room school) and then County Line (a one-room school with seven grades in one room).

The edge of our farm dropped off steeply to the Callaway–Ferrum–Endicott area, and we could see more than fifty miles on a clear day and the lights of Martinsville at night. I thought it was one of the most beautiful places on earth and still do.

Our area was very different from life thirteen miles away, in the town of Floyd. One big difference was that the town had been hooked up to electricity since about 1922. Over two decades later, we (and others in our area) were still using oil lamps and battery radios—and would continue to do so until about 1949.

Sometimes I talk with people a generation older than me, and their upbringing was not very different from that of my early years. Not having electricity was the common thread that made our lives similar—that, the isolation, and poor roads.

One of my earliest memories is of the ghost-like dead chestnut trees standing on the hill behind our house. I had questioned that memory for years because by the time I was old enough to remember them, the fungus-stricken trees would have already fallen down—lying there as logs and a place for me to play.

In 1999, my husband and I built a home on the farm. One day, I was looking at old photographs and came across one of me as a toddler. The quality of the photograph was poor, but I could still make out the details. There in the picture, behind me up on the hill, the camera lens had captured the standing chestnut trees of my early memory.

Recently, we named the homeplace "Chestnut Ridge Farm" in memory of the majestic species that once made up 50 percent of the Eastern hardwoods—a memorial to a tree that meant so much to people and the local economy during the 1930s and earlier.

Like the chestnut trees, other scenes from my childhood come back to me in snapshots that seem to belie a more modern time. I remember washtubs and our non-electric wringer washing machine. I see my mother ironing clothes with heavy black irons she heated on our wood-burning cookstove. I also see her sewing on a treadle sewing machine. I see my father using a cradle/scythe to cut small fields of grain, and I picture him pushing a plow behind a horse. I see our family getting up loose hay with pitchforks and tramping around the haystack, making sure the hay was packed down.

Jean's father, Max Thomas, around 1944, plowing
with horses, "Bob" and "Gypsy."

All was not hand labor, though, and I also recall some rather sophisticated machines, such as our mowing machine and dump rake—both pulled by our horses, "Bob" and "Gypsy." Even our corn sheller was an amazing little tool that made short work of shelling corn when farm animals were waiting to be fed.

I remember the hot sun while we hoed corn, an all-day job done twice in the summer and taking a week or more each time. I recall the brown rustling stalks of corn at harvest time. I can still feel the paper-like cuts of rough fodder on my skin as we worked our way through a forest of corn, cutting stalks and making them into shocks. And I remember the November cold as we sat there by the shocks, shucking corn and talking about every subject imaginable.

We grew most of our food, and our big garden was an important part of summer, as was the canning my mother did. Our fruit trees bore well and each fall we made a huge kettle of apple butter outside over an open fire. At one point, we grew "cane" (sorghum) and made our own molasses, and I remember our horse going round and round the sugar cane mill. I can still see my mother and others at day's end, filling gallon buckets from a lava-hot vat of molasses. There must have been twenty-five or thirty buckets.

Besides raising our food, we sometimes ate fish we had caught or a squirrel or rabbit from one of Uncle Monroe's morning hunts. There were no deer in this area when I was growing up. We also foraged for watercress, walnuts, chinquapins, wild strawberries, huckleberries, and blackberries. In addition to a bucket full of berries, I sometimes came back from the berry patch with a dose of chiggers. Probably no creature on earth can cause as much torment, for its size, as the larval stage of this tiny mite. Chiggers don't burrow in the skin, but they feed on fluids in the skin cells, leaving their host itching like crazy.

Jean's father in the mid-1940s on top of haystack, stacking hay with a pitchfork.

We always butchered hogs on Thanksgiving Day. That was a good time, for the weather was cold enough by then for the meat to keep, and my parents had four days off from teaching school. We didn't raise turkeys and we never had turkey at home to eat for Thanksgiving or at any other time. Following Thanksgiving, we always had fresh sausage, though.

And there's more to tell. A summer morning comes to mind and the memory at sun-up of sitting on a stool, milking—my head against a cow's warm body as she eats grain from a feedbox and my trying to make sure milk goes into the bucket instead of on me. I also remember our cats hanging around, hoping for a dish of warm milk. And afterwards there was the process in the springhouse of straining the milk and getting it ready for Raymond West, our milkman, to collect.

5

It is feeding time and cows make their way toward Jean's father and bales of hay he has for them on this snowy day—April 11, 1992.

The Thomas farm near the Blue Ridge Parkway is beautiful year round. Pictured are two other snow scenes there.

Either before or after such a busy morning, my mother would find time to prepare breakfast on our wood-burning cookstove. The results were worth waiting for: fresh eggs from our hens, fried ham from our meat house, fried apples, homemade biscuits, fresh-made butter ("cow butter," we called it), homemade jam, white or red-eye gravy, fresh-churned buttermilk, and coffee. On special occasions, we had fried "salt" fish for breakfast. Stored in barrels of a brine solution, those fish (lake herring) could sometimes be purchased at nearby country stores.

Life became easier after we acquired electricity and a Ford tractor. We got electricity about 1949 and a tractor in the early 1950s. Still, anyone who has ever lived on a farm knows there is always a lot of hard work to do, regardless of electricity and a tractor. As a kid on the farm, I never worked overly hard and I truly enjoyed much of the work we did. It gave meaning to every day and there was still time for play. But I know both of my parents worked hard, as did my grandparents and others who came before.

Even after we quit milking cows, we rarely traveled more than an hour from home. We shopped at stores in the town of Floyd and often made purchases at country stores near our home. Those country stores were run by Tom Agee (near the Parkway where the Wormy Chestnut store was later located), Winfield "Field" West (near the Parkway where a pottery shop now stands), Beulah Nichols (near Parkway milepost 151 where the Floyd County Dry Goods store was later located), Esley Ingram (on the Franklin Pike), Leonard Smith (on the Franklin Pike), and Cam Turner (my grandpa, whose store was also on the Franklin Pike). Besides those stores, we sometimes went down Five-Mile Mountain or Cannadays Gap Road to shop or do business in Ferrum or Rocky Mount.

We sometimes went to Check or Copper Hill and stores near there, but we rarely went to places on the other side of Floyd County—places like Willis, Indian Valley, Pilot, and Alum Ridge. And we had little reason to go to Christiansburg since Roanoke was closer and offered more options for shopping and medical care. Trips to Roanoke were always a big deal, especially at Christmas, and we usually spent the day when we went. We also ordered from the Sears and Roebuck and Montgomery Ward catalogs. Even our baby chicks sometimes came to us by mail.

Like some others who were raised on local farms, I am privileged to have experienced the life I did, for we are the very last of a few of our generation to know first-hand about an earlier age in the county before the time of electricity and modern conveniences. We also experienced community life before the consolidation of schools, stores, and churches. This is our precious heritage, and I write about it because I don't want the story to be lost.

Based on Jean's article published in the Floyd Press *on April 14, 2005*

Jean and her mother, Clara Turner Thomas, in 1945 at the house where Jean grew up.

Jean and her father, Max Thomas, in 1948, are ready to go fishing as the family dog and cat vie for attention.

Jean and her little sister Janet pose in 1953 by an old-time Blue Ridge Parkway sign for Smart View Park—a park two miles from their family's farm.

Chapter 2

The Threads of Time

Back in the late 1940s when I started school, I wore pretty dresses my mother made. Trimmed with rickrack or lace, some of my dresses were sewn from colorful cotton feed sacks recycled from our family farm. I can still see the designs of that unique dual-purpose cloth, now archived for posterity in pieced family quilts.

An old spinning wheel interests me, too, and I try to picture my great grandma working by the firelight, turning wool into thread. I wonder what it was like for her, already tired from a long day of work, to keep going at night.

I look out my window at hillsides now green and imagine sheep, not cows, the way it was back then. From shearing sheep to spinning yarn, and all steps in between, I'm awed by a way of life that seems impossible to me now. But mostly I wonder about the women back then, with hands never idle and wheels never still.

I consider the next steps after yarn had been spun, and I think about weaving and how it was done. It was cold-weather work, my dad told me, for most looms were kept in unheated outbuildings. My great grandma's "weaving house" was about 11 x 15 feet, and she was able to weave several yards of cloth per day. I would have been interested in the colors of her yarn—some from black or white wool, and some made vivid from pokeberries and other natural dyes.

Except for shoes, which men usually made, women made most of the clothing in the late 1800s. One of my great grandmas was a proficient tailor, and her specialty was men's suits. Using wool she had spun and woven herself, she sewed each suit by hand. Along with the other work she did, it took her about a month to make a suit. According to my dad, her suits looked like those worn by Abraham Lincoln. She was paid $12 for each one—good money in those days. She was sixty years old before she saw a sewing machine. My dad remembered watching her work:

> She would measure the man and then cut out a paper pattern. Then there would be long hours of fine needlework. To make the lapel, layers of white cloth held together by a flour paste were pressed with a hot iron. The coat lining was made from a muslin-like material, and lining and padding had to be exactly the right size, or there would be a wrinkle. The suit would be basted together and then tried on the man. For buttons, round

wooden pieces were covered with wool cloth. Most suits were dark blue or black, and all were made of wool. They were warm in winter and hot in summer. A suit would last a man twenty years if he stayed the same size.

Peddlers from New York had needles, thimbles, and scissors, which they packed on their backs and brought to the mountain people. My dad said, "The peddler stayed from Saturday night through Monday. To pay for his keep, he had combs and other trinkets for children, and he gave needles to the women. He sold spectacles for $15."

Today, Floyd County is home to a wide variety of artisans. But unlike today, people years ago didn't have many arts and crafts. "They did have their loom-woven coverlets and other needlework," said my dad. "Even so, people were practical artisans. They had to be. They also were frugal," he said. "They wore their clothes until they were no longer worth patching, and most children had only one change of clothes. Not to be wasteful was almost like an eleventh commandment, and people tended to make do or do without."

Jean holding a red coverlet that her great grandma Delilah Ann Moran Vest wove on a weaving loom in the 1800s. *(Photo courtesy of Pat Boothe)*

Jean learning to spin using her great grandma Vest's spinning wheel.

In time, advances in technology offered some help for repetitive home textile work. In the late 1800s, some people took their wool on horseback to a wool-carding factory in the Burks Fork area of Floyd County. There, the wool fibers were combed by a process called "carding" and made into large rolls, ready for home spinning. About 1900, the factory's services expanded to include wool washing, spinning, and weaving. At one point, a 300-spindle spinning machine was added to the operation.

That first textile factory was still in operation in the 1930s, and it set the stage for an emphasis on commercial textile production in Floyd County. As a child, I remember many people working at the shirt factory. Owned by J. Friezer & Son, it was located in Floyd where Winter Sun is today. Later on, the Donnkenny Company took over that location and one other, and those companies were known as Skyline Sportswear and Fabric Cutters, respectively. None of those factories exist in Floyd County today. Another textile company, Cross Creek, closed in 1998. Since 1994, the North American Free Trade Agreement (NAFTA) has been a major factor in those closings and in closings elsewhere. (Continuing the textile tradition today are two companies in Floyd County: Legacy Linens makes upscale linens and D&K, LLC, makes mattress tape and narrow knitted elastic.)

Besides commercial endeavors, many people in Floyd County continue to create with thread. Whether for art, practical purposes, or both, many people still knit, embroider, quilt, or sew clothing. A few people even spin, weave, braid rugs, or make lace by crocheting or tatting.

Supporting that textile tradition for over thirty years (since 1971) has been a wonderful store called Schoolhouse Fabrics. I first went to that building as a student, but I now go there for fabric. It's one of my favorite places to get in touch with memories and dreams as I plan my next sewing project.

Today I am struck by all we can learn about ourselves and our past from the textile record. Earlier people worked harder than I can imagine, but somehow they managed. Their tools were simple, but sufficient, and everything people did focused on family and day-to-day life. Even children kept busy carding wool and doing other useful tasks. "A boy reached manhood at age fifteen," said my dad, "and, symbolically, his clothes changed from knickers to long pants. At age thirty-five, a woman was considered middle aged and started covering her head with a bonnet. Older women wore enormous black muslin bonnets with stiff, quilted brims."

I am struck by the mutual dependence between farm and home back then: the family farm put food on the table and clothes on their backs. Such simplicity of purpose! Yet, they must have lived on the edge of survival at times.

About 1910, sewing machines and printed cloth started to become available, and the raising of sheep started to decline in this area. That was the beginning of major textile changes in the home and on the farm. About 1920, women quit using the loom and spinning wheel. Some, I'm told, burned them—trying to forget the hard work they represented.

I'll never know, firsthand, what it was like for them. Yet, I do know that the loom and spinning wheel meant everything to those who first settled in this area—for they came here carrying looms and spinning wheels in their wagons or on their backs.

As for me, I am grateful to have a few threads of the past, and I treasure each one because it helps me connect with my family and this place.

Based on Jean's article published in the Floyd Press *on April 18, 2002*

Chapter 3

The Greatest Fire

The Floyd Fire – 1896

When we read about disasters in other places, there is a tendency to think, "That couldn't happen here." Yet, it could and it did—eleven days before Christmas on a Monday morning, December 14, 1896. Fire broke out in Mr. A. J. Lee's hotel on Main Street in the town of Floyd (currently the site of Blue Ridge Land and Auction). "Two hotels, four stores, the post office, law offices and many other buildings" went "up in smoke," according to the *Floyd Press,* published three days later. Although no one died in the fire, an estimated loss of $40,000 was reported—a lot of money in those days.

Discovered soon after midnight, the fire appeared to have started in and over the old pool room in the basement of Mr. Lee's hotel. According to the *Press,* " Mr. Lee had several barrels of brandy stored in that room and it may have been that a liquor fiend broke in to steal the brandy and accidentally or intentionally set fire to the building." Evidently, Mr. Lee's hotel had been a landmark, one of the oldest buildings in the area.

Many people in town and nearby heard the fire alarm, saw the "brilliant light," and helped fight the fire from the ground, from ladders, and from rooftops. A strong west wind exacerbated the damage, and ashes from the fire settled in the surrounding countryside, as much as five miles away. The next day, Mrs. John Cannaday, who lived 3½ miles from town, found a "half-burned leaf of the Bible—an unusual way of spreading the Gospel, to be sure."

Water from a town well was used for fighting the fire, and many heroic efforts were reported by the *Press*. The Peter Howard residence—a building with four floors located where Farmer's Foods stands (now Village Green Shopping Center)—was the scene of much danger. Quoting from the *Floyd Press*:

> Daring men . . . spread blankets over the roof . . . while young men and old men, white men and black men, and women, too, carried water in buckets up the high winding stairs . . . and placed them in the hands of those brave fellows who stood up in the glare of the red flames, with grim and desperate determination pictured on their faces. . . . Mrs. Carrie Dobyns was made quite sick by her efforts. She stood at the well [probably a hand-dug well in front of the courthouse] . . . and

filled buckets . . . getting her clothing wet, from which she contracted a severe cold.

Mr. S. R. Brame (*Floyd Press* owner) almost succumbed while trying to save the Howard residence. Exhausted and overcome with fatigue and heat, "he lay helpless on the high roof, towards which the flames from the burning building licked their fiery tongues."

Among those helping fight the fire were Rev. John Kellogg Harris and his Oxford Academy pupils. "Even the young ladies [students] exerted themselves to the utmost carrying water."

Several prisoners were in jail at the time and Sheriff Slusher let them out, fearing the fire would endanger them and the jail. According to the *Press* article, "All [prisoners] worked hard to save property and all returned to prison after the fire was under control." The jail (thought to be made of logs) caught fire twice but was saved each time. The following Tuesday, a large crowd of people attended Court Day in town and "there were many expressions of regret and sympathy" over losses from the fire.

Besides damage from the fire, many goods were stolen. "Messrs. Jett and Spangler, who had no insurance on their stock, estimate their loss from stealing and removing as $400 or $500, and others suffered heavily in the same way."

Some buildings were insured, but others, such as the Tompkins and Howard law office, had no coverage. Howard and Huff's store, located at the site where Farmers Supply now stands, had $2,500 in building coverage but no insurance on merchandise destroyed or stolen during the fire. According to the *Press*, four insurance companies were listed as insurers for some of the damaged buildings: Virginia Fire and Marine, Liverpool Globe Co., Hamburg-Bremen Insurance Co., and the Phoenix Company of London. The *Press* article concludes with the following description of the aftermath:

> The wide and long gap in the very heart of our pretty little mountain town now presents a sad and dreary waste—piles of blackened rocks, bricks and mortar, and charred timbers. Sheets of crumpled sheet and tin roofing lie strewn over the ground; cellars half-filled with debris open wide their black mouths here and there; and tall and bare chimneys stand like silent sentinels watching over the ruin and desolation.

This was the town of Floyd's most damaging fire, but at least two other major fires occurred a few years later, one in 1912 and the other in 1924.

14

The Town – 1896

I tried to imagine people in this isolated, mountainous town fighting that 1896 fire—by hand! This was before the county had cars, radios, telephones, or electricity. The best transportation was a horse and buggy on dirt roads. I remember my own family's hand pump (used in emergencies), so it was easy to identify with the hard work of pumping water and carrying buckets through that cold December night.

I wanted to become familiar with this town that has been the county seat since 1831 and incorporated since 1892. I wanted to explore, historically, a place that had been called Jacksonville until four years before the fire. As I walked around town, I began to picture my surroundings 115 years earlier when the fire took place.

At that time, the town of Floyd was laid out in a manner similar to today. Single-lane roads, sometimes snow-filled or muddy, were located approximately where Routes 221 and 8 now run. Called Main and Locust Streets today, the latter was referred to as "Cross Street" in those early days. Another road ("Back Street" and now called "Oxford Street") went down toward the prestigious Oxford Academy. The courthouse and jail stood in the general vicinity of the current courthouse, and the jail probably sat forward toward the street on the lower side of the courthouse.

Many of the buildings along Main and Locust Streets are quite old, but most were built after 1896—the time of the fire. In fact, several, such as the Howard Building (where Farmers Supply is located), were built immediately after the fire.

Also built soon after the fire were the V. M. Sowder Building (where Blue Ridge Restaurant stands) and the Tompkins law office at 111 W. Main Street.

A few buildings in town pre-date the 1896 fire and are still in use today. Irish brick mason Henry Dillon built several of them, including his own family residence that he built in 1852. The Dillon home, still used as a private dwelling, is located at 209 W. Main Street.

Even older is another brick home just up the street at 204 W. Main. Also built by Dillon, it was originally the home and office of Dr. Tazewell Headen and was built in 1849. The bricks were locally made and the house walls are three bricks thick. I understand that Dr. Headen was married to the sister of Confederate General J.E.B. Stuart. Both the Headen and the Dillon homes were spared from the 1896 fire.

Two of the oldest buildings in town are the Ferdinand Winston house at 203 S. Main Street and the A. J. Kirby house at 209 N. Locust

Street. The Winston house is a simple wood-frame structure built in 1845 for Moses Clark. Later, the house belonged to Ferdinand Winston, sheriff and cabinetmaker, who made fine furniture and coffins. The Kirby house (later owned by Evelyne Rutrough) is a wood log-frame home beside Blue Ridge Bank (now Carter Bank) at 209 N. Locust Street. Early records show that a Mr. Kirby was living there before 1831. Evidently, he had owned a large amount of land here at that time.

This was the home of Dr. C. M. Stigleman and the building is still standing on Main Street in Floyd.

On the east side of town are the historic Stigleman house and the old Floyd Presbyterian Church. Located at 406 N. Main, the Stigleman family's brick-stucco, wood-frame house was built in the 1850s. Besides practicing medicine, Dr. Stigleman was the first superintendent of Floyd County Schools. He also raised the first Floyd County company (Company A, 24th Virginia Infantry, " Floyd Riflemen") in the Civil War. According to historian Marguerite Tise, Stigleman surrendered the town when General Stoneman arrived with his Union troops in 1865. Capt. Stigleman rode from his house, carrying a white surrender flag, to the center of town.

The old Floyd Presbyterian Church, built by Henry Dillon, was also spared from the fire. Built in 1850, this church is on both the

State and the National Historic Registers. Although the congregation moved elsewhere in 1974, the Early Greek Revival building still stands today on East Main Street.

Another landmark pre-dating the 1896 fire is the Old Jacksonville Cemetery—located behind Farmer's Foods grocery store (now Village Green Shopping Center). That cemetery dates back to the 1790s, and several prominent people are buried there.

Patrick Henry's seventh son, Nathaniel Henry (1790–1851), was a local schoolteacher and he is buried there in an unmarked grave. (Members of the Floyd Courthouse Chapter, NSDAR, have recently erected a monument in the cemetery for Nathaniel Henry.) The grave of Harvey (Hervey) Deskins, a signer of the Articles of Secession, is there as well. He represented Floyd County in the Virginia General Assembly.

Brick mason Henry Dillon and his wife Harriet (Harriet A. Helms Dillon) are buried in the old graveyard, along with some others in their family, including their son, John Dillon. John, a physician, was killed in the Civil War in 1863 at Mine Run. Henry Dillon travelled alone to the Mine Run burial site and brought his son's body back to Floyd in a wagon.

The People – 1896

As I concluded my walk through time, the philosopher in me wondered about the influence of the outside world on Floyd during those days. Certainly the Civil War had made an impact, and Confederate veterans were recognized each Fourth of July when they lined up in formation at the site of the current Turman Yeatts Motor Company and marched in parade to the beat of a single drum. They marched to the courthouse square where they joined others from the county, caught up on the news, and enjoyed a complimentary meal. Yes, war touched people here, but what about the influence of other events on Floyd County?

I wondered if there had been talk of national politics and the Grover Cleveland administration. I wondered if the Depression of 1893 that caused unemployment rates of 20 to 25 percent in some cities had affected people here. Had people come here from those cities, asking local people for food and jobs on farms? Were Floyd County people talking about women's suffrage issues, and were they aware that three states out west had recently passed laws giving women the right to vote? And what about prohibition laws elsewhere that decades later would still be a joke for this "moonshine capital"? Were people interested in such recent inventions as electric lights, typewriters, telephones, and sewing machines? Did some people own and ride bicycles or go up in hot air balloons? Were people reading Tom Sawyer and Horatio Alger stories?

Certainly, such information was available locally, for county newspapers ran stories and ads on a variety of topics. For about 150 years, Floyd County has had a newspaper, and the oldest newspaper I have seen, the *Floyd Intelligencer*, was established in 1850.

Some schools, such as the Oxford Academy, offered a fine education back then. It was a private secular school that had been in operation since 1875. Other schools, both private and public, existed, too, and some of those teachers were excellent as well.

Besides formal schooling, some children were taught at home and others were self-taught. And since 1876, public schools had provided a free public education to children ages seven to sixteen.

In addition, we also know that literary groups discussed and debated issues and events of the time. I have heard about two such societies in Floyd County. One was the Jacksonville Literary Society (started in 1890) and the other was the Gray Bluff Literary Society (started in 1894). Mostly debating groups, they pondered and argued over such topics as women's suffrage, the treatment of North American Indians, and whether Washington was a greater general than Napoleon. Another debate topic was "Ambition is a Virtue." With the rise to power and wealth of families like the Rockefellers and Carnegies, people here were asking questions about the limits of personal ambition.

Many travelers came through Floyd in those days, bringing news from the outside and mingling with the locals. A crossroads at the time, Floyd must have been a bustling place of ideas, entertainment, gossip, and services. We also know that the county population was greater then than at any time in history and that more people lived here than in most neighboring counties. According to the 1900 census, 15,388 people lived in Floyd County—10 percent more than today (year 2000), and 34 percent more than in 1970. (According to the 2010 census, the population for Floyd County was 15,279.)

In 1900, a variety of stores, hotels, eateries, and professional services served the people. Without knowledge of antibiotics or germ theory, several local doctors used homeopathic methods and often made house calls on horseback. Later on, doctors made use of drugs and any other measures that proved of value in treating disease—an allopathic approach.

Compared to other places back then, Floyd County "was quite an accomplished place," said Gino Williams, local historian, "but events set in motion by the Civil War and lasting well into the twentieth century dropped Floyd behind some of its neighbors."

Long a Republican stronghold, Gino Williams said, "The County fell further behind as Democrats ascended to power in Richmond. The Byrd Machine controlled Virginia politics for the first half of the twentieth century, and Floyd found itself excluded from road building and industrial progress; a railroad easement was never used either."

Besides politics, Gino said at least three other factors led to economic decline in Floyd County: cars, better roads, and the American chestnut blight. Roads and cars made it possible to get supplies and jobs in other places, and the chestnut blight affected the economy and the spirit of the people for years to come. Max Thomas, historian, expanded on this:

> Floyd County had a big variety of natural products. The people were self-sufficient and did not need progressive changes. The American chestnut was a cash crop and could be bartered at the store for such products as soda, salt, and lamp oil. Chestnuts provided food for animals, and chestnut wood was used for building houses, tools, and fences. . . . Other natural resources included arsenic, copper, zinc, soapstone, and clay suitable for molding bricks. The people also had plenty of water power and the land was well suited for growing cabbage, buckwheat, rye, and corn. . . . Home weaving was still in progress and people made most of their own clothes. Except for gingham and shoes, not made by local cobblers, families relied on themselves for such needs.

Yes, the people were mostly self-sufficient back then, and perhaps they were unwilling to picture things any other way. Yet, changes and a decline did come, leading ultimately to dependence and a shrinking population. Meanwhile, a state of inertia seemed to occur and many people tried in vain to hold on to self-sufficiency and old ways—trying to keep the outside at bay.

I believe my ancestors liked relying on themselves rather than depending on neighboring counties and other parts of the state. With a wide variety of skills, services, and natural products, they felt they had everything they needed or wanted. Perhaps the greatest fire of all back then was an inner fire of a people who wanted to be in charge of their own destiny.

Based on Jean's article published in the Floyd Press *on June 21, 2001*

People in the Turtle Rock–Pizarro community built and attended Harvestwood Church on the Franklin Pike from 1916 to 1967. Only the cemetery remains there today. The church was named for three men in the community: R. O. (Bob) Harvey, Lincoln Vest, and Greenville Wood.

Chapter 4

Remembering Harvestwood Church (1916–1967)

My mother, Clara Turner Thomas, grew up in the Pizarro community, and—except for where we lived, a few miles to the east—Pizarro was the part of Floyd County I used to know best. Our house was near the Blue Ridge Parkway, but we traveled the Franklin Pike often and visited friends and relatives along the way. My parents knew everyone along that road and so did I. My grandpa, Cam Turner, ran a country store on the Franklin Pike, and we often stopped by to get groceries and gas and to visit. That old store had two large rooms on the main floor and an upstairs attic. The front room had floor-to-ceiling shelves filled with canned goods and other grocery items. A big potbellied stove stood in the middle of that room, and my grandpa stood behind the store counter, serving neighborhood customers. Glass jars of candy separated him from me as I tried to choose from chocolate drops, coconut bonbons, and stick candy.

Stored in the back room were sacks of cattle and chicken feed, along with other supplies farmers needed. Feed sacks in those days were bright, colorful cotton prints, and my mother took an interest in selecting ones that were suitable for sewing projects. During the 1940s, she made pretty feed sack aprons for herself and dresses, trimmed in rickrack or lace, for me.

My grandparents' white two-story house, with a wrap-around porch, was near the store. Both buildings (originally built and owned by Greenville Wood) are still standing along the Franklin Pike.

Close by, within sight of my grandparents' house, was Harvestwood Presbyterian Church. In later years, it was considered a chapel, but those of us who went there always called it Harvestwood Church. Although Harvestwood had a few expenses and was "kept up" by the local people, I always knew that the mother church in town provided the pastor and a little financial support.

Harvestwood Church was a basic, one-room rectangular design, without indoor plumbing. At first, there was no electricity, and I remember the remnants of hardware on the walls that once supported kerosene lamps. Concrete steps led to the double front doors, and about 125 people could fit inside.

I remember that tall sanctuary with three windows on each side. They provided natural light and a pastoral view of fields and trees outside. Inside, the church had a center aisle. Twenty-four pews filled part of the room—mostly in two rows, with the rest up front in the "amen corners." Those bench seats were painted white, with brown trim. Two wood stoves were situated midway, on either side of the room. In winter, my grandpa arrived at church early and built a fire. I'm told oil heat was installed in the early 1960s, but I remember wood heat before that.

Up near the altar, a low white wooden fence cordoned off a raised pulpit area behind. A large open Bible was on the lectern, and two chairs for ministers were at the back. A display table in front of the pulpit was useful during communion and at other times.

Also up front and to the right was the old pump organ, played by my Aunt Thelma Turner Houchins. She was in charge of the music, and we all sang along with her as she played that old 1914 Epworth organ, made by the Williams Organ Company of Chicago. (That organ is now owned by the Floyd County Historical Society and is on display at the Old Church Gallery in Floyd.)

Back then, we sang old-time hymns over and over: "At the Cross," "What a Friend We Have in Jesus," "The Old Rugged Cross," "In

This is the old pump organ that was played by Thelma Turner Houchins at Harvestwood Church. The organ, now owned by the Floyd County Historical Society, is on display at the Old Church Gallery in Floyd.

Thelma Houchins played the organ and led music at Harvestwood Church. She was also a teacher for Floyd County public schools.

the Sweet By and By," "Amazing Grace," "Holy Holy Holy," "We're Marching to Zion," and others. For funerals, we sang "Rock of Ages."

Behind the pulpit area was a heavy, velvety maroon-colored curtain that was stretched across an alcove in the back of the building. That curtain provided a backdrop to the pulpit, and it gave privacy to my Sunday school class.

My parents remembered when Harvestwood was built, and my dad said that the white wooden building, with a crimped-tin peak roof, was made of pine and poplar with oak framing. He thought a Mr. Underwood had built the church, along with help from Andrew Graham.

Besides a place of worship, Harvestwood was always used by the community as a meeting place. Back in 1928 when my mother graduated from Pizarro High School, the baccalaureate and commencement exercises were held at Harvestwood. I can't begin to express what it meant to an isolated, rural community to have a convenient place for gathering and worship. When Harvestwood was closed, records listed it as having eighteen members of the mother church who considered Harvestwood their place of worship. Sunday school enrollment was listed as thirty-five. Harvestwood Church is no longer standing today.

I will always think of Harvestwood as my church, and I was baptized and married there. My wedding in 1966 was just five months before Harvestwood was closed. I was not aware of any plans to close the church at that time and was sad when it happened in February 1967.

Built in 1916, Harvestwood Church and Cemetery were named for the three men who helped found them: R. O. (Bob) Harvey, Lincoln

Vest, and G. D. (Greenville) Wood. Bob Harvey was a postmaster who also ran a store at the crossroads of Franklin Pike and Poor Farm Road. Lincoln Vest was a farmer in the community, and Greenville Wood was a storekeeper who lived near the church.

For the church site, the three church founders personally paid J. P. and Annie Turner $50 for one acre of land near Pine Creek. That transaction took place on January 4, 1915 (Floyd County deed book 40, page 438). The property had previously been surveyed by J. A. Sowers on November 16, 1914. Besides that donation of land for a church, the three founders—and many other people in the Pizarro community—donated free time, labor, and money to help build Harvestwood. On August 28, 1945, Frederick and Ida Wood gave additional land so the burial ground could be enlarged. (Floyd County deed book 63, page 299)

The Reverend Dr. R. Gamble See helped start Harvestwood Church. He had been a missionary in Brazil where he met and married his wife, Louisa Spear, who was also a missionary. They came to Floyd in 1912. He was active in the church and community for over fifty years.

Dr. Robert Gamble See was the minister I always associate with Harvestwood. He had been in Floyd County for only four years when Harvestwood was built in 1916. He was heavily involved in starting the church and for keeping it going.

We shared Dr. See with the other congregations, but we were always pleased when he came to us—usually on the fourth Sunday. After preaching, families would take turns inviting him for Sunday dinner (lunch). I remember that it was a big deal when Mama cooked for him. She would usually have fried chicken, mashed potatoes,

24

white gravy, green beans, rolls, and a cake or pie—usually both. If it were summer, she would also serve fresh vegetables and fruit from our garden. I never could understand how she found time to cook a big meal on Sunday morning before going to church.

Dr. See's birthday was on August 15, and the women of Harvestwood used to host a birthday gathering for him at the church. Later on when Rev. Robert Link was pastor, he was included in the celebration, for he was born on August 15, too. Recently, I have seen a quilt made in 1922 for Dr. See's 44th birthday. The quilt, pictured below, is dated and contains forty-one squares—each done by a woman or girl in the Harvestwood community. My mother would have been twelve at the time, and one of the squares is hers. I recognize many of the names and initials, but some are a mystery to me. Appendix B in this book has a detailed description of that quilt.

Although Dr. See was later honored as a doctor by his alma mater, we usually called him "Mr. See." Even after he "retired," he ministered to us. When he was eighty-three, I asked him to baptize me; when he was eighty-eight, I asked him to officiate at my wedding.

I have not seen a complete list of persons who considered Harvestwood their home church. No doubt, it was a long list during the early and mid-1900s, when the Pizarro community flourished. According to files at the Floyd church, the following are some of the people who were part of the Harvestwood congregation in 1961: Mrs. Moyer Huff, Mrs. Edna Huff, Miss Irene Houchins, Mr. C. L. Turner,

Mrs. Cobra Houchins, Mrs. Max Thomas, Mrs. Ralph West, and Mrs. W. F. Nichols.

Judy Huff Sweeney has fond memories of Harvestwood and especially enjoyed attending Sunday school and Bible school there. Minnie and Marvin West were probably the last to be baptized at Harvestwood. They, and others, had recently completed a church membership preparatory class with Rev. William Young. Class participants were to be baptized at the Floyd church on Easter Sunday. Marvin was unable to be there on Easter morning because of his milk truck schedule, so he and Minnie were baptized on May 2, 1965. Rev. Young arranged an evening service for them at Harvestwood.

Minnie remembers the electric light fixtures at Harvestwood and how they hung down from the tall ceiling. She especially remembers a precarious cleaning project. A stepladder was placed on a table, and she climbed the ladder to clean the lights. Minnie helped out at Harvestwood in other ways, too. At one point, she taught a children's Sunday school class.

In addition to the Reverends See, Young, and Link, I remember two other pastors who preached at Harvestwood: the Reverend Bob Childress, Jr., and the Reverend Al Burdette. I also remember Miss Frances Alexander, who worked with our Bible school in 1954. She was not a minister but had been a missionary.

About fifteen years after Harvestwood was closed due to consolidation, another congregation built a pretty white church nearby on the adjoining lot. That later church is called Harvestwood Covenant Presbyterian Church, and it has an active congregation today. Although it is also Presbyterian and has a similar name, it is unrelated to the old 1916 Harvestwood Church and its mother church, The Presbyterian Church of Floyd. Harvestwood Church and The Presbyterian Church of Floyd were/are affiliated with the Presbyterian Church (U.S.A.). The newer Harvestwood Covenant Presbyterian Church is affiliated with the Presbyterian Church in America.

My own personal connection to the 1916 Harvestwood Church goes back to 1943, when I was a baby. In addition to neighbors and friends, my grandparents and other relatives would be there each Sunday. It was a nurturing place for a child. Preaching ("church") was once a month, but Sunday school was every week. Women within the Harvestwood congregation ran the Sunday school. During the summer, the church could be warm, and I remember stiff paper fans donated for our comfort by Wood Funeral Home. There on the benches, along with hymnals, were the fans.

Besides the religious part and seeing everybody, my earliest memories of Harvestwood had to do with my behavior and clothes. I was supposed to be still during church services, and my mother would quietly make suggestions to me. Sometimes she would give me a stick of gum and smile at me to reinforce my good behavior. I also remember wearing my "Sunday clothes" to church: a pretty dress, black patent leather shoes, a pocketbook, and sometimes a hat. For Easter, my sister Janet and I usually had new outfits.

Church services at Harvestwood were traditional and similar to Presbyterian services today. Eventually, we had printed programs, but we could also refer to a metal plaque on the wall up front. That plaque had movable numbers that told us the hymn page numbers, as well as last week's attendance and offering. Sometimes when church turnout was small, Dr. See began the service by quoting, "For wherever two or three are gathered in My name, I am in the midst of them."

Sunday school was held year round, and all ages would start out together each week with opening exercises. Then we'd each go to an age-appropriate class. Being a small congregation, we had just a few classes with a wide range of ages within each group. We didn't have a lot of extra activities at Harvestwood. In fact, I would use the word "simplicity" to describe what it was like—and we liked it that way. I do remember an occasional picnic, Christmas programs with parts to learn, and my mother's Circle meetings.

My memories of Bible School at Harvestwood mean a lot to me. I would stay with my grandparents, who were conveniently located next door to the church. Besides going to Bible school, I "helped" my grandpa in his store, and I talked with my grandma while she cooked and worked around the house. I especially liked her molasses "sweet cakes" (cookies) and her corn cakes (cornmeal pancakes).

Bible school lasted a week, and about twenty-five of us attended. One summer in the late 1950s, my class made a wooden cross for the front of the church. That cross was placed up high, over the front door, as a permanent part of the building.

Years after Harvestwood was closed, the trustees of the Harvestwood Cemetery Association asked if the Presbyterian Church of Floyd would deed the Harvestwood property to the Cemetery Association. That request was granted and the deed was signed on April 17, 1987. (Floyd County deed book 794, page 547)

These days, the Harvestwood property has been returned to nature, and only a cemetery sign and tombstones call attention to a sacred place where my parents, grandparents, and some of my other ancestors are buried. Not so private anymore, the surrounding neighborhood is more built up now. Yet, the Harvestwood grounds are still peaceful, with a wooded area in back and a view of Buffalo Mountain to the south. Maples, oaks, and a cucumber tree grow on the site, and the taller trees may have been growing back in 1916 when the church was first built.

Harvestwood was a special place. Although it existed twenty-seven years before I was born, I have been associated with it since 1943. A part of me will always be connected to this place.

Based on Jean's article published in the Floyd Press *on August 7, 2003, and on her article in the book* The Presbyterian Church of Floyd: Celebrating 150 Years of History, *Nov 2003*

Chapter 5

Turtle Rock

When I was growing up, I used to hear about a place called Turtle Rock. I knew it was near the Pizarro community in Floyd County. I also knew Turtle Rock included the area surrounding the intersection of Poor Farm Road and the Franklin Pike. According to my parents, the home of R. O. (Bob) Harvey was at that intersection, as was his store, with a post office in back. On Election Day, people in that precinct came to Mr. Harvey's store to vote.

For that geographic area, there were actually two post offices within walking distance of each other, one called Pizarro and the other called Turtle Rock. Turtle Rock was older and was open from April 14, 1871, to July 31, 1906. Jacob T. Helms was a postmaster there.

The Pizarro post office was open from April 17, 1886, to January 11, 1939. Bob Harvey was a postmaster there. From 1886 to 1906, both Turtle Rock and Pizarro post offices were open for service. Perhaps two post offices were needed at that time, for many people lived in those adjoining communities.

People sometimes ask how the Pizarro post office got its name. It turns out that personnel at the Post Office Department in Washington came up with the name Pizarro (a random choice, possibly from the name of an early Spanish explorer who had no connection to this area). Local people here had submitted the name Harvey, but Harvey was rejected in favor of the assigned name, Pizarro. The Turtle Rock post office was named for an unusual rock formation nearby—a large rock that looks like a turtle.

So Turtle Rock was the name of a rock, a community, and a post office. It was also the name of a Presbyterian church. As for the Turtle Rock Church, I knew nothing about it until I did some research and saw the Floyd County Historical Society's photo of the church. The photo's quality is poor, but the church building appears to have been a one-room, unpainted gray structure. Garfield Radford, a local farmer, remembered it that way. He also recalled being inside the building once when he was a small boy. He remembered handmade benches and two large windows on each of two sides of the building. The front door faced down the hill to the east. He said the old church building was on the west side of Poor Farm Road, about a mile from the Franklin Pike.

From what I know, the Turtle Rock Church had an interesting story. Its history began with the old Jacksonville Presbyterian

Church in Floyd—later called Floyd Presbyterian Church. Founded in 1850, the Jacksonville church on Main Street had no regular pastor until 1866. After that, two ministers each served successively for a short time. Then, the Reverend John Kellogg Harris responded to the church's call on May 15, 1872.

In all, Rev. Harris served as pastor of the Jacksonville church for thirty-one years—from 1872 to 1882 and from 1889 until his death in 1910. According to church records, Rev. Harris also founded the Turtle Rock Church in the Pizarro–Turtle Rock community on June 25, 1882. According to a 1930s *Floyd Press* newspaper article, "a colony of members at Jacksonville Church supplied charter members for Turtle Rock Church."

A few months after starting the Turtle Rock Church, Rev. Harris and his family responded to a mission call for the Indian tribes in Red Cloud and Scotia, Nebraska. During their seven-year absence, some members of Turtle Rock Church returned to the Presbyterian Church in town, but there is evidence that a congregation continued to meet at Turtle Rock for over thirty years—until about 1913, when the building fell into disrepair.

According to the early session minutes of the Jacksonville Presbyterian Church, William Cannaday was a member and ruling elder of Turtle Rock Church. It seems a ruling elder could preach and assume some of the other duties of a pastor. Perhaps he helped fill in for a while after Rev. Harris left. According to Susie Vest (David Vest's wife), Emma Thurmond also attended Turtle Rock Church. Emma Thurmond was David Vest's grandmother.

I have no idea if Sunday school was held at Turtle Rock, but we do know that Sunday school was being held in the 1860s at Dillon's Chapel, a Presbyterian Church in the Kemper community of Floyd County. According to session minutes for the Jacksonville Presbyterian Church, Sunday school in the late 1800s was referred to as "Sabbath school."

I don't know about music at Turtle Rock Church either, but I expect hymn singing was unaccompanied. Perhaps the congregation followed along in books with shape notes or just sang hymns from memory. From what I know of successive generations in the Pizarro–Turtle Rock community, music was an important part of life.

After Turtle Rock Church closed, a couple of things happened to continue Presbyterian work in that part of the county. In 1916, Harvestwood Church was built nearby. Besides that, a mission school called Cannaday School had recently been started several miles away.

We know that people in the Pizarro–Turtle Rock community gave land and donated free time, labor, and money to build Harvestwood Church. Harvestwood was an active place of worship for over fifty years.

Neither church building is standing today, but together, Turtle Rock and Harvestwood served the Pizarro–Turtle Rock community for more than eighty years.

Based on Jean's article published in the Floyd Press *on August 14, 2003, and on her article in the book* The Presbyterian Church of Floyd: Celebrating 150 Years of History, *Nov 2003*

Located on the Franklin Pike, this was the home of Dr. J. Wilton Thurman and family. The building is still standing and continues to be used as a private residence. Dr. Thurman rode horseback day and night to visit the sick in this area. *(Photo courtesy of Susie Albert Vest)*

Chapter 6

Plagues – Then and Now

Since October 2002, when some Americans died from malicious exposure to anthrax, the problem of bio-terrorism has been on my mind. I wonder if other dangerous diseases like smallpox could be next. Since Bible times, and before, people have been terrified of plagues. Scientists have provided help, but some germs and viruses elude modern science, and diseases such as AIDS remain pandemic in scope. Germ warfare raises the stakes and is a warning call.

I make no attempt to understand the senselessness and immorality of germ warfare, but I wanted to try to understand more about disease itself and how it can impact and take a people down. Especially, I wanted to get a historical perspective on how people in our Floyd County area coped years ago during such difficult times.

Some diseases, I remember first-hand: measles, rheumatic fever, tuberculosis (TB), and influenza (flu). I also recall the panic and fear of polio during the 1940s and the coffin-like "iron lungs" used for treating seriously ill children. It would be several years before the Salk and Sabin polio vaccines would be available.

People had only a primitive knowledge about cause and treatment of polio, and it was thought that rivers and swimming pools were possible sources of infection. Sometimes young people would slip out and swim anyway without their parents' knowledge.

Older people talked about smallpox, diphtheria, scarlet fever, typhus, and typhoid. They also talked about TB, pneumonia, and influenza. Few resources were available in those days, and plagues of various kinds were devastating to our ancestors.

Like today, flu outbreaks occurred often back then, and the toll was high. Unlike today, a flu vaccine did not exist. Some flu epidemics were regional, such as the one in Virginia in 1793. Others were much wider in scope, covering the entire country or world.

The years 1918–1920 were especially bad years for flu in many places, including Floyd County. According to my dad,

> Entire families would be sick at once. Doctors didn't know what to do, so they recommended whiskey. Some of the older women thought the disease was similar to "grippe" and doctored with quinine. They were right and most of their patients lived. Neighbors fed and milked stock for sick families, and cut firewood, stacking it on their porches, but they would not expose

themselves to the disease. Dr. J. Wilton Thurman rode horseback day and night to visit the sick in our area. He would look in and ask how our family was. Then he'd go to the springhouse and bring a big jar of buttermilk to the house. He chopped wood and piled it behind our stove. He provided food and warmth.

An October 1918 State Board of Health report, cited in the *Floyd Press*, spoke about the influenza epidemic and its impact on our entire region: "The situation is such as to give the health authorities serious concern. Indeed this section [Southwest Virginia] appears to be the worst afflicted of any part of the state." The article went on to describe conditions in one far-western part of our region: "Conditions in St. Charles could not be worse. The great majority of the people are sick and the rest are panic stricken and completely disorganized. It is said that the sick and the children in some houses are suffering for food because there is no one able to prepare it. . . . Diphtheria has been added to the fearful influenza conditions."

I heard of a family struck down by diphtheria, with the entire family sick. They went off to bury one of the little girls and when they came back, her sister had died.

"Many people in this area had diphtheria," said my dad, "and some were sent by doctors to the hospital where many patients died. The poor usually made out better than those who could afford medical care in a hospital; many survived at home." He went on to say,

> Diphtheria had not been a problem in the Floyd County area since the 1920s when a vaccine had become available. Yet, in 1940, a strange sickness with similar symptoms was killing many children. Ruling out diphtheria as a "disease of the past," doctors called the strange illness "membranous croup." Children continued to get sick and die. Finally, a couple took their child to Dr. John Woodrow Green at Ferrum and he diagnosed the child as having diphtheria. People had gotten careless about immunizations, and the disease had come back. Dr. Green wired Richmond and had massive amounts of vaccine sent to this area. He worked for seventy-two hours and the scourge was over.

My dad also told me about TB, saying it was a "dreaded disease of the mountains, for it always meant a slow death. Family members usually became infected, too, and flies probably spread the TB germ," he said. "Cows were unvaccinated so some people may have gotten the bovine type of TB. People didn't know what to do for TB, but some used cod liver oil to help build up mucous membranes." A vaccine is now available, but, according to my dad, "It was used ten years in Europe before our medical profession would allow it here. Now we have drugs to treat and cure this dreaded disease."

As I think about disease and suffering back then, I wonder how they managed at all. "Information about germ theory did not reach the mountains until 1890," said my dad. "Vaccines were slow to arrive, and modern drugs had not yet been discovered." Yet, the people must have felt some degree of control, for they knew about herbs, home remedies, and good nursing care.

Thankfully, there was always someone in the mountains who knew about doctoring—often a woman. "It was not unusual for mountain nurses to go to homes and stay until the family was better," said my dad. "None of these women were paid. It was done out of kindness."

My great grandma, Delilah Ann Moran Vest, was one of those mountain women who cared for the sick. My dad told me that two of her remedies for colds and bronchitis were hot boneset tea and mustard plasters.

Although I never knew her, I understand from my dad that she seemed to have an intuitiveness about medicine and sanitation. She understood about spreading disease and she was careful not to carry it home to her family—and never did. Coming home from tending the sick, she would stop at an outbuilding before coming in the house. Her family would bring boiling water, lye soap, and a change of clothes.

Her youngest child, Sadie Vest Troxler, remembered her cleaning her shoes by pouring lamp oil over them and then leaving them out in the sun. Later, she rubbed her shoes with tallow and beeswax.

Finally, one more disease of note was smallpox. It is one of the communicable diseases we seem to fear most, particularly in light of recent bio-terrorism. "In the mountains this disease was rare," said my dad, "but it was feared because there was no plant that would give other than symptomatic relief. Although Dr. Edward Jenner had already discovered a cowpox vaccination to prevent smallpox, people here knew nothing about it, and vaccination was delayed. Beginning in the 1930s, smallpox vaccination was required by school immunization laws."

In 1979 the World Health Organization announced that smallpox had been totally eliminated. Except for those in the armed forces, the U.S. ceased routine vaccinations at that time. A few side effects of the vaccine also influenced the decision to stop inoculation. Stockpiles of the smallpox virus were either destroyed or sent to research centers in Atlanta or Moscow. At the time, my dad was concerned about this overconfidence and feared we could become as vulnerable to small-pox as Native Americans once were.

In doing research for this article on plagues, I came across a 1925 book by the Virginia State Board of Health. It contains an assortment of bulletins on various health topics and disease. The bulletin on smallpox caught my attention. The first paragraphs provide insights that may be as applicable today as back then. I quote them as a con-clusion, and offer those words from the 1920s for consideration:

> Men measure danger by its proximity. The nation, which sees war as a distant, uncertain cloud will do little to protect itself; the people before whose homes the storm of battle is breaking, will make any sacrifice for safety. The same rule applies with added force to the warfare on the enemies of a man's health. Those diseases, which he most fears, and those against which he protects himself are those that are imminent. If typhoid fever is in a distant county, he will take no precautions; but if fever sweeps the house of his neighbor, the average man will boil his water and screen his kitchen and dining room.
>
> Particularly is this true of smallpox. As long as its ravages were but myths, men were unafraid; but when this ancient enemy of the race stalked in every street, and when his mark was on the face of every man, smallpox was the daily fear of all. Anything that the wildest fancy prompted for protection was done on the instant; any sacrifice would be made to escape this awful plague.

Based on Jean's article published in the Floyd Press *on January 10, 2002*

Chapter 7

Graveyards

Years ago, people in the rural, mountainous areas of Appalachia buried their kin in small family cemeteries near their homes—a necessity, for transportation was difficult. That was the case in Floyd County, where hundreds of small graveyards dot the countryside— many of them in remote, forgotten places, and not recorded at the courthouse. Since at least 1990, Genevieve Starkey has been sleuthing out and documenting these cemeteries. Her cemetery work in the Burks Fork magisterial district is in book form and includes over 100 cemeteries. She and Phyllis Goad Phillips published that book in 1992. Since then, Genevieve, Jo Parr, Judy Blackwell, Rhonda Smith, and others have been documenting graveyards in other parts of Floyd County. That information is now on the Internet.

One of my earliest memories was being awakened well before daybreak Christmas morning in 1945 when I was almost three. Santa Claus had already come, but I was hurried out the door to stay with my grandma.

One of our neighbors had died and my parents were called to help with burial preparations—preparing the body and digging the grave. The ground was frozen, but neighbors pitched in and dug graves by hand in those days. At the conclusion of a burial service, mourners watched as shovels of dirt covered the casket and filled in the grave. Burials were hands-on without a backhoe to do the work.

People here have always cared for family graves, and I recall regular trips to the cemetery, especially during the summer. While my parents mowed, I clipped grass around tombstones and walked around the graveyard, reading tombstone inscriptions. It was not a morbid time but just something we did, and a time of remembrance.

In my mother's and father's families, I know of twelve different small cemeteries where they, their parents, or their grandparents are buried. The twelve cemeteries I know about are the **Brammer Cemetery** in Floyd County; the **Charles and Violet Hall Turner Cemetery** in Franklin County; the **County Line Church Cemetery** near the Floyd–Franklin line; the **County Line Church Cemetery** (older) near the Floyd–Franklin line; the **Harvestwood Cemetery** in Floyd County; the **Jack Martin Cemetery** in Patrick County;

This is the tombstone of Nathaniel A. Thomas, Jean's great grandpa. He is buried at Radford Cemetery on Silverleaf Road near the Floyd–Franklin County line. In 1862, at age 32, Nathaniel was drafted into the Confederate army as a private in Company D of the 51st Regiment of the Virginia Infantry. In 1865 he walked home from the surrender.

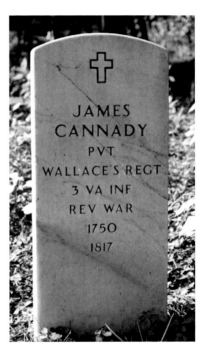

This is the tombstone of James Cannady, Jean's great great great great grandpa. He is buried on the west side of Cannadays Gap Road, near the bottom of the mountain. James served in the Revolutionary War and was a private in Wallace's Regiment, 3rd Virginia Infantry. The name Cannady was spelled by some descendants as Cannaday.

the **James–Via Cemetery** in Franklin County; the **Peter Cannaday Cemetery** near the Floyd–Franklin line; the **Radford Cemetery** near the Floyd–Franklin line; the **Samuel L. Vest Cemetery** in Floyd County; the **Walter H. Thomas Cemetery** in Patrick County; and the **Walnut Grove Cemetery** in Bluefield, West Virginia. Appendix D in this book has additional cemetery information.

Some parts of this piece are based on Jean's article published in the Floyd Press, *September 23, 2010.*

Chapter 8

The Story of Dillon's Chapel

I had heard of Dillon's Chapel all of my life, but it became real to me after Henry B. and Maude Shelor took me there a couple of years ago. Located on Black Ridge Road about five miles southwest of Floyd, the white, one-room chapel still stands as a focal point in the Kemper community.

This is the second location for Dillon's Chapel. The first building was nearby on land owned by Henry Dillon, the chapel's founder and namesake. The earlier building was used from 1860 to 1916. After that, the congregation moved to the current location on Black Ridge Road. Although closed for Presbyterian services since 1967, Dillon's Chapel is a landmark and a reminder of 143 years of history.

A few steps away is another landmark: the old two-room Kemper School, now used for hay storage. Both the chapel and the school were a short walk from home for Henry B. Shelor, and he and his family spent many hours in both buildings. Henry B. attended school at Kemper until he was twelve, and he remained a faithful member of the congregation at Dillon's Chapel until it closed. He was baptized there on August 8, 1926, when he was 11½ years old. After he married Gracie Maude Boyd of Patrick County, they attended Dillon's Chapel together.

It is fitting that Kemper School and Dillon's Chapel remain side by side today, for their past histories are intertwined. In fact, the Chapel was originally a school building. From schoolhouse to Chapel—how did all of this come about? Enter Floyd County Public Schools and a need for a bigger Kemper School. The school board donated the old one-room school building to the Presbyterian Church with the understanding that the building had to be moved from the premises to make room for a bigger school.

Rufus and Maggie Hubbard gave land adjoining the school lot for the church site. (Maggie was a granddaughter of Henry Dillon, the original founder of Dillon's Chapel.) The church building and lot were to be used according to Presbyterian Church regulations. When no longer used "for the purpose of a church lot," the deed states that the land and building were to revert back and become the property of the Hubbards. So on Valentine's Day 1916, an agreement was made, and the deed was drawn up.

Once school was out that spring, the moving process began. But how to move the old school to the adjoining Hubbard property so the building could be used as a place of worship? Well, somehow the schoolhouse was jacked up and two logs were slid underneath the building. The front ends of the logs had been tapered to look like runners on a sled. Then a steam engine, owned by Henry B. Shelor's father, Carl, was used to pull the building. Besides help from the steam engine, people in the community pushed. Yet, the old school building would not budge. What to do?

It was a farming community and people were used to relying on their own ingenuity. This challenge was no exception. They had an idea. Away they went for a good lubricant for the skids: fresh cow manure! They slathered it on and started the project again. Now the pushing and pulling were easier, and the school building made its way to the Hubbard land—where the building still stands today.

Once the wooden schoolhouse was moved, the log runners were removed, and a few changes were made to make the building more suitable for a place of worship. New siding was added and the overall building was enlarged. To increase the sanctuary size, a twelve-foot section was added to the front of the building. To accommodate a pulpit, a small bay was added to the back. "The extensions cannot be detected from the outside," said Maude Shelor, "but they are clearly visible from inside."

Maude continued to talk about Dillon's Chapel and described the interior: "The pulpit area had a lectern, love seat for the minister, and a small table in front of the lectern. All remain in the building today." She said the old-style pump organ, which was always played by Mrs. Henrietta Dillon Shelor, has been removed. The pews were handmade by local people and Maude said those benches were "very uncomfortable." Two wood stoves provided heat.

She described two improvised Sunday school rooms in the back. "They were separated by curtains, supported by wires that stretched from one side of the sanctuary to the other. The adult Sunday school class met at the front of the sanctuary. If weather permitted, the junior class moved outside. Otherwise, they met behind the curtain area." In addition to weekly Sunday school, there was "preaching" once a month.

Carl Shelor's sawmill was used to saw lumber for remodeling the building. Without the help of Carl's sawmill and steam engine, the moving and remodeling of the building would have been much more difficult—perhaps impossible. Carl made his profession of faith and was baptized at Dillon's Chapel on March 10, 1935.

Carl's wife, Henrietta Dillon Shelor, had been a member of Dillon's Chapel since she was a young girl. She was devoted to the chapel and the Kemper community. In fact, she did everything she could, said Maude, to keep the chapel going. "Miss Henrie," as she was affectionately called, would call around before services, encouraging people to come. Besides serving as church organist, she did mission work and served the church in many other ways. At one point, the Presbytery's Board of Women's Work officially recognized her efforts. Mrs. Shelor lived to be ninety-one years old and was a church member for about seventy-nine years.

As a small congregation in an outlying area, Dillon's Chapel had been one of three congregations served by the pastor from the "mother church" in town. Once the chapel closed in 1967, consolidation of the four congregations took place. Meanwhile, at Dillon's Chapel, "Mrs. Shelor kept right on with Sunday school and getting preachers from other denominations to come occasionally to preach," said Maude. "Due to health conditions, she finally had to quit, and the Chapel closed."

Maude remembered two wedding ceremonies being held at Dillon's Chapel. In addition to religious services, she said the building was frequently used during the week and at night for Home Extension and other club meetings. In recent times, the building has been rented to other denominations.

When Dillon's Chapel closed, there were sixteen members of the mother church in town who considered Dillon's Chapel their place of worship. In addition, there were thirty-five on the Sunday school roll at Dillon's Chapel. At that time, an artist named Lillian Overstreet did a very special drawing of the chapel. Lillian had gone to church at Dillon's Chapel and also had been a student at Kemper School, next door.

To understand more about Dillon's Chapel, it is important to know something about the original Dillon's Chapel building and its founder, Henry Dillon. Maude Shelor knew about Henry Dillon, firsthand, from her mother-in-law, Henrietta Dillon Shelor. Henrietta was Henry Dillon's granddaughter. Much of the following information is from conversations Maude had with Henrietta.

It is not known, for sure, who built the original chapel, said Maude, but "Henry Dillon was a religious man and the chapel was built on his land." Floyd County property records show that Henry Dillon and his wife Harriet had a lot of land, and their acreage was located in the Kemper community where Dillon's Chapel now stands. Records show that Henry and his wife owned 1,005 acres on Howell

Creek, in Floyd County. That property, along with three slaves, was inherited by Henry and his wife from her father, Jacob Helms.

Henry Dillon built many fine houses in the Floyd County area and "there are clues that indicate he also built the first Dillon's Chapel," said Maude. "Henry Dillon's last home was a wooden structure and it still stands today, near the chapel's location."

Maude understood that the original chapel was a wood-frame building, big enough for about twenty-five people. George Shelor, brother of Henry B. Shelor, remembered the two of them as children playing on a large flat rock. George said he always heard that rock had served as a doorstep for going in and out of the old Dillon's Chapel building. Maude never saw a photograph of the old church and doubts if one exists.

The existence of the first Dillon's Chapel building is important, said Maude, because the "first Presbyterian Sunday School in Floyd County was conducted there." Although Sunday school seems to have been held regularly in those early days, preaching was not so regular. "If a preacher came at all," said Maude, "it would not have been on a regular basis." Presbyterian records are silent about the old Chapel—probably because "the land and building were not owned by the Presbytery at that time."

Just who was this Henry Dillon, founder and namesake of Dillon's Chapel? Turns out he was born in Cork, Ireland, in 1808, and left with his parents one year later for America. The family began a new life together in South Carolina, but their happiness was cut short. Both parents died early, and Henry was "taken in" said Maude, "by a Bacot family." Later on, young Henry was apprenticed to Mr. Bacot and learned the trade of masonry and plastering. Henry left South Carolina when he was twenty-one and ended up in Floyd County. At age twenty-six, he married Harriet A. Helms of Patrick County, and they had eight children. He and Harriet remained in Floyd County for the rest of their lives. Harriet was born in 1813 and died in 1871. Henry Dillon died in 1886.

From all accounts, Henry Dillon certainly made a contribution to Floyd County architecture. He erected the old Academy, his own brick house in town, and the colonial mansion across the street. Then, too, he built the early Lutheran and Presbyterian churches in the county. The Jacksonville Presbyterian Church (later called Floyd Presbyterian Church) was built by him in 1850. No longer used as a church, the old building is still standing and is on both the state and the national historical registers. According to historian Marguerite Tise, Henry Dillon also built the second county courthouse in 1852. That second courthouse building replaced the one built twenty years earlier and was used by the county for the next one hundred years. The third, and current, courthouse was built in 1952.

Information from the *Henry Dillon Genealogy* describes Henry as "a tireless worker and consecrated Christian gentleman." According to session minutes of the Jacksonville Presbyterian Church, Henry Dillon was a dedicated member of the church and served as a ruling elder for several years. As "ruling elder," he would have been able to perform many of the same duties as a minister—both at the Jacksonville church and also at Dillon's Chapel.

Maude called attention to a special feature of the Jacksonville church on Main Street: a separate front door leading to a balcony. Maude thought that Henry, as builder, "had a hand in that balcony design. . . . He was a very caring man and promoted Christianity for everyone," she said. Maude thought the balcony was built "so the slaves would have a place to worship."

In addition to Henry Dillon's becoming an orphan at an early age, Maude said that two other unusually sad things befell him. One was the loss of his oldest and very promising son John, who had been a graduate of the Richmond School of Medicine. Serving as a Confederate Army major in the Civil War, John was killed at the Battle of Mine Run on November 27, 1863, at age 28. Learning later on about his son's death, a devastated Henry Dillon traveled alone by horse and wagon to the battlefield, north of Richmond. It was a two-week trip each way. He dug up the grave and brought the body back to Floyd for burial.

Another sadness for Henry Dillon, according to Maude, had to do with Henry's daughter Emma, and her move to Texas. On October 4, 1866, when Emma was nineteen years old, "she married a Yankee soldier," explained Maude. The couple tried living in Floyd and also in his home state of Connecticut. Unable to find acceptance at either place, they moved to Texas—never to return to Floyd County or be with her family again. Letters between them are evidence of their pain of separation, said Maude. Emma died of consumption while still young.

With these stories in mind, I try to imagine what it might have meant to have a little Chapel called Dillon's in the Kemper community years ago. It must have meant everything. No doubt, people's lives during the 1800s were hard and isolated. To say the "old days were hard" seems like an overworked cliché today. Yet, it was true. Even decades later, times were difficult. Maude Shelor spoke from personal experience as she described what life was like in the early 1900s when she grew up at Rock Castle Gorge, near Meadows of Dan: "Work at home and on the farm was done by hand. No electricity existed, so kerosene lamps were necessary. Kerosene lanterns were used for outdoor work at night—to check on young animals on cold winter nights. Lanterns were also used when visiting neighbors or to go coon hunting."

As one example of indoor work, Maude talked about "wash day" and trying to clean really dirty clothes with a washboard, homemade lye soap, and water. "Water had to be carried from a spring and then heated in a large iron pot outside. Clothes were hung on the line and would freeze during the winter. Ironing was done with heavy irons that were heated on a wood-burning stove, or on the fireplace hearth." Maude said that her mother liked to wash and iron on the same day. She thought the clothes would iron better if they were still damp.

Besides the hardships of home and farm work, many families lost loved ones to illness.

A bleak picture, yet many have told about the joys, too. Nostalgia takes them back to a simpler time and simpler pleasures. The heart is warmed with memories of family stories, community corn shuckings, apple butter making—or just the simplicity of a fried chicken dinner on Sunday. A strong faith and indomitable spirit often accompany those stories.

Regardless, the isolation surely was a major problem. Roads were dirt and mud with deep ruts. "We didn't travel very much, especially during the winter," said Maude. "We had five children in our family and we had to travel in a wagon."

No doubt, Henry Dillon and others were aware of the isolation people felt in the community, too. The need for a church nearby would have been obvious. What a comfort Dillon's Chapel must have been for people in that community—a place to come together to worship and to share joys and sorrows with one another. Even later, after roads were better, a local chapel would have been important.

I am so impressed by the ones who worked hard for Dillon's Chapel. In particular, I am inspired by Henry Dillon, the chapel founder, and by his granddaughter, Henrietta Dillon Shelor, who tried as long as she was able to keep the little chapel going. And finally, I am amazed to learn about a community of people who wanted a church building so much that they used every effort and resource they had to physically move a building to its current place on Black Ridge Road.

Based on Jean's article published in the Floyd Press *on July 26, 2003, and on Jean's article in the book* The Presbyterian Church of Floyd: Celebrating 150 Years of History, *Nov 2003*

Chestnut rail fences in
the area

Chapter 9

Legacy of the American Chestnut

When I was a child, the ridge behind our house was strewn with chestnut logs. Those huge logs had been majestic trees when they succumbed to blight. My elders always mourned their loss and spoke of them with reverence.

I took the logs for granted and they served as a wonderful, open-air playhouse for me. Each log was unique and I played on every one—many times. I remember their smooth gray exterior and the pithy orange inner wood that looked like railroad cars. I used to play store with that transitional wood, breaking off pieces for my "customers."

Besides play, those logs served other purposes for me. One time I hid inside a hollow log during a dangerous thunderstorm. Another time, I managed to scramble over a log, using it as a barrier between a raging bull and me. Later on, as a teenager, I'd climb the hill, sit on a log, and think. Problems seemed less worrisome when sitting on a log.

Half a century later, I walk where those logs used to be. I imagine them upright and dominating the forest canopy—as they did when my parents were young. I imagine their pungent smelling blossoms in springtime and their prickly covered nuts ready for harvest in September. I try to grasp what that tree once meant to my family and others.

"Chestnuts were the leading crop in the Blue Ridge and the main source of income," said my dad. He went on to explain:

> The rich soil here was perfectly suited for hardwoods and they grew fast. In a few years, a good chestnut orchard could pay for a farm. Stores gave due bills for chestnuts—cardboard money that families could use throughout the year to buy such things as clothes, lamp oil, salt, and bicarbonate of soda. Some cattle buyers bought chestnuts and hauled them to Ferrum where they were shipped by rail to Baltimore, the chestnut market of the world. Everyone liked to eat chestnuts and we ate as we picked. They were also roasted and sold as a special treat at Christmastime.

> Chestnut wood was the perfect lumber. It resisted decay and warping, and it was easy to saw, plane, and polish. It was fairly soft and easy to work and made good fence posts. Chestnut

rails were ten feet long and easily split and handled, the best of wood. Many chestnut fences lasted over a hundred years and some are still around, especially along the Blue Ridge Parkway. The last crop of chestnuts in this area was in 1922 and that was only half a crop. Chestnuts sold for thirty cents a pound that year—the most ever.

Tragically, the mighty American chestnut is gone from our landscape. An Asian blight fungus, *Cryphonectria parasitica*, was responsible for the death of about 3.5 billion chestnut trees in the first forty years of the twentieth century. The imported Chinese chestnut had been resistant to the disease but served as a carrier to infect our native tree. The first blight was detected in New York State and it worked its way south from there. The American Chestnut Cooperators' Foundation put it like this: "What had been the most important tree in our Eastern forest was reduced to insignificance. . . . No comparable devastation of a species exists in recorded history." Chestnut saplings can occasionally be found today, but they usually succumb to the virus once they reach about twenty feet.

After the chestnut blight, the local economy suffered greatly and the way of making a living changed forever. At first, there was a market for dead chestnut wood. Trees, eighty feet tall and three feet in diameter, were turned into something called "acid wood." The wood was hauled to Radford and used by a tanning factory. According to my dad, it took two men all day to cut a load of acid wood, and the pay for a load was $12—half of which went to the trucker. Cutting acid wood was hard work for meager pay, but times were hard and people needed any money they could get. Soon after, people started leaving this area for jobs in other places—places like Roanoke and the cotton mills at Danville and Spray (across the state line in North Carolina).

Although I could never fully understand such a loss, I, too, grieve for the special tree that meant so much to people here. A few years ago I ordered three chestnut seedlings. I know the prognosis, but I've planted them anyway and will pamper them along, appreciating every year they survive. It's a thrill to see them growing and to see what the leaf looks like.

I believe the mighty tree can be brought back in a vital way to the Appalachian region. I am hopeful, but I worry that environmental conditions are more hostile now than a century ago. Deer have increased dramatically in this area, and air pollution is now a serious threat to all living things. A Sierra Club book titled *An Appalachian*

Tragedy tells about the impact of pollution on our Eastern forests.

Still, there are reasons to be encouraged, and some scientists believe the American chestnut could be restored to economic importance. They are supported in that hope by The American Chestnut Cooperators' Foundation (ACCF)—an organization "dedicated to restoring the American chestnut to its former place in our Eastern hardwood forests." The ACCF focus includes breeding for blight resistance, cloning resistant American chestnuts, and reclaiming the habitat needed to rescue the species. The ACCF supports educational projects for schools, 4-H, and other groups. Seed-nuts are available to ACCF members following harvest in October, and people sign up each year to plant seeds and be a part of supervised projects and ongoing research.

Based on Jean's article published in the Floyd Press *on November 22, 2001*

Cecil Reed, rural mail carrier, first used a Model A Ford to deliver mail in Floyd County. (Photo courtesy of Maurice Slusher, who received it from Twila Reed.)

Chapter 10

Postal Service in Floyd County

When I was a small child, my family's focus was generally within a twelve-mile radius of our farm in the Walnut Knob area. Our closest town was twelve miles away in Floyd.

Occasional trips to Roanoke, Ferrum, or Rocky Mount took us farther in our 1940s black Chevrolet coupe.

The outside world came to us, though, through the U.S. mail. Cecil Reed was our rural mail carrier on Route 4, and we looked for him every day except Sunday. John Hylton was our substitute mail carrier. No matter what we were doing, we always stopped when the mail came with news from the outside world.

Besides letters from family and friends, the *Roanoke Times* and *Floyd Press* came to our mailbox, as did the Montgomery Ward and Sears and Roebuck catalogs. At one time, a person could order almost anything from those catalogs—even a kit for building a house. I loved getting the catalog "wish books" and spent hours looking at toys and working on my Christmas list for Santa Claus.

Occasionally, baby chicks came to us by mail, and I'm told that some people ordered hives of bees and even a queen bee, packaged separately.

My dad remembered that Mr. Reed originally carried the mail in a Model A Ford that had "a high clearance over deep, rutted, mud roads." He said that in bad weather people would ask Mr. Reed to do their banking and bring items from town. "They seemed to think such services were part of Mr. Reed's job."

My nostalgic memories of the mail system were fresh in my mind as I headed off to meet with Maurice Slusher. It was an enjoyable afternoon, and I learned a lot from him about postal history and his years with the postal system.

❧❧

Since he was a boy helping out in the store run by his Aunt Zula and Uncle Rollie Phillips, Maurice Slusher has been interested in post offices, including the Indian Valley Post Office located in the Phillips' store. In June 1947, Maurice started as a clerk at the Floyd Post Office, but he had always wanted to be a rural mail carrier—as had his friend Vasco Hylton, who was a clerk at the Willis post office.

Finally, the opportunity occurred for them. "We both transferred to rural routes in 1962," said Maurice, "and purchased four-wheel-drive International Scouts for the job." The severe winter of 1960 was on their minds and they wanted to be as prepared as possible for their back road, mountainous routes. Maurice carried mail for Route 1, an area that included Haycock Mountain. He spent an average of 55 hours and 37 minutes per week at his job.

Maurice Slusher, rural mail carrier, is pictured about 1980 delivering mail in Floyd County. *(Photo courtesy of Maurice Slusher)*

Since then, he has been researching postal service history and has done in-depth research on Floyd County post offices. A big part of his research has focused on locating over one hundred local post offices on an old Floyd County map.

Maurice owns many postal service artifacts, including photographs, an old mail pouch, a scale for calibrating postal weight, various types of mailboxes, metal divider trays for organizing mail, a 1947 registered mail stamp (used with heated wax and not used after the early 1950s), and a solid oak desk once used by postmaster Archa Vaughn. Mr. Vaughn's oak desk was replaced at the post office when metal furniture was issued.

Maurice has a large stamp collection and his airmail stamps are his "pride and joy," he said. He has all but five of the airmail stamps ever issued, including one of the first issued—a 1918 six-cent stamp. He has a thirty-two cent stamp for Rural Free Delivery, marking the 100th anniversary of Rural Free Delivery (RFD), and he has common stamps from the 1930s onward. His collection comprises more than twenty large books. He also has a collection of post cards, and one is made of leather. Its postmark is Bluefield, West Virginia, with a 1907 date.

"The first official Rural Free Delivery (RFD) routes began on October 1, 1896, in Charles Town, West Virginia," said Maurice, "but RFD came later to Floyd County." Citing some old *Floyd Press* articles, Maurice said the "real beginning of Rural Free Delivery in Floyd County seems to have been November 6, 1902. At first, there were three routes. Today, and for over seventy years, home mail delivery through RFD has been a service available throughout Floyd County.

When RFD started here, people did not understand, explained Maurice, "and they thought they'd have to buy a box and then pay rent on it, too." He said people weren't sure if the mail service was here to stay, "so they put out whatever they had on hand for a mailbox. Feedboxes and lard buckets were sometimes used—anything that would keep the weather out."

Later, manufacturers produced a variety of types of mailboxes. In time, mailboxes became more standardized and Maurice showed me five different styles. All but one was embossed with a stamp of approval by the Postmaster General, a requirement after 1901. To get the stamp of approval, Maurice said a mailbox had to have good metal workmanship, be weatherproof, have a signal (flag), and preferably, open from the side or top.

Early rural boxes were designed so they could be locked, either with a built-in box lock or with a padlock. While the use of locks was not widespread among rural patrons, the ones that were locked added to the rural carrier's workload. There were fourteen approved mailbox manufacturers using different style locks, and the rural carrier had to carry an assortment of keys to unlock and lock the boxes.

Pictured about 1900 is Jasper Light, rural carrier in Simpsons. Also shown is an early mailbox outfitted with padlock. *(Photo courtesy of Maurice Slusher)*

The use of locks was gradually phased out during the intervening years. Top and side loading boxes were not to be used after 1957. Today's rural mailboxes are tunnel-shaped, with a front opening. Some families have large-size boxes to accommodate parcel post packages.

During the early days of Rural Free Delivery, some mailbox manufacturing companies looked to rural carriers in some places for help with marketing, said Maurice. As a result, those rural carriers found themselves with a conflict of interest. "Company reps would contact them, asking for help in selling mailboxes, or they would ask the carriers for names of new people on their routes." This led to a new postal ruling on July 19, 1901, which stated that rural carriers could not act as agents or sell for a company.

"Rural carriers used to be required to wear uniforms," Maurice told me. "Those were woolen garments and the carrier had to pay for them out of pocket, a cost of $15.95 to $25.00 for a uniform. The original blue color was changed to bluish gray, for rural carriers complained that the original color showed dirt." The wool uniforms were hot in summer and impractical the rest of the year. Rural carriers needed a flexible dress code so they could deal with unpredictable weather and road conditions—dust, mud, ruts, snow, ice, and streams to cross. In the mid-1920s, rural mail carriers were no longer required to wear uniforms. In city and urban areas, mail carriers must still wear the bluish gray uniform.

Until 1925, rural carriers did not have an equipment allowance. On a salary of about $2,000 per year, a rural carrier during the 1920s had to furnish gas, a vehicle, and food for the horse (if that were the mode of transportation). There was no reimbursement for mileage, Maurice said. In 1925, rural carriers started getting a maintenance allowance of four cents per mile. In those days, many rural carriers were also farmers, and carrying the mail was compatible with that lifestyle. According to Maurice, 57 percent of rural carriers today are women.

"Another thing rural carriers didn't like," he said, "was picking up unstamped letters with coins for postage. That was especially hard in bitter cold weather when fingers would be numb from the cold as they felt around in the box, trying to locate loose change." Maurice showed me a little poem someone wrote about that tedious process. Part of it goes like this: *It's all right in springtime / Or when summer breezes blow, / But a different proposition / When it's thirty-two below. / When all your fingers / And all your toes / Are frozen hard as rocks, / It's anything but funny / Scratching pennies from a box."*

In 1903, rural carriers formed the National Rural Letter Carriers Association (NRLCA) and began to speak with a unified voice about the concerns of the profession. Foremost among their concerns was salary. In 1902, a carrier received $600 per year without any equipment maintenance allowance.

According to Maurice, the Floyd County carriers formed a county-wide organization in 1921 and became dues-paying members of the NRLCA. Although he does not know the exact number, Maurice said there probably were about twenty carriers in the county at that time. The local minutes reflect thinking and resolutions of that local Floyd County group. For example, members went on record as supporting a bill in Congress for an equipment allowance for rural carriers.

County road conditions were another big concern with both rural mail carriers and the general public. Maurice has researched old copies of the *Floyd Press* and said there were many comments back then from local citizens, complaining about poor roads and the need to work together on improvements.

In 1928, the local rural carrier organization put forth a resolution regarding county road conditions, a primary concern, said Maurice. In 1932, the Floyd County RLCA asked the State Highway

Pictured around 1923, is the Model T Ford of rural mail carrier, C. M. Epperly. Road conditions were a big concern for rural carriers and everyone in those days.
(Photo courtesy of Maurice Slusher)

Commission to give special attention to local roads. Six rural carriers were appointed to study the county road situation. A year later, local minutes of the rural carriers expressed "appreciation to road engineers and road camps for splendid road work done on rural roads."

Maurice said that, until 1969, post office and rural carrier jobs were political patronage appointments. After candidates qualified on the civil service exam, the local political committee would make a recommendation to their congressional representative, who would then submit the application to the Post Office Department to finalize the appointment. "Even though they were political appointments, the local political committee would not pick someone who was dishonest or untrustworthy," Maurice said. "Generally, good individuals were chosen."

While still a rural carrier, Maurice and other rural carriers became part of a big organizational change for the U.S. mail. On July 1, 1971, the mail service was placed under an independent agency called the U.S. Postal Service. Until then, the mail service had been under the U.S. Post Office Department and had been led by the Postmaster General, who was part of the President's Cabinet.

As a rural carrier, Maurice was active at all levels of the rural carrier organization. In 1975, he was appointed state steward for the Virginia RLCA and served in that capacity until he retired in 1988. During his tenure as steward, Maurice worked out of his home. He was in charge of the state steward system and assisted at the state level in resolving contractual disagreements and grievances between management and carriers.

At one point, Maurice testified before Congress on the topic of equipment allowance. He talked about the cost to a rural carrier of operating a vehicle on the job. On the 100th anniversary of Rural Free Delivery in Virginia, Maurice was invited to be keynote speaker at the anniversary observance at Palmyra, Virginia, where RFD had first begun in the state.

ᡱᢀᡱ

Before 1902, there was no house-to-house mail delivery in Floyd County. Even as late as the 1920s and early 1930s, some areas did not have house-to-house mail delivery. Instead, mail was delivered to the various small post offices, and people had to call for their mail there, said my dad. Some people were not able to collect their mail on a regular basis.

Until 1903, rural carriers were required to cancel stamps on collected mail and had to use a furnished hand stamp or an indelible pen. After August 1, 1900, letters cost two cents to mail, rather than one cent.

Since 1832, there have been over 100 small post offices in Floyd County. Maurice showed me a list of those post office names. Thirty-one had the same names as nearby one- and two-room schools and, like the small schools, most of the post offices were discontinued by the early 1900s. "It was common for post offices to be located in country stores," said Maurice, "and the store wouldn't do much business, once the post office closed. A post office closing would impact the entire community." This book, in Appendix A, contains Maurice Slusher's list of early post offices in Floyd County.

Along with the list of Floyd County post offices, Maurice showed me a 1930s post office map. I was especially interested to see the locations of the Turtle Rock and Pizarro post offices in the vicinity of the Franklin Pike, close to where my parents grew up. Although Turtle Rock was the older post office, they were both open at the same time, from 1886 to 1906.

Maurice said that in 1831, when Floyd County became a county, there were only two post offices here. At that time, Patrick County had four post offices, Franklin County ten, Montgomery County four, and Roanoke three. The area that would later become Carroll County had a post office located at Hillsville. The first post office in Floyd County was Simpsons, although at that time, Floyd County was still part of Montgomery County. The second post office in Floyd County was at Floyd Court House—referred to as "Floyd C. H." Floyd County would soon outnumber adjoining counties in number of post offices.

In 1890, according to Maurice, there were 54 post offices and 14,405 people in Floyd County. In 1900, there were 63 post offices and 15,388 people. In 1910, there were 23 post offices and 14,092 people. In 1920, there were 16 post offices and 12,115 people. In 1930, there were 14 post offices and 11,698 people. In 1940, there were 11 post offices and 11,987 people. In 1950, there were 10 post offices and 11,351 people. In 1960, there were 8 post offices and 10,462 people. In 1970, there were 8 post offices and 9,775 people.

I wondered why Floyd County had so many post offices. Maurice said, "Population was increasing and people wanted the convenience of having a post office nearby. People here put in applications for post offices and the Post Office Department approved them. Few applications were turned down."

Someone, or several people in a community, would initiate the idea for a post office and then started gathering signatures on a petition to be submitted to the Post Office Department. In addition to signatures, the petition had to have a proposed name for the post office, say who the postmaster would be, and describe the post office location.

The Post Office Department already had some guidelines for naming a post office, Maurice said. For example, the name of a post office and name of postmaster could not be the same. Still, twenty post office names approved for Floyd County had the same name as the postmasters. For example, Akers was the name of a post office with a postmaster named Washington Akers.

If a submitted name for a post office was turned down by the Post Office Department, the application would be returned, asking for another name. Or, in some cases, Post Office Department personnel came up with another name entirely. For example, persons along the Franklin Pike submitted the name Harvey for a post office. The Post Office Department rejected Harvey and named the post office Pizarro.

Names for some other post offices were turned down, too—names such as Farmer's Friend, Ida, and Duncan's Mill. The Post Office Department chose Santos instead of Ida, and Duncans instead of Duncan's Mill. Maurice still wonders about some of the names chosen by the Post Office Department. How did the Department come up with the name Santos, for example?

One petition from a community in Floyd County called for naming a post office Earls. That name was turned down by the Post Office Department and the local postmaster asked his wife, "What other name could we submit?" She thought a bit and said, "I've always liked nasturtium flowers. Maybe the post office could be called Nasturtium." That name was accepted.

Maurice talked about an application submitted to the Post Office Department from Botetourt County. After proposed post office names from patrons were rejected twice, the name Purgatory was assigned by the Post Office Department. The name came about after a Department clerk noticed a mountain called Purgatory on a Botetourt map. After the local petitioners were notified of the new name, they wrote back to the Department with the name "George God Be There" as postmaster.

Maurice said that as time went on, the Post Office Department put out additional guidelines for naming post offices—guidelines for making names more uniform. For example, the final "h" was to be dropped in names like Lynchburgh. In 1892, "C. H." for courthouse was dropped. Floyd C. H. became Floyd. Names like Pulaski City became Pulaski.

A post office in a community could have been in a home, in a store, or at a stand-alone location, said Maurice. Sometimes the location of a post office within a community would change. For example, the Willis post office was first called Greasy Creek and then Hylton. Maurice said each was probably at a different location within the same area.

Today, five post offices in Floyd County offer service to residents—the ones at Floyd, Willis, Check, Copper Hill, and Indian Valley.

Evelyne Rutrough, post office clerk, is shown emptying a postal box at the post office in Floyd. That post office was across from the courthouse, but the Floyd post office was located at several different places in town over the years. *(This photo, courtesy of Maurice Slusher, was taken about 1941.)*

At one time, the town of Floyd was known as Jacksonville, and Maurice said Jacksonville is mentioned in post office records. Still, there was never a post office by that name. The oldest post office shown on Maurice's list is Floyd Court House (Floyd C. H.). It was established on January 3, 1832. Later in 1892, its name was changed to Floyd. According to Maurice, by 1892 there were 68 post offices in the county, serving a population of over 15,000.

The Copper Hill post office was established in 1854, the Check post office in 1883, and the Willis post office in 1894. One of the oldest

This first Copper Hill post office was near the current Copper Hill post office on Route 221. *(Photo courtesy of Maurice Slusher)*

postmarks Maurice has is on a letter sent to the post office at Topeco. It is postmarked Tuggles Gap and dated October 17, 1890.

A few of the old post offices, such as Nasturtium, are still standing. In operation from 1897 to 1905, Maurice said the old building is on Route 221, not far from Willis Elementary School. The old Copper Hill post office is still standing, too. It is located along Route 221, not far from the current Copper Hill post office.

A post office called Smart was located near the Blue Ridge Parkway (at the confluence of Smart View Road, Cannadays Gap Road, and Silverleaf Road). Sparrel Tyler Turner was the first postmaster at Smart, a community located just south of Parkway milepost 155. Nearby Smart View Park, closed for now, was probably named for the old Smart post office, although some people say the park got its name from having a "right smart view."

My four hours visiting with Maurice Slusher went quickly, and I sensed in him a true dedication to his profession. I also gained a renewed respect and appreciation for the unique role the rural carrier has played and continues to play in the everyday life of local people.

Indeed, the rural carrier may be one of our best safeguards today for rural security. Certainly, the rural carrier is aware of conditions along the way and would notice anything out of the ordinary. "A mail carrier passes a house every day and there is a bond," Maurice said. "I miss that kind of contact."

This chapter contains parts of Jean's articles that appeared in the Floyd Press *on January 29, 2004, and August 18, 2011.*

Chapter 11

Thrash Home and Family

Effie King Brown, educator and historian, used to talk about the historic Thrash family home in the Copper Hill area. She was related to that family and, at age twenty-one, boarded at the Thrash home for a time while she taught at the old Pine Forest School nearby.

The Thrash home is one of the oldest in Floyd County and was built in the 1830s by John Thrash and his father, Squire Valentine Thrash. The large brick house, now painted red, is still standing. Effie could remember large Norway spruce trees in the yard, but only their stumps remain today.

Built in the 1830s by the Thrash family, this house is one of the oldest in Floyd County. It is located in a remote part of the Copper Hill area—about six miles west of Route 221. It is near both the Montgomery and Roanoke County lines.

According to Gladys Conner King, wife of Howard Ward "Chip" King (a sixth generation descendant of John Thrash), the Thrash family was originally from southern Germany. The beautiful Copper Hill location probably reminded them of the German countryside.

Gladys said the Thrash family obtained the first land grant for the property in 1794—a land grant on sheepskin signed by James Monroe for 2,400 acres. The Thrashes received additional land grants in 1795 and 1799. A survey of the property was done in 1800.

Prior to the time Floyd County became a county in 1831, the Thrash property was part of Montgomery County. The house is in Floyd County today and the land is in both Floyd and Montgomery counties. The property is also near the Roanoke County line.

John Thrash married Lydia Cole, daughter of John Cole, a Revolutionary War soldier and an early settler to the Copper Hill area. John and Lydia Cole Thrash had two sons: John Thrash, Jr., who moved to Missouri, and Valentine Thrash, who remained nearby and married Harriett Gray. Valentine and Harriett Thrash's two daughters, Mary Ann and Mahala, lived with their own families in the Copper Hill area, too. Mary Ann married William Sowder and Mahala married Jonathan Conner. Both men served in the Civil War.

Tammy King Simpson, a seventh generation descendant of John Thrash, grew up listening to family members talk about the Thrash family and property, which has been in the Thrash family and farmed since 1794. Today, descendants farm part of that original land under the business name of "King Brothers Farms."

Tammy's paternal grandparents, Howard Ward King, Sr., and Eloise Angle King, bought the property in the 1950s and farmed it. Tammy has fond memories of listening to her grandmother King tell about those times.

The Thrash home is six miles from Route 221. Thrash's Mountain is nearby but not part of the Thrash property. Tammy thinks nothing of making the forty-minute drive to the town of Floyd today, but she said her grandmother went to town about once a year. The area is still remote, as it was in her grandmother's day. Still, "lots of people lived in that part of the county back then," Tammy said.

Sugar Run Road cuts through the Thrash property and continues down the mountain to Shawsville. "Today, the road to Shawsville has grown up, " Tammy explained, "but years ago people used the road regularly." She said people also drove their cattle down Sugar Run Road to Shawsville, where they were shipped to market by train.

Tammy said the Thrash family was very religious and attended the Primitive Baptist Church, as did many early settlers of the area. The Thrash family cemetery is located on the Thrash property, not far from the Thrash house. Some graves are unmarked, but some of the marked graves are those of Priscilla A. Conner Manning, Walter B. Manning, William P. Manning, Shelton Leak Conner, Sallie B. Hall Conner, Lula E. Conner, Valentine Thrash, Harriett Gray Thrash,

Mahala Thrash Conner, and Jonathan Conner.

Recently, Floyd County Historical Society archives personnel have learned some additional information about the Thrash family from an undated paper written by Thrash descendant Valentine M. "Marion" Sowder. Marion had connections to the Thrash, Sowder, and Huff families, and his parents were William and Mary Ann Thrash Sowder. In the paper, Marion said that their graves are located at the Huff Cemetery.

Amos D. Wood's book *Floyd County: A History of Its People and Places* confirms that Marion Sowder's grandparents on his mother Mary Ann Thrash's side were Valentine Thrash and Harriett Gray. Dr. Wood's book says that Valentine Thrash "was one of the early justices of the peace when the Locust Grove district was formed; he was a member of the Legislature of Virginia during the Civil War and was of much service to families of soldiers in Floyd County."

Although Thrash descendants live in the Copper Hill area today, as far as is known, no persons with the Thrash surname live in Floyd County today.

This piece, in part, is based on Jean's article that appeared in the Floyd Press *on April 10, 2008.*

Head of the River Primitive Baptist Church, also known as Salem Church, was established in 1784. Located by Route 221 in the Locust Grove district, it is the oldest Primitive Baptist Church in the area. Pictured here is the second building—built sometime before 1884. The third and current building was built in 1984 and is still in use. *Courtesy of Mary Poff*

Paynes Creek Primitive Baptist Church, organized in 1804, is on River Ridge Road near Blue Ridge Parkway milepost 151. Services continue to be held at Paynes Creek today.

Chapter 12
Primitive Baptist Churches – Introduction

The Primitive Baptists, also known as Old School Baptists, had their start in the 1600s in Europe as a Separatist movement. Not long after that time, persons of the religious group began arriving in North America. By the 1700s, many had settled in Appalachian areas, including the southwestern Virginia counties of what are now Floyd, Franklin, and Patrick. In the nineteenth century and the first half of the twentieth century, Primitive Baptist churches dotted the rural countryside, usually away from the county seat. Some of those churches continue to hold services today.

The oldest Old School Baptist Church in the United States is the Welsh Tract Baptist Church. That church was first organized in south Wales, but soon after, its members immigrated to Philadelphia. They arrived there in 1701 and built a church near what is now Newark, Delaware.

Years ago, we sometimes went with my grandma, Lila Vest Thomas, to preaching at Paynes Creek, County Line, Head of the River, or to some other Primitive Baptist Church. Besides monthly services at individual churches, there'd be annual association meetings in which churches within an association group took turns hosting a three-day gathering for the other congregations. Even though churches were small, a large crowd of people attended those summer association meetings. I especially remember the singing. Following a song leader, we sang old-time hymns without instrumental accompaniment. My father and some other people could sight-read any hymn, following shape notes in the hymnal.

Many elders attended those services and took turns preaching during the three-day weekend. I always remember that their hats hung in a horizontal row to one side of the back wall, behind the pulpit. Sometimes preaching took place outside "in the grove" (grove of trees), especially during the afternoon. Midday, there'd be "dinner on the grounds." I also remember long wooden tables of food outside, with roofs overhead.

A *Floyd Press* article tells about an "old-time Primitive Baptist" association meeting held at Paynes Creek Church on September 3–5, 1943. According to the article, 375 people attended on Friday, 900 on Saturday, and 2,050 on Sunday. Thirty sermons were delivered that weekend. According to the article, park rangers directed traffic.

Paynes Creek Church, organized in 1804 as an "arm" of Salem

Church, is one of the oldest Primitive Baptist churches in this area; it is located next to the Blue Ridge Parkway near Parkway milepost 151. Services are still held there on the first Sunday of the month. As I understand it, Lewis Payne, who came to this area in the late 1700s, donated land for Paynes Creek Church. The church and nearby creek must have been named for him.

A 1937 *Floyd Press* article tells about an association meeting held at the Primitive Baptist Church in Floyd September 10–12, 1937. According to the article, it was estimated that 5,000 people attended and that preaching was outside in the grove. Many were from out of town, but "there were more invitations extended for guests, than guests for the invitations," said the article. "A number of state police were a great help in directing traffic." Early deed records show that the Primitive Baptist Church in Floyd was started in 1877 or earlier. Services continued to be held there on the fourth Sunday until a few years ago, when that church on Howard Street closed.

Head of the River Church, also known as Salem Church, is the oldest Primitive Baptist Church in Floyd County. That church was established in 1784 and is located on Route 221 near Copper Hill. Preaching continues to take place there on the second Sunday of the month.

The current church building, built in 1984, is the third place of worship on the site. The previous building was used for over a hundred years. The original building was made of logs. The cemetery on the church grounds is old and, on a recent visit, I especially took note of Littleberry Vest's grave. He was my great great great grandpa. He died in 1868.

Another Primitive Baptist Church we sometimes attended years ago was County Line Church by Thomas Farm Road. That church was on the Floyd–Franklin line and it was organized in 1869 by Asa Shortt, Richard J. Wood, Judy Shortt Wood, Violet Turner, the Cockram family, and others. Services at County Line were usually on the third Sunday. Although County Line Church is now closed, descendants gather each summer for a picnic, worship service, and fellowship.

Before starting the church on top of the mountain (at County Line), some of those members had attended services down in Patrick County at the church at Charity. Originally known as Smith's Run, that Primitive Baptist Church was established in 1778. It became known as Charity in 1806.

Pine Creek Church was established not long after Head of the River (Salem) Church. Considered an "arm" of the Salem Church, Pine Creek was started about 1795. According to Robert Baylor

Semple's 1810 history, forty members from Salem Church helped start the Primitive Baptist Church at Pine Creek.

The Pine Creek Cemetery is historic because of the number of Revolutionary War and War of 1812 graves. The Pine Creek Church has been closed since 1996.

I am familiar with the above churches, but I know of other Primitive Baptist churches in the Floyd–Patrick–Franklin area, too. Services are still held at some of them. As in the past, people still talk about "going to meeting" when referring to going to church, and refer to the church as a "meeting house."

I am interested in the Primitive Baptist Church because of my family connections in early times. A number of my ancestors, including Charles and Judy Thomas in the Charity area, attended those services. I am also interested because it was the predominant denomination in this part of the country during the 18th and early 19th centuries.

Pine Creek Church and Cemetery are located near Spanglers Mill Road. The Pine Creek Church (1795–1996) was once heavily attended, and the cemetery is historic—with a number of Revolutionary War and War of 1812 graves. (Recently, the Floyd Courthouse Chapter of NSDAR, erected this monument in memory of Revolutionary War and War of 1812 veterans buried in the cemetery.)

Chapter 13

Pine Creek Primitive Baptist Church

An effort is underway to obtain a historic designation for a little white church and cemetery located on Spangler Mill Road in Floyd County. Called Pine Creek Church, it is the second oldest Primitive Baptist Church in the county and was started in the late 1700s. The cemetery there is also old and contains a number of historic graves.

Pine Creek Church was constituted in 1797 by some members from Salem Church (also known as Head of the River Church). Salem Church, on Route 221 at Copper Hill, was constituted in 1784 and still has an active congregation.

According to Robert Baylor Semple's 1810 history, Salem Church "dismissed forty members for the purpose of forming a new church at Pine Creek." Pine Creek Church was always considered an "arm" of Salem Church, said Mary Poff, a current member of Salem Church.

In the Pine Creek minutes, it says that Peter Howard was licensed to preach in 1802 and was ordained in 1804. He was the first preacher at Pine Creek and took over pastoral care of the church in 1807. He and his wife, Sarah Howard, were received from Meadow Creek Church and were the first Pine Creek members. They joined Pine Creek in 1795 before the church was constituted two years later.

In 1803, fifty-one communicants were listed in the Pine Creek minutes. Down through the years, a list of at least 150 Pine Creek members has survived, although there are periods of time with gaps in the church minutes. In later years, Pine Creek services were held on the fifth Sunday, with the gathering ending with a watermelon feast.

Mattie Moore Martin was the last person to join Pine Creek Church, and Elder B. Odell Thompson baptized her on September 14, 1958. According to the minutes, Pine Creek closed after its last service on July 4, 1996.

Early members of Pine Creek listed in the minutes include Abigail Boothe, Alse Wells, Ambrose Briant, Annie Becket, Charles Simmons, Daniel Boothe, Ealoner Howery, Ealoner Simmons, Elizabeth Farif or Farris, Frances Briant, Ira Howard, Isaac Boothe, Jane (or Jone) Wells, Jemima Dickison, John Shortt, Judith Shortt, Lavica Rose, Lettice (Letty) Howard, Lidia Short, Lott Shelor, Martha Graham, Michael Howery, Nancy Boothe, Owen Sumner, Permelia Howard, Peter Howard, Sarah Howard, Rhoady Booth, Rhoada Shelor, Romelio Howard, Sarah Howery, Sarah Sumner, Sarah West, Susannah Beckett, and Thomas Simmons. Some Pine Creek members, such as Lidia Short and John and Judith Shortt, transferred from Charity Church in Patrick County.

Of the early church members at Pine Creek, the following were listed in the 1822 minutes as black: Alse Wells, Jane or Jone Wells, Lettice (Letty) Howard, Lott Shelor, and Squire Howard. They "joined in full fellowship," according to the minutes. Appendix C in this book has a more complete list of early Pine Creek members.

In addition to Peter Howard, some other early elders/moderators at Pine Creek were H. V. (Valentine) Cole, Thomas L. Roberson, Amos Dickerson, Michael Howery, and Owen Sumner. It was said that, at one time, Elder Michael Howery performed about half the marriages in Floyd County and Elder Owen Sumner performed most of the others.

Some other elders listed in the Pine Creek minutes who preached there were Thomas Simmons, John Lester Cole, Benjamin Clarke, Sam Moore, T. S. Roberson, Asa D. Shortt, Henderson Dodd, Posey G. Lester, David Sumner, J. F. Spangler, T. H. (or J. H.) Howard, I. F. Martin, David Spangler, S. L. "Sam" Moran, B. Odell Thompson, Amos Hash, J. P. Helms, B. V. Spangler, Hale Terry, and Roy Agee. In 1874, Asa D. Shortt applied for a letter of dismissal from Pine Creek to continue helping with County Line Church, which had started five years before.

Typically, Primitive Baptist churches function as independent entities, and members take care of their own needs and expenses as they arise. A Primitive Baptist Church is usually part of an association group that includes other churches in the area. Once a year, one of the churches would serve as host, and members from within the association—and from other associations—would attend a weekend gathering with preaching, business meeting, and "dinner on the grounds." Years ago, hundreds (sometimes thousands) would attend a weekend Primitive Baptist Association meeting. Association meetings are still held today.

Pine Creek Church was originally in the New River Association, but in the later 1800s, Pine Creek became part of the Smith River Association. In 1866, Pine Creek Church hosted the Smith River Association meeting and hosted a number of future association meetings as well.

Three deeds are described in the Pine Creek minutes book: one for five acres in 1804, one for three acres in 1939, and one for ¾ acre in 1951—making a total of 8 ¾ acres of land for the church and cemetery, with rights to a spring cited in the 1939 deed.

The Pine Creek Cemetery has hundreds of graves and is historic in its own right. Over the years, Charlie Wood and Wilton Sutphin, among others, have cared for the Pine Creek Cemetery. In more recent times, Jimmy Howery has served as caretaker. Like some others who have cared for the cemetery, Jimmy Howery has ancestors buried at Pine Creek. Jimmy and his daughter, Kendra Arthur, have recorded tombstone information from Pine Creek and have also documented soldier graves there. Their work has provided a valuable historic record.

Buried there are soldiers from the Revolutionary War, the War of 1812, and the Civil War. (According to a monument recently erected at the cemetery by the Floyd Court House Chapter, NSDAR, Revolutionary War soldiers buried at Pine Creek Cemetery include John Banks, Moses Dickerson, Major Thomas Goodson, Thomas W. Goodson, Peter Howard, Robert Howard, William Howard, Captain Daniel Shelor, and Daniel Spangler. The monument also lists the following War of 1812 soldiers buried there: Thomas Goodson, William Goodson, Isaac Moore, George Shelor, and William Spangler.)

Pine Creek minutes provide a snapshot of what was going on at the time. For example, no services were held in December 1896 and January 1897 "due to rough weather and sickness." Later, the minutes say that no services were held from August 1918 to January 1919. Probably services were cancelled because of the influenza epidemic.

The Pine Creek Church building is still standing, but it is unclear whether an earlier log building in the late 1700s was on the premises. One clue: The September 1881 church minutes state that a committee was appointed to raise money to build a new meeting house. No follow-up information could be found in the minutes.

A very special chinquapin bush continues to grow in the middle of Pine Creek Cemetery. Chinquapins and their small nuts, encased in burrs, were common in Floyd County during much of the twentieth century but are scarce today. It is believed they were somewhat affected by a disease similar to the one that caused the American chestnut blight at the start of the twentieth century. This one bush at Pine Creek Cemetery is a treasure.

Based on Jean's article published in the Floyd Press *on November 24, 2011*

The winter of 1960 was unusually hard in Floyd County due to power outages and snow falling each Wednesday for about six weeks. When scraping roads, highway crews ran out of places to put snow. This local photo shows what the roads and mountains of snow looked like during that time. Floyd County Schools were closed for twenty-one days straight.

Chapter 14

Floyd County Weather

In early December 2009, I watched the weather and wondered if the winter might turn out like the winter of 1960 when Floyd County schools were closed twenty-one days straight. In 1960, we had about sixteen inches of new snow every week for six weeks during February and March. During that time, there was no transportation in parts of Floyd County. Prior to February, we had already missed school. To make up lost days of school that year, we went to school on Saturdays through most of June. Finally, the state excused us from making up all of that missed time.

Laurence Wood, of Wood Funeral Home in Floyd, remembered about ninety inches of snow that year and the hardships people endured. Except for a few four-wheel-drive jeeps and trucks, people drove two-wheel-drive vehicles in those days. A *Floyd Press* article (March 10, 1960) reported a sixth heavy snow since February 12th that winter.

When school finally opened again, our snow-covered dirt road was barely passable. I remember my father and mother, both teachers, on their way to school with us kids in the back seat of our pink Studebaker. After making our way to the paved Franklin Pike, my father, dressed in suit and tie with overalls to protect his suit, would lie down by the Franklin Pike pavement and take off car chains. Coming home, he'd put the chains on again.

He'd do that and teach school between caring for livestock before sunrise and after sunset each day. Throughout the spring, the Franklin Pike looked like the far North with piles of snow in twenty-foot mounds on either side of the road. It felt as if we were driving through a tunnel.

In those days, our electric power lines still came up the mountain from Franklin County, and our electricity was often out—sometimes for a week or more. We never had a generator back then. Our wood-stoves provided heat for warmth and cooking, and we used oil lamps at night. It was amazing what good food my mother could turn out using our wood stove.

Food in our freezer sometimes spoiled during long power outages, but, in desperation, we could put frozen food outside in nature's icebox, which would be near zero degrees at times. We didn't have bears and some of the other varmints we have today, so we didn't have to worry so much about wildlife getting into food stored temporarily outside.

Finally, in the 1980s, after years of lobbying from local people here, Blue Ridge Parkway officials allowed our electric power lines to be rerouted. Instead of coming up the mountain from Franklin County, our lines came from Floyd. The lines came across the Parkway to us (actually under the Parkway) at milepost 151.

My father, Max Thomas, devoted a chapter to weather in his book *This Pleasant Land: A Blue Ridge History*. He told of hearing old people talk about the year of 1884—"the cold year that had no summer." He wrote:

> The winter of 1884 was rougher than the summer for there was barely enough food and little variety. Some livestock starved. The reason for this cold year was the eruption of a volcano in Japan, but the hill people knew nothing about it. So much debris was in the air that the sun could not warm the land. . . . A lesser cold year was 1910, when little was raised, but it was not nearly as severe as 1884. The year of 1918 had a normal summer but a terrible winter. Drifted snow lay on the land from November until April, and a number of days had temperatures below zero. This may have been a factor in the [severity of the] flu plague [influenza pandemic] of that winter.

My dad said that later cold winters were 1935, 1960, 1961, 1962, and 1963. (And for the record, the winter of 2009–2010 here was snowy with low temperatures, but the weather was not nearly as severe as the winter of 1960.)

Based on Jean's article published in the Floyd Press *on February 18, 2010*

Chapter 15

Snowed in with a Dog

When I was a kid, we always had a dog—a farm collie with its own doghouse outside. Except during severe weather, dogs did not set foot in our house. Our cats, too, lived outdoors and took shelter in the hay barn or granary.

Since I became an adult, arrangements have been different, and our pets have always lived in our house with us. That began years ago when we returned from a year in California. We had promised our daughters, ages four and seven, that we would get a puppy after we settled back in Virginia, so we did.

Bo smiles for the camera, oblivious to the trouble he caused in 2010 after being sprayed by a skunk.

Over the years, all of our cats and dogs have landed in the proverbial lap of luxury. We've provided good lives for them and, in return, they've given back to us, too. We've had our problems, at times, though. Our border collie was way too smart for us, and our Labrador retriever puppy almost never became housebroken. But our last dog probably provided the greatest challenge.

Prone to wander and chase any moving object off our property,

Bo, our twelve-year-old Australian shepherd, had his first encounter with a skunk one morning. He reeked and looked ashamed as he came to the door. We had been snowbound for five days in a row, and the last thing my husband and I wanted inside with us was a skunk-smelling dog. Even our cat ran and hid. We felt like shunning Bo, but it was too cold to leave him outside. Still, I was keenly aware that everything the sprayed dog touched would immediately smell like skunk, including our clothes and the dog's leather collar. The air was heavy with skunk odor.

By now, Bo was in a holding pattern in the garage while we tried to figure out what to do. I wondered if the legendary tomato juice bath would work, but a quick survey of the pantry turned up only one small can.

I called our local vet and was told about a couple of commercial products at the office—not an option for snowbound folks twelve miles away. Barring that, I could try the following recipe mixture: one quart of 3 percent hydrogen peroxide, ¼ cup baking soda, two teaspoons of liquid dishwashing detergent, and a quart of warm water. We were told to protect Bo's eyes and to leave mixture on him for five minutes. Then rinse well.

Before treatment, I checked out Bo for obvious oily skunk spray. I also gave him the sniff test—a mistake causing me to heave as I inhaled that strong scent up close. The entire dog smelled like skunk, big time!

With the house shut up tight, we wondered where and how to bathe this stinking dog, who seemed oblivious to our predicament. We decided on the laundry tub by the window in back of our basement. For this messy project, we opened the window, wore rubber gloves, and tried to scrub away the odor. After bathing with the recipe mixture, we rinsed and then bathed him again with a regular dog shampoo. After towel drying, we put him in a dog crate in the basement to dry off some more in front of a heater.

Meanwhile, I opened windows throughout the house, washed our towels and clothes, lit pumpkin-scented candles, and started baking a chicken to, hopefully, add a pleasant aroma back in the house. Bring on spring!

In late spring, we had Bo's tresses clipped and, after that, he was back to being his sweet-smelling self.

Based on Jean's article published in the Floyd Press *on February 18, 2010*

Chapter 16

A Drive Through Time on the Blue Ridge Parkway

It is a spring morning and I am driving a familiar route—the Blue Ridge Parkway. Built in 1936, this part of the scenic road is near my house, and it ribbons through these mountains as if it were always here. Sometimes, I drive this road on automatic pilot, but mostly I see it anew, for its beauty is ever changing—no matter the season.

On this morning—back in 2005—I am on a mission as I drive south toward Rocky Knob Park. I want to revisit Parkway history and try to visualize the area as it was before the Parkway was here. I am also looking for remnants of the Appalachian Trail that used to go through this area.

The Trail family once owned this cabin near the Floyd–Franklin County line. Since the 1930s when the Blue Ridge Parkway was built, this cabin has been part of Smart View Park—a park near milepost 154 and enjoyed by tourists and local people alike.

My first stop is Smart View Park near my house. The park is still closed for winter, but I park my car, walk past the gate, and follow the one-way circular road. From habit, I stop at the old cabin, once owned by the Trail family in the late 1800s. I enjoy the view and then veer off into the woods, following the three-mile Loop Trail. I end up at the large picnic area where we used to meet for family reunions, a game of baseball, and a spread of food that always included home-made fried chicken and lemonade. (Both Smart View Park and the Rocky Knob Park visitor center were closed recently, due to cuts in the Parkway budget. We hope they will reopen soon.)

I end my walk back at the park entrance where we used to buy ice cream cones from the little park store. As I leave, I reflect on the park's name. We always called it "the Park" but I've heard opinions of how Smart View Park got its name. Most likely, it was named for a nearby post office at Smart, Virginia. But some say it got its name from having a "right smart view."

Back in the car, I drive south past Haycock Mountain, Rakes Mill Pond, and the Rocky Knob visitor's center. Just after that, I turn left and park at Rock Castle Gorge overlook. Acquired by the Park Service when the Parkway was built, the 4,000-acre Rock Castle site must be one of the most stunning views along the Parkway.

Named for the quartz crystals in the area, Rock Castle was a thriving community of farm families in the early 1900s. After that, the population gradually declined, but many people continued to live there. It must have been hard for them to give up their land and homes when the Parkway was built in 1936. Floyd resident Maude Boyd Shelor grew up in the Rock Castle area and part of her family's land was acquired for the Parkway.

Continuing south on the Parkway, I arrived at Mabrys Mill. Located on the edge of Floyd County, the mill is one of the most photographed and popular tourist sites along the Parkway. (Historian and Park Ranger Michael Ryan has recently written and published a book about the mill. His well-researched book is comprehensive and focuses on the couple who built and ran the mill, Ed and Lizzie Mabry. The book is titled *Ed and Lizzie: The Mabrys and Their Mill, A Blue Ridge History*.)

The entire Parkway took fifty-two years to build and was finally completed in 1987. As late as the mid-1950s, only half of it had been completed. Yet, much of the Virginia section was finished by January 1, 1940. After twenty years of negotiation, the last 7.7 miles of the Parkway were completed in the Grandfather Mountain section of North Carolina. An engineering feat known as the Linn Cove Viaduct made completion possible—that, and an agreement with the local landowner, Hugh Morton, who had opposed building the Parkway because of environmental issues.

What an undertaking it must have been to build the Blue Ridge Parkway—a road 469 miles long that went through some of the most rugged terrain imaginable. A Cornell graduate and landscape architect named Stanley Abbott was chosen as the lead architect for the project. What a visionary idea to plan a road with landscaping as the focus!

At first, local people were excited about a good road coming through, a road the width of four wagons! People had been hauling produce to Martinsville and Roanoke and thought a good road would be a godsend. They didn't realize, at first, that it was a road for tourists and that farm and commercial vehicles would not be allowed on it.

People here used to refer to the Blue Ridge Parkway as the "Parkway," "Skyline" or "Skyline Drive." Calling it the "Skyline," though, is confusing, since the road that goes through Shenandoah National Park is also called the Skyline Drive.

In the Parkway building process, much of the scenic road traversed private property, with thirty-one miles in Floyd County. When I tried to measure the Floyd County miles, it seemed like more than that. I realize, though, that the county lines of Floyd, Franklin, and Patrick weave back and forth across the Parkway. The thirty-one mile figure for Floyd is from the National Park Service tally. Only one county (Buncombe County in North Carolina) has more miles of the Parkway than does Floyd County.

For the new road, state personnel were charged with getting each right-of-way and doing each land appraisal. The federal government was in charge of building the road. Typically, Parkway right-of-ways were several hundred feet on each side of the road, but widths varied considerably and some, such as the Rock Castle area, were much larger.

The Parkway affected almost everyone who lived near it when it was being built. For some, it meant jobs. For others, it gave them extra money for land they weren't using anyway. For still others, it gave them an excuse to move. Most, though, did not want to sell any of their property. This was home and the land, in many cases, had been in their families for generations.

It was through a legal process known as *eminent domain* that state and federal governments justified their actions to take private property for public use—provided owners received just compensation. However, local landowners often disagreed with the government about what was "just compensation."

Right-of-way appraisals were often low, and sometimes land was first condemned before being appraised. Sometimes farms were bisected by the Parkway, cutting off farm animals from water. One landowner in the Rocky Knob area made out better than most. His cows were able to get to water on the other side of the Parkway by going through an underpass built by the Park Service.

Jean stands beside a Parkway underpass near Rocky Knob Park. The underpass was created for a local farmer so his cows could walk from one side of the Parkway to the other to get water. Such an accommodation was rare.

Sometimes people sold their land to the Parkway and then rented it back for farming. Even today, some people pay rent to use the land that once belonged to their families. I sometimes look for roses and other cultivated flowers along the Parkway. That's one way to tell where a house used to be.

Decades after the Parkway was built in Floyd County, those of us on the east side of the Parkway continued to have problems with the Park Service—especially problems with electricity. We'd had electricity since the late 1940s, but the power line route had continued to be unsatisfactory. The Park Service withheld permission for the power line to cross the Parkway, so the line had to come up the mountain to us from Franklin County. That is steep, rugged terrain, and power outages would often last for a week or longer.

Appalachian Power Company personnel tried hard to repair our lines, but working conditions were often difficult and dangerous. In summer, leafed-out trees were heavy, and hard rain and windstorms often brought them down on power lines. In winter, deep snow and ice caused trouble.

Working conditions were hard in such steep, wooded, snake-infested terrain. Sometimes, after working in snow and ice storms, power-line workers would come to our house, hungry and very cold. While they warmed themselves by our wood stove, my mother would fix them something to eat.

Finally, people here complained so much about the hardships that the Park Service acquiesced and the power line was re-routed under the Parkway from the opposite direction at Parkway milepost 151. Our electric service has been better ever since.

Building the Parkway involved much hand labor, but the Park Service also brought in rock crushers and other large machines. Rocks were needed and local people were paid in cash for them. My grandma was paid a total of $100 for fifty dump-truck loads of rocks—all from her cornfield, just after harvest. She said it was the only time she ever "got something for nothing." Some people were also paid fifty cents for each fence rail. Even today, some of the old rail fences can be seen along the Parkway.

President Franklin Roosevelt's New Deal "make work" programs were a big help in getting the Parkway built, especially before World War II. The Civilian Conservation Corp (CCC) was one of those programs, and CCC camps were located at Rock Castle Gorge and Fairy Stone Park. Some local people were hired for CCC jobs and other jobs connected with the Parkway. CCC workers built the Rocky Knob cabins.

Near the cabins, and still standing, is the two-story log home once owned by the Thomas Whorley family. Their son, John Whorley, is referred to as the "king of Slate Mountain" in Richard C. David's book *The Man Who Moved a Mountain*.

As I think back on the years since the Parkway was built in this part of Virginia, I have mixed emotions about the process and how it came about. And I understand local people saying back then that city people wanted recreation at country people's expense.

Still, I am grateful for the beautiful road that is here now—a national park road that I travel every week. I know the time and place where wildflowers bloom along its edge and take pleasure as each tree decks out in the spring. And it is a true gift when I see a pileated woodpecker, red-tailed hawk, or flock of wild turkeys.

Living near a road like this allows me to appreciate anew this beautiful place I call home. I like driving the Parkway for errands and enjoy showing it off to visitors. I especially like being able to drive partway on it to my sister's house in Lynchburg. Although it was not always so, I think my parents eventually came to appreciate the

Parkway, too. And I am glad for the ease of travel it afforded them in their later years.

I conclude my day's outing by making one last stop—near Parkway milepost 168 at the Saddle Overlook. I pause briefly to enjoy the view and then start up the trail to the right. I walk on a well-worn path, a path once followed by the Appalachian Trail. After some climbing, I come to a log structure that once served as an Appalachian Trail shelter.

This Appalachian Trail shelter remains in place and is pictured here near Saddle Overlook and Parkway milepost 168.

The shelter looks the way I remember it from years ago when I came here with classmates. It sits solidly on the edge of the mountain like a balcony looking down on a stage below. It is a beautiful setting and it is easy to see why both Park Service and Appalachian Trail personnel chose this site. The Appalachian Trail was here first, though. The two routes coexisted near each other until 1954. After that, 160 miles of the Appalachian Trail were moved to Giles County and other points west.

As I stand by the Appalachian Trail shelter, on the summit of the Blue Ridge, I am struck with a sense of awe as I recall my dad saying, "The high ridges of Floyd, Grayson, and Carroll Counties are some of the oldest mountains on earth. Once as high as the Rocky Mountains, they were probably never underwater." He thought mountains here were originally formed during the Pre-Cambrian era, some two billion years ago.

I also remember his talking about a later geologic force about 250 million years ago. Known as the Lynchburg Thrust, that sixty-degree thrust was a powerful force from the east toward the Floyd peneplane. It caused buckling, folding, and faulting—leaving deep streams, waterfalls, and canyons in its wake.

Not only am I standing on ancient land, but I am also standing on a watershed divide. Raindrops falling in front of me, and down the mountain to the east, flow to the Atlantic; raindrops falling in back of me toward the west make their way to the Gulf of Mexico.

Finally, as I stand on the border of two counties—one formed in 1831 (Floyd) and the other formed in 1791 (Patrick)—I am reminded of the early people who came to the foothills and valleys just down the mountain from where I stand. They came on foot, on horseback, in wagons, or in flat boats called bateaux during the eighteenth and nineteenth centuries to what is now Franklin and Patrick Counties.

I imagine those early explorers and settlers coming here from the north and east and seeing this rugged terrain for the first time. No doubt, something drew them to this place the way it draws us still. Perhaps it looked like England, Scotland, Wales, Ireland, France, or Germany—places they, or their ancestors, had left behind. In time, some of them would make their way up the mountain to what is now Floyd County, and points beyond.

Some of us think of ourselves as natives of this place, citing ancestors who lived in this area for over 200 years. Some can even trace their roots to the Cherokee and other people who came before. Regardless of our roots, we all follow a long line of people who were here first—thousands of years ago. As a kind of benediction, I am reminded of words from Ecclesiastes: "One generation passeth away, and another generation cometh: but the earth abideth forever."

Based on Jean's article published in the Floyd Press *on May 12, 2005.*

In years past, families often played music in their homes. Pictured by the piano in 1964 are Max, Clara, and daughter Janet Thomas.

Years ago, in the 1800s and early 1900s, many people attended singing schools in this area. This photo is believed to have been taken at the old Iddings School in the Locust Grove district. Jean's great grandpa, Sam Vest, is in the second row, fifth from right. Sam and his family lived near Iddings School and spoke about attending singing schools when Henry Graham was the song master.

Chapter 17

Our Musical Heritage

Some of the most magical memories of my childhood relate to music. Whether it was front-porch pickin' and singing on a summer evening, singing in the car, or something more organized at church or elsewhere, the melodies were always uplifting and the fellowship was enjoyable.

To accompany our informal singing at home, Daddy played the violin (fiddle) and banjo, Mama played the piano, my sister played the mandolin, and I played the flute. Mostly, the songs our family sang at home and in the car were hymns and old-time secular songs. We especially liked singing songs from a 1915 songbook called the *Golden Book of Favorite Songs*—songs like "When You and I Were Young, Maggie," "Long Long Ago," "Old Folks at Home," "My Old Kentucky Home," "Little Brown Church in the Wildwood," "Juanita," "Home Sweet Home," and so many others. We knew those lyrics by heart. At Christmastime, we sang holiday songs.

My parents had heard the Carter family, but other groups performed around here, too. We sometimes went to hear performances at a country schoolhouse or a neighborhood church. Even though we had a lot to do on the farm, my family made time in the summer to attend John Hancock's singing school at Silver Leaf Church. And I marveled at the way John Hancock and others, like my dad, could read shape notes and get the pitch right every time. My dad and his Grandpa Sam Vest had attended singing schools years before when Henry Graham was the singing master. Sam Vest said singing schools in the Floyd County area were being held by the mid-1800s or earlier.

In his two books, *Walnut Knob* and *This Pleasant Land*, my dad devotes sections to music. In the latter, he writes, "The fiddling records of Tommy Jackson and the banjo picking of Charlie Poole are perfect examples of mountain music—its tempo and the method of playing and singing."

Music is such an important part of the heritage of this area, and that love of music continues today. No wonder Floyd County has always been known for its music. And it seems that we hear of more musicians and musical venues every week in the *Floyd Press*.

Over the years, the historic Floyd Country Store has attracted musicians and visitors from both near and distant places. People pack the store every week to hear traditional Appalachian music at the "Friday Night Jamboree" there. And, since 2002, FloydFest has drawn huge crowds each summer for its four-day event.

In the year 2000, I asked Marie Gallimore of WGFC Radio to help me put together a list of musicians from our area. Marie, a singer and musician in her own right, came up with a long list. Her list included gospel groups, bluegrass groups, country bands, instrumentalists, singers, and songwriters.

She singled out Randall Hylton, "a great songwriter, guitar player, and singer from Willis," she said, "who ended up in Nashville." Randall received the Bluegrass Music Songwriter of the Year award and will always be remembered as a beloved native son who accomplished so much in music.

Several years ago, I spoke with Arthur Conner of Copper Hill, who makes violins. For over thirty years, he has worked at his craft— "a hobby," he said. His customers have included Ricky Skaggs and George Strait.

And finally, I must mention that the largest distributor of bluegrass, gospel, and old-time music in the world is located in Floyd County. Located near the Floyd stoplight, County Sales (also called County Records) is a retail store that serves walk-in and mail order customers.

Several years ago, I stopped at the Blue Ridge Music Center at milepost 213 along the Blue Ridge Parkway near the town of Galax. I especially wanted to see the interpretive center's temporary exhibit arranged by the Blue Ridge Institute and Museum of Ferrum College. With notepad in hand, I made my way around the exhibit hall, learning about thirty-seven old-time musicians from Southwest Virginia during the 1923–1943 time period.

The first thing that caught my eye, though, was a floor-model phonograph made in the 1930s by Monroe Simpkins of Floyd County. It was a lovely dark wooden unit, about four feet high. The exhibit label said that Monroe Simpkins was the only Southwest Virginian known to have made phonographs as a business enterprise back then.

Monroe Simpkins was a friend of Elder Golden P. Harris, a Floyd County musician from Indian Valley. For a while Elder Harris helped Monroe Simpkins build and sell phonographs for the Blue Ridge Phonograph Company.

Born in 1897, Elder Harris was a Primitive Baptist preacher, old-time fiddler, and recording entrepreneur. He did most of his recording from 1931 to 1933, and he was one of two Southwest Virginians known to have created their own recording labels before World War II. (The other was William Myer of Tazewell County.)

In 1931, Elder Harris traveled to New York and recorded two hymns on the Melotone label for the Brunswick Company. Later on, he recorded hymns on labels of his own—Harris, Bottomley, and Dunlap—and sold the records out of his home for 75 cents apiece. Elder Harris played and sang music for as long as he lived.

The Parkway exhibit also featured Sam and Banks McNeil of the Floyd County Ramblers. According to the exhibit, the McNeils signed with the Victor Recording Company in 1930 "on the strength of a local murder ballad" they had sung on a Roanoke broadcast. Victor brought them to New York where they recorded six songs. They quit playing professionally after that but continued to play together, informally, for years.

As I continued to walk around the exhibit hall, learning about early recording history, I looked at an old 1915 Edison cylinder player. There were only two Southwest Virginia groups who made cylinder recordings: The Fiddlin' Powers Family of Russell County and Ernest Stoneman's bands in Carroll County. Cylinder players were soon followed in the 1920s by machines that played 78 rpm recordings. Those record players remained popular for several decades.

I learned that some Southwest Virginians recorded on smaller labels, but the major record labels before World War II were Victor, Brunswick, Columbia, Paramount, and Okeh. According to the exhibit information, record sales surged for large and small companies until the Great Depression of the 1930s, when most small companies were "wiped out."

The last thing that caught my eye at the Music Center was an old-time radio. People here in the mountains started listening to radio in the early 1920s when country records were beginning to sell.

Even in the 1940s, we were still listening to a battery-powered radio at our house. We listened to *Amos and Andy, Gangbusters, Ma Perkins*, and the Saturday morning *Cream-of-Wheat Story Hour*—my favorite program. We also enjoyed listening to music from *Renfro Valley* and the *Grand Ole Opry*.

Radios, phonographs, and recording companies all played important roles in promoting local music in the Blue Ridge. Still, according to the exhibit information, only a few local musicians, such as the Carter Family of Scott County, stand out in the early 1900s for their great success and impressive recording careers.

According to the exhibit, "Few other parts of the country produced so much commercially recorded music prior to World War II as did Southwest Virginia. Still, only a handful of Southwest Virginia performers saw real fame or money. Most were simply hometown stars, playing music locally and living average lives."

Radio, and then television, helped change the music available to us here in the mountains. As a teenager in the mid-1900s, I listened to our AM radio at night and picked up station WLS out of Chicago. Radio signals bouncing off a layer of the atmosphere late at night made it possible to pick up that distant station that played rock and roll music. I especially recall a disc jockey named Dick Biondi and another one named Wolfman Jack.

Today, music here in the Blue Ridge has come full circle and many people are once again playing old-time music, along with a vast assortment of other genres of music.

Some of the information in this chapter is based on Jean's article published in the Floyd Press *on August 24, 2000.*

Chapter 18

Old-Time Stores

In the days before good roads, people in remote sections of Floyd County depended greatly on country stores. Those stores sold groceries, household supplies, hardware, animal feed, and most other necessary things. Besides that, the country store served as a meeting place and sometimes as a post office.

My dad said that lamp oil used to be delivered to country stores in a wagon pulled by mules. "It was hard work," he said, "but mules held up better than horses." He thought lamp oil might have come from Christiansburg. Later, gasoline was delivered to local stores run by Cam Turner, Winfield "Field" West, Esley Ingram, Leonard Smith, and Tom Agee—and to some other local stores.

This photo, taken in the 1950s, is of a store owned by Cameron Lee Turner (called C. L. or Cam). Cam also farmed and was elected to the county board of supervisors for three terms. Originally, the store was built and run by Greenville Wood. The building is still standing.

When I was growing up in the 1940s and 1950s, we often shopped at country stores. Beulah Nichols' store was one mile from us at Parkway milepost 151, and Field West's store was near Parkway milepost 156, where a pottery shop is now located. We sometimes stopped at stores run by Leonard Smith and Esley Ingram along the Franklin

Pike. And we often stopped at a store located at the intersection of the Franklin Pike and Paradise Lane. That store was run by Cam and Dora Turner—my grandparents. I loved spending time at their house and store. That store building and nearby house were originally owned by Greenville Wood, my Grandma Dora's uncle.

Tom Agee built this store about 1912 and and was a storekeeper there for about fifty years. *(Photo courtesy of Ray and Martha Smith)*

Tom Agee's store at Parkway milepost 159 was also a convenient store for us, and we sometimes stopped there, too. That store was built by Tom Agee about 1912 and was owned by him for about fifty years. Later on, Ray and Martha Smith ran a store there and called it the "Wormy Chestnut." The Smiths had a lovely store filled with Appalachian-type crafts and much more. I once purchased a hand-made quilt as a gift for someone, and I still have the old-time school desk I bought there. Behind the counter was a beautiful hutch that had once been at the Hotel Brame in Floyd.

These days, the stores closest to us in this part of the county are along Route 221, north of Floyd: Ingram's, Smith's, J & J's, and the Country Store at Check.

The G. J. Ingram & Son Store has been in the Ingram family since 1945 when George and Doris Ingram purchased it from O. R. (Oscar) and Daisy Sweeney. The Sweeneys had owned the store since the early 1920s. The Ingram store continues to sell general merchandise and farm supplies.

Smith's Grocery & Hardware Store, beside the Copper Hill Post Office, was built in 1948 by Sherman Smith. It has continued to be owned and run by the Smith family for sixty-five years. That grocery–hardware store sells gas and an assortment of other things, including food for a quick lunch. The store has some vintage woodwork inside, including a glassed-in candy case.

The J & J Market & Deli is located at the intersection of Route 221 and Daniels Run Road. The first businessman on that site was Tyler Prillaman, who helped build an octagon-shaped building in 1927-28. He ran a garage for repairs there and a community grocery store. In 1937, Glen Vest traded twenty-five acres of land for the building and ran it as a grocery store. Glen was joined by Raye Janney in running the store in the late 1930s and then again after Raye came back from World War II. After the building burned down in 1975, Raye Janney built another store there in its place, and he and his wife, Helen McNeil Janney, ran it until Raye retired. Raye won an Exxon dealer award for fifty-six years of Exxon service. Glen Vest went on to run the Vest Drive-in Theater nearby, and I remember that drive-in from the 1960s.

The Country Store at Check was known as Simpson's Store when I was growing up. That store also has an interesting history. It was built by John Gray and located near the Check post office. After that, Joseph J. Poff owned and ran the store. Willard C. and Garnett Poff Simpson owned the store after that and moved it to its current location on Route 221. After he came back from World War II, Basil Poff Simpson, Sr. (Willard and Garnett Simpson's son) ran the store.

King's Store was also located along Route 221 on the corner of Route 221 and Kings Store Road. The store closed some years ago, but the building is still standing. The store was originally owned by Peter M. King. Later, it was owned by Peter's son, Wallace King.

I know of another store in this part of the county—the Clyne Angle Store on Daniels Run Road. The Simpsons post office was located at that store with Clyne Angle as postmaster. That store is no longer in use, but the Simpsons post office was one of the oldest in the area, dating back to 1823. All of these stores are the way I remember country stores, and I love them still.

Of course, a number of stores were in the town of Floyd and, like now, they met many of our shopping needs. During the 1950s, Mr.

Ayers' dry goods store carried toys at Christmastime—as did Western Auto. Woolwine and Rutrough's drug store had a soda fountain where ice cream cones cost five cents each. Before then, Purcell's (a department store) got its start, but I remember it later, during the 1950s when it was still part of the Hotel Brame building. Since the 1920s, Farmers Supply has been in operation, and its windows at Christmastime are beautiful—the way I imagine stores looked back in Charles Dickens' time. I remember more modern looking stores in town, too—for example, Ben Franklin (five-and-ten) and Piggly Wiggly (grocery store) during the 1950s and after.

This photo, taken in 1964, shows three stores on Main Street in Floyd: Western Auto owned by Jessie and Herman Heafner; the Farmers Supply store on the corner of Main and Locust Streets; and Woolwine and Rutrough's drug store between Western Auto and Farmers Supply. Only Farmers Supply is in operation today. Built in 1897, that building has housed Farmers Supply since the 1920s. Jack Lawson owns Farmers Supply today.

Moses Restaurant was a popular family restaurant in Floyd during the mid-1900s. It was owned by Roy and Willie Moses and was on north Locust Street where Oddfella's Cantina is located today. Purcell's was a department store located in the Hotel Brame building. Among other items, furniture was sold at Purcell's. *(Photo courtesy of Citizens Cooperative)*

The Ben Franklin five-and-ten store opened in 1952 in Floyd and was located on the corner of Main and Locust Streets—where Blue Ridge Land does business today. To the left is the Farmers Supply store.

Pictured is 1964 is the Piggly Wiggly grocery store located on Main Street on the east side of town where Floyd Pharmacy does business today. At one time, the store was owned by Gene Williams.

This view along north Locust Street is from the 1925 time period. The Hotel Brame is located on the left and the side yard of the courthouse is on the right. The Hotel Brame was built by Samuel R. Brame in 1904 and was located on the corner of Main and Locust Streets. By 1912, the building was being used for lodging, dining, and dancing. Besides the hotel and restaurant, other businesses were housed in the building from time to time. Waitman Slaughter, the last basement occupant, ran a grocery store and hotdog stand—the forerunner of today's Slaughter's Supermarket. The hotel building was razed in 1965. *(Photo courtesy of Susie Albert Vest)*

Chapter 19

Local Telephone History
"Can you hear me now?"

Our telephone ring was **two shorts** and **one long**. I remember that all these years, even though I was little when we had a crank telephone on the wall in our parlor. Those old-time phones are sometimes referred to as "crank and holler" because a crank was used to "ring" someone and then it was sometimes necessary to holler (shout!) in order to be heard. "Can you hear me now?" was a common question callers asked back then. Today, a wireless phone company named Verizon has a television ad of a test man asking the same question.

Electricity was slow in coming to many parts of Floyd County, but people had telephone service in the early 1900s. Primitive, compared to the phone I use now, that early crank phone—along with a battery radio and daily newspaper—connected my family to the outside world. That real-time communication also connected us to family and friends and was especially useful when emergency help was needed.

I wasn't yet born when telephone service began in Floyd County, but I have experienced each stage as it progressed, starting with the "crank and holler" wall phones and continuing with rotary dial phones, party lines, private lines, touch-tone phones, fax machines, answering machines, voice mail, cell phones, modems for dial-up Internet, and high-speed Internet.

During the 1950s and 60s, telephone communication was an integral part of our day-to-day life. Still, we tried to keep long-distance calls to a minimum. Long-distance calls were expensive so we relied more on letter writing. In 1964, I spent six months overseas and never once talked with my family on the phone. I sent them a telegram when I arrived and wrote weekly letters after that. International phone calls were very expensive and service was sometimes unreliable.

The first telephone service in Floyd County began about 1910 in Locust Grove and was provided by Locust Grove Mutual. The first switchboard there was at the home of the G. W. King family, who ran the switchboard twenty-four hours a day. Over the years, the switchboard was located in several different houses, depending on who was the telephone operator at the time. For over forty years, Locust Grove Mutual continued to provide telephone service—until Citizens Telephone Cooperative purchased it on August 24, 1956.

I remember seeing telephone poles along roadways—tall,

sometimes leaning poles with rows of inverted, cup-shaped, green glass insulators on top. Those glass insulators are now collector's items and a reminder of an earlier time.

Lineman Connie Browning works on a telephone pole, making line repairs. This 1961 photo was taken on Webbs Mill Road near the old Webb's Mill. *(Photo courtesy of Citizens Cooperative)*

For decades, people kept up their own telephone lines in Floyd County. In 1915–1916, Zephine Graham worked on the Locust Grove lines and rode a motorcycle between repair jobs. Some others who worked on the Locust Grove lines were Vent Austin, Albert King, and Leonard Craighead. At one point, about 300 customers were part of the Locust Grove system, with up to fourteen customers on a line. Effie Brown told me there were nineteen phone lines in Locust Grove.

Effie's family acquired telephone service in 1916 when she was six years old. She remembers her father installing their phone. He put it "high up on the wall so young ones wouldn't play with it." Her mother was only five feet tall and could barely reach it. Effie said that whenever someone on her family's line received a call, every phone on the line would ring. It was clear from the ring who was being called, but eavesdropping often occurred on party lines.

When wanting to make a call, a person was supposed to listen first to see if there was a "message on the line" (someone talking).

In order for Effie's family in Locust Grove to call out of the area, they had to crank **one long** and the central operator at Lilac would pick up. Lilac is a community near Kelley School and the Blue Ridge Parkway. Effie said the phone ring at their house was **one long** and **two shorts**. It was listed in the phone book as "**17_1 J**" (line 17, **one long,** and **two shorts**).

Rather than having phone numbers listed in the phone book like today, a phone number would be in code. The first number would tell the line number. Vertical lines stood for "longs." Letters of the alphabet served as codes for **shorts**. The code for letters was: B=1 short; J=2 shorts; R=3 shorts; and W=4 shorts. If a family was on line 10 and their phone ring was 3 longs and 3 shorts, it would be listed in the phone book as "**10_lll R**."

Besides Locust Grove Mutual, there were several other telephone companies in Floyd County back then, according to Gerald Gallimore, General Manager at Citizens (and now retired). Each locality had its own telephone service. There were two telephone companies in Floyd: Citizens Mutual and Floyd Telephone Company. P. L. Shelor operated the Floyd Telephone Company whose switchboard was located at the Hotel Brame.

The most enduring telephone company in Floyd County has been Citizens. With switchboards at Black Ridge and Floyd, Citizens Mutual began providing telephone service on February 28, 1914. Citizens Mutual was the predecessor of Citizen's Telephone Cooperative.

It must have required a lot of community cooperation in order for early telephone systems to work. "At first," Gerald told me, "those above-ground lines were made of iron wire. Iron is heavy and you can just imagine the repairs needed when two to three inches of ice added additional weight to lines during winter storms. Iron wires also attracted lightning."

In 1925, Citizens Mutual started replacing the iron wires with copper wire. That process was completed in 1976. Copper is a better conductor of electricity but was more expensive than iron. "Lines were always in various states of repair," Gerald said. "People built and kept up their own lines. Some lines were even nailed to fence posts." During the 1930s and 40s, each household paid about $2.50 per year to connect to the switchboard for phone service.

Being on a party line was interesting because people were able to "listen in" on one another's phone conversations. That was a good way to learn the latest news and gossip, but there was no privacy. The 1914 bylaws for Citizens Mutual addressed eavesdropping as follows: "Anyone listening while others are on the line must put his hand over the transmitter to prevent noise from being heard on the phone."

People would ring "central" (ring the operator) when they needed to reach someone who wasn't on their line. The operator would then plug in the switchboard connection. Operators were instructed to say "number please" and people were supposed to give the number so the operator didn't have to look it up. An exception was made for people who couldn't read or write. In case of emergency, one long crank would be a signal for everyone on the phone line to pick up their phones.

Typically, eight households were on a party line at first, then six, and finally four. It would have been too expensive to offer everyone private lines back then. Still, most doctors had private phone lines, as did banks. At the insistence of the superintendent of schools, Effie Brown also obtained a private phone line. She was a school princi-pal, and the superintendent said he could never get through to her on the party line. Others with private lines included Jessie Peterman, Rev. R. Gamble See, the Farmers Supply store, and the Floyd Hack Line—an old-time taxi service pulled by horses, between Floyd and Christiansburg.

Effie remembered what communication was like before people had telephones. People had to go in person, send a messenger, or write a letter. "People wrote a lot of postcards," she said. "The mail was faster than today. A person would send postcards to several friends, saying there would be a gathering on Saturday night at so-and-so's house." Phone service made communication much easier.

Maude Shelor was raised in Patrick County near the Floyd line, and she remembered problems with telephone lines during the 1920s and 30s. Lines were often broken, and her dad and another man tried to repair them. Their central switchboard operator was at Ballard in the Conners Grove community. She said her family's telephone ring was **one long, one short,** and **one long** and that there were about eight families on their line. "Our phone was used sparingly," she said, "and children were not allowed to use it at all. Batteries were expen-sive and the phone was used only for important matters." Maude said there wasn't much time to talk on the phone because her family was always working. She said she was a teenager before the phone "impressed" her.

Margaret Smith, former teacher and longtime county resident, said that years ago she was in Washington, D. C., visiting a friend. She tried to call home collect, going through various central switchboards down the line. It was hard to hear, so each operator would tell the next one: "Margaret's coming home." When the message finally got to Margaret's family, her grandfather was listening in on the party line and also heard the message. "If you had to go through three or more operators, you couldn't hear," said Gerald Gallimore, "and you had to get the operator to pass along the message."

Telephone communication was certainly a collaborative event back then and, at times, humorous. During the late 1960s, actress Lily Tomlin played the part of an old-time telephone operator on a popular television comedy program called "Laugh In." Her celebrity pseudonym was Ernestine.

The last telephone operators in Floyd County were Ilene Carr of Locust Grove and Ada Weeks of Willis. According to a *Floyd Press* article, both operators were replaced in December 1958 by a "mechanical gadget" that enabled telephone subscribers to dial numbers for themselves.

Ada served as an operator for the Willis exchange for over thirty years. Her daughter, Eula Weeks Hurd of Radford, remembered the switchboard in their house. "It was in my parents' bedroom near the

Ada Weeks (Mrs. Will Weeks) was a switchboard operator in Willis for over thirty years. *(Photo courtesy of Citizens Cooperative)*

kitchen—convenient for calls, night or day." Her older sisters helped with the switchboard and sometimes Eula helped, too. "My mother was a community lifeline for the area," said Eula. "People would call asking about the weather, who was sick, who had died—all the news."

Eula remembers switchboard batteries. "They were different from batteries today. Seems like there were two of them for our switchboard—crock-like batteries with liquid and prongs in them. At first ours were in the house and later they were outdoors."

The old crank-style telephones were run by batteries, too—batteries that were similar to ones farmers now use to power electric fences, according to Gerald Gallimore. "Sometimes people took the batteries out of their phones and used them in their battery-operated radios to listen to the *Grand Ole Opry*." This, of course, drained energy from the batteries—as did eavesdropping on party lines.

It is interesting to look at old telephone directories, for they serve as a snapshot of history for the time. Besides names of people, names of communities were included—some familiar to us and some, such as High Peak, long forgotten. Telephone books also had interesting advertisements that reflected the times. One Farmers Supply ad had information about "Fordson" tractors for sale. Some other local ads were ones for the Floyd County Bank, Hotel Brame, Citizens Bank, and Floyd Drug Store and for photographer D. L. Cole. Ads for Roanoke included ones for Propst Childress Shoes and Henebry Jewelry. I remember both of those stores.

Telephone companies had rules for participants and those rules were stated in their bylaws. Rules varied from company to company. For example, some companies required members to put in their own lines or hire it done. A 1915 Locust Grove Mutual bylaws booklet included the following rules:

> (1) No person shall be allowed the use of the telephone for more than five minutes at any one time. Any person . . . who shall refuse to cease talking at the expiration of five minutes, when requested to do so by any member wishing to use the line, shall be fined ten cents for each offense. (2) No abusive, profane or obscene language shall be permitted to pass over the line. Any person so offending shall be fined one dollar, and shall be deprived the further use of the line until fine is paid. (3) Persons under the influence of liquor must not use phones. (4) Operators of Switchboards shall be selected by the Board of Directors and the compensation is not to exceed seventy-five cents per year

for each phone in their zone. (5) No person shall ring central between the hours of 9 p. m., and 5 a.m., unless on urgent business. On Sunday central shall not be called except between the hours of 8 to 10 a.m., and 4 to 6 p. m., except on urgent business. (6) No extra phone shall be added to any line without the consent of three-fourths of the stockholders on that particular line. (7) The company shall furnish all poles, wire, and fixtures; plant the poles, and the stockholders shall keep up the said line at their own expense . . . .It shall be the duty of stockholders to keep the line in good repair. (8) All lines including poles, wires, fixtures, are the property of the company. The phone is the property of the owner.

Telephone lines were here before electricity and before the Blue Ridge Parkway was built. Once Appalachian Electric Power (AEP) came to Floyd County, AC lines caused interference—a humming sound on the phone lines. Finally, on October 28, 1938, AEP paid Citizens Cooperative $4,000 to remedy the humming problem by adding an extra wire to telephone lines.

During the 1930s Depression years, people were relieved of having to keep up their phone lines; instead, Citizens Mutual took over that task. By the end of World War II, "the old telephone system had aged out," said Gerald Gallimore.

Meanwhile, the U. S. Congress enacted the Rural Telephone Act in 1949. That legislation made it possible for companies and cooperatives to obtain low-interest loans. The act enabled telephone systems to reconnect the more isolated rural areas and provide service at affordable member rates. Soon after, Citizens Mutual applied for and received a Rural Electric Administration (REA) loan to update the telephone system. The $470,000 loan to Citizens Mutual was approved in February 1952.

"Every time technology is replaced, it is expensive," Gerald explained. Still, "rural families wouldn't put up with an inferior telephone system. Families worked together to get what was needed. That was the rural way."

Citizens Mutual provided local telephone service until 1953. Around then, Citizens Mutual and the Floyd–Montgomery Mutual Telephone Company merged to form Citizens Telephone Cooperative. The Cooperative purchased or absorbed several additional companies in the 1950s.

In January 1956, a dial telephone system began in Floyd and Alum Ridge. Touch-tone and other calling features began in 1980, the same year Citizens made available the 911 emergency services. Beginning in 1973, the phone company started putting phone lines underground; that project was completed during the 1970s. In 1976, there was still a party line system in Floyd County with four shareholders on each line. After the late 1980s, party lines were eliminated entirely and everyone had private lines. About 1984, Citizens Coop began replacing copper cable with fiber optics. In 2003, Citizens went from being a stock-issuing cooperative to a membership (user-owner) organization.

Finally, Gerald talked with me about the families and generations of families who have worked for Citizens over the years. In particular, he listed the Hylton, Weeks, Huff, and Whitlock families.

Gilbert Hylton served two separate terms as president of Citizens Mutual. His first term began in 1914 at the start of Citizens Mutual, and his second term began in 1937. Later, his son Maynard was elected president of Citizens Mutual and then elected president of Citizens Telephone Cooperative. Maynard's son, Donald Hylton, worked for Citizens, doing excavation work and putting phone lines underground. And now, Donald's daughter, Donna Hylton Smith, works for Citizens, carrying on the family tradition. Also, Ralph Hylton, Maynard Hylton's nephew, worked for Citizens until he retired.

Clarence Weeks is pictured here testing a telephone line in 1976. *(Photo courtesy of Robert Weeks)*

Manager Bill Dunn (right) briefs a Citizens Cooperative line crew in 1961 before they start out along country roads. Making up the team were, from left, Maynard Hylton, P. D. (Posey) Weeks, Connie Browning, and Clarence Weeks. *(Photo courtesy of Citizens Cooperative)*

P. D. (Posey) Weeks worked for Citizens Mutual and later worked for Citizens Coop, retiring in the 1960s. Posey's nephew was Clarence Weeks, who worked for Citizens. Now, Clarence's sons, Robert and Paul Weeks, are Citizens employees.

Clarence began working for Citizens in 1957, the year his son Robert was born. Clarence died on June 3, 1996, two days after Robert began working for Citizens. "He knew I had gotten the job before he died," said Robert. "I think he was just waiting around to make sure I had a good job."

Ravanal Nixon Huff worked for Citizens, and her daughter-in-law, Sandra Conner Huff, works there today.

Lena Richards Whitlock was a telephone operator and secretary for Citizens Mutual and Citizens Cooperative, working for the coop until she was in her 70s. Currently, Dennis Whitlock works for Citizens; he is a distant cousin to Lena's husband and is married to Lena's grandniece.

Gerald told me "the core families who settled Floyd were involved with early telephone service, but that's another story for another time." In 2013, Citizens Telephone will celebrate its centennial. This will be a time to pay tribute to all who have helped Floyd County come so far with technology and telecommunications. Alexander Graham Bell's "electrical speech machine" has come far indeed—both locally and worldwide.

Based on Jean's article published in the Floyd Press *on March 17, 2007*

Lena Richards Whitlock was a telephone operator in Floyd, and she is pictured in 1961 by the switchboard. *(Photo courtesy of Citizens Cooperative)*

Chapter 20

The French Connection

It has been said that the French and Welsh are the forgotten settlers of Southwest Virginia. Let's shed some light on the French connection to Floyd County, and also explore the accuracy of a local legend about movie star Joan Crawford and her possible French connection in Floyd County.

I have been interested in family history for years but have only recently learned of a French ancestor of my own. Uncovering this information made me want to know more. It turns out that many people in this part of Virginia have connections to 17th century France.

So how did the French come to be in this part of Virginia? Well, like so many of our ancestors, French emigrants back then were escaping religious persecution in their homeland. During the reign of King Louis XIV, it has been estimated that as many as two million Calvinists (known as French Huguenots) fled from France. They were first given refuge in Germany, Switzerland, Holland, and England.

In time, King William III of England helped make it possible for some of those French Protestant refugees to sail to the colonies—especially to Virginia and the Carolinas. During the year 1700, five ships set sail at various times. The first to depart was the Mary Ann (also known as the Mary and Ann). It sailed from Gravesend, England, on April 19, 1700, and arrived at the mouth of the James River (now present-day Hampton, Virginia) three months later, on July 23.

Virginia Governor Frances Nicholson went to greet the Mary Ann and those on board—207 men, women, and children. Approximately 350 would arrive on the other four ships.

Arrangements had been made for their arrival in the new land by King William III and also by Nicholson's government in the colony of Virginia. Provisions and protection were to be made available, as well as land. Colonel William Byrd took an interest, too, and tried to help the immigrants get established.

The refugees disembarked and traveled by way of Jamestown, but it had already been decided by their hosts that they would settle on land west of Jamestown. Some settled along the Rappahannock River and other places. But 66 individuals were given land patents for themselves and their families along a stretch of the James River. Some 87 land patents (comprising about 10,000 acres in all) were distributed among the 66 individuals. This was near present-day Midlothian, an area that came to be known as Manakin Town. The area may have been named for the Monocan Indians who had once inhabited the area. Today there is a town called Manakin on the north side of the James River, but that is in a different location from the original Manakin Town (which was on the south side of the James River).

Not long after they arrived, the newcomers set about building a house of worship—the first of five churches that would be built by them and their descendants in the area. According to written anecdotal records, family worship was held three times per day.

By the time they arrived in Virginia, they had already survived many dangers. Still, nothing in their past could have prepared them for life on the frontier. In France, they had led prosperous lives, working in professional positions or as skilled tradesmen. They had no experience carving out a home and farm and raising a family in such an untamed wilderness.

To make matters worse, the immigrants were quite a distance from protection promised by the colonial government. They did not have horses and had to walk many miles to obtain provisions. It was a twenty-mile walk to the nearest gristmill and even farther to Jamestown. They also traveled up the James River by boat and probably transported goods that way. Many of those first settlers took sick or died their first year in Virginia.

In time, though, the survivors made a life for themselves in Manakin Town. They learned how to raise crops and cattle and attempted to domesticate the buffalo. Later on, they manufactured cloth and made claret wine from wild grapes. Eventually, some of them—and especially their children and grandchildren—made their way to other places, including the Southwest part of Virginia.

Early French settlers in the colonies had surnames like Agee, Bernard, Bilbaud, Bondurant, Brooke, Chastain, Chastion, Clarke, David, Duval, Fontaine, Foushee, Gardner, Grahame, Gwinn, Henley, Howard, Jordan, Lacy, LeSeur, Martin, Maury, Michaux, Michel, Moriset, Munford, Patterson, Perry, Porter, Powell, Richard, Robinson, Rogers, Smithe, Soblet, Trent, Watkins, Williamson, Woodson, and others. Some names were later Anglicized or took on variations in spelling. For example, Bilbaud or Billiabo became Bilbo. LeSeur was usually spelled LeSueur by descendants.

I know of several people in the Floyd County area who have ancestors with some of these names. One person has an ancestor whose surname was Foushee (Forcee). My own ancestor was Jacques (James) Bilbaud/Billiabo from the west central part of France. My more recent connection is through his granddaughter, Marie "Mary" Bilbo, who married John Young Shortt.

Movie star Joan Crawford also had French ancestors, as well as a possible connection to Floyd County. She was born in Texas in 1905 and was named Lucille Fay LeSueur. I had read in the 1937–1938 Works Project Administration (WPA) oral history records that Joan Crawford's great grandparents had lived in Floyd County and were buried at Camp Creek Cemetery. Their names were listed in those Depression-era records as Martell and Catherine LeSuear.

So I started from the post office in Floyd and headed out the old Christiansburg Pike (Route 615) toward Camp Creek Cemetery. On the way, I crossed Little River on a modern bridge and tried to imagine the old wooden covered bridge (1850–1944) that had been there before. As I drove on, I passed the 19th century Camp Creek Church on my left. I had read in the WPA records that the LeSueurs and other local families had worshiped at that little church and that Martell LeSueur and his son Bert served as trustees there in 1883.

Shortly, I arrived at Camp Creek Cemetery, located on a pretty knoll to the right. According to WPA records, the cemetery has been in use since 1887 and originally was known as the "Bouman Burying Ground," named for the land's original owners, Mr. and Mrs. Asa Bouman.

The 1930s WPA records describe the cemetery as overgrown and unkempt. Not so on the day I was there! In fact, the graveyard was lovely and well cared for on that recent spring morning. Birds were singing, and white and purple violets provided part of the ground cover. Dogwood trees were budding, and a huge maple tree was already in flower. Around the edge of the graveyard were "rock lilies" (yucca), a blooming spirea, and daffodils.

It took me only a few minutes to find the gravestones of Martell and Catherine LeSueur. The dates were difficult to read but concur with the WPA records. Martell's date of birth was listed as May 16, 1821, and his date of death was listed as November 28, 1904. Catherine's date of birth was September 19, 1801, and her date of death was August 27, 1887. On the tombstone, Catherine's name appears to be spelled Catharine (with an "a"), although it is spelled Catherine (with an "e") in the documents I've seen.

I wondered about the twenty-year difference in Martell's and Catherine's birth dates. My research, though, has led me to conclude that Martell is buried beside his mother, rather than his wife. His mother's name was Catherine "Kitty" Goodykoontz LeSueur (daughter of John George Goodykoontz and Mary Beaver). "Kitty" was married to Moseby LeSueur (Martell's father) on February 6, 1819.

Martell LeSueur was married to Sarah Phlegar on March 3, 1853, in Floyd County, and their home was near the Camp Creek Cemetery and Church. According to WPA records, Martell LeSueur built a weatherboard house in 1874 and lived there until 1900. After his wife Sarah died, Martell married Elizabeth "Lizzie" S. Howell Carter on September 11, 1891, according to historian Polly Dixon. Martell died in 1904 and is buried between his mother and his daughter, Eliza Alice LeSueur Howery. Eliza was born on November 6, 1861, and died on September 9, 1935. Eliza shares a tombstone with her husband, Johnathon Howery, who was a minister. Johnathon was born on April 19, 1855, and died on February 9, 1931. I am not sure where Martell's wives are buried.

It is my understanding that the following were children of Martell and Sarah Phlegar LeSueur: Emma Catherine (married Rev. Samuel Bowman/Bouman), Elbert Joseph "Bert" LeSueur (married Amanda Stuart and their children were Clara and Elbert LeSueur), Nancy A. (born June 14, 1859), Elizabeth "Eliza" Alice (married Johnathon Howery), and Flora Ann (married Galusha A. Van Fleet).

To find out more about Joan Crawford (Lucille Fay LeSueur), I contacted the Huguenot Society of the Founders of Manakin in the Colony of Virginia. After that, I learned additional information from the Texas Historical Society. And finally, I spoke with Polly Dixon of Houston, Texas. Polly is a descendant of David LeSueur, and her knowledge about the LeSueur family is extensive.

Joan Crawford's parents were Thomas E. LeSueur and Anna Belle Johnson LeSueur. Thomas's parents (and Joan Crawford's grandparents) were James Howell LeSueur and Permelia D. "Amelia" James LeSueur. James Howell and Permelia LeSueur are not buried in Floyd County, nor are James Howell LeSueur's parents. James Howell and Permelia LeSueur are buried in Davidson County, Tennessee. Joan Crawford's father, Thomas E. LeSueur, died in 1938 and is buried in Abilene, Texas. (His tombstone has Thomas L. LeSueur but, according to Polly Dixon, it should be Thomas E. LeSueur.)

With her French Huguenot ancestry, Joan Crawford does have a small connection to Floyd County, but we have to go back several generations to explain it. It seems that David LeSueur came from England as a single man. The name of the ship and the date of his arrival are unknown. The first record of David LeSueur in King William Parish, Virginia, shows him there in 1724. He married Elizabeth Morrell/Morrill, daughter of French Huguenot William Morrell/Morrill. They had a daughter, but apparently both mother and child had died by 1730. About 1732–1733, David LeSueur married his second wife, Elizabeth Chastain, daughter of Pierre Chastain and Anne Soblet. David LeSueur and Elizabeth Chastain LeSueur had eleven children, including sons Martell and Chastain. Joan Crawford descends from the Chastain LeSueur line and Moseby LeSueur of Floyd County descends from the Martell LeSueur line.

To explain further about Moseby LeSueur (and the Floyd County line), Moseby married Elizabeth Bacon of Franklin County and they were the parents of the later Martell, who is buried at Camp Creek Cemetery. They were also the parents of James William LeSueur. (James William LeSueur married Nancy Caroline Yearout. One of their children was named Eliza and she married James Asa Sowers.) It is the later Martell LeSueur and his mother, Catherine Goodykoontz LeSueur, who are buried beside each other at Camp Creek Cemetery in Floyd County. (This Martell LeSueur was named for his grandfather Martell LeSueur, son of David LeSueur and Elizabeth Chastain. As noted above, Martell and his mother Catherine are not the direct ancestors of Lucille Fay LeSueur, aka Joan Crawford.)

To summarize, there is a strong French connection in Floyd County, and some people here are direct descendants of Moseby LeSueur, Jacques Bilbaud, and others. Joan Crawford's grandparents are not buried at Camp Creek Cemetery, nor are they from Floyd County. Joan Crawford does have ties to Floyd County—indirectly.

According to Effie Brown, Joan Crawford paid a visit to Floyd County in the late 1950s. Effie, a school principal at the time, was at the school board office in the courthouse for a meeting. While there, she and others saw a black limousine pull up out front. Evidently, Joan Crawford stopped at the courthouse that day to inquire about the location of Camp Creek Cemetery. Effie assumed she was looking for information on the LeSueur family.

Thinking back to the early 1700s, it is interesting to me that my ancestor (Jacques/James Bilbaud) would have been a neighbor of David LeSueur and Elizabeth Chastain LeSueur in Manakin Town and that they would have known one another.

In 2007, Virginia will celebrate the 400th anniversary of the settlement of Jamestown. As part of that anniversary, it is worth noting that the LeSueurs, Bilbauds, and others from France came through Jamestown on their way to Manakin over 300 years ago. They and their offspring, went on to help settle other parts of America, including Floyd County.

For years now, I've been trying to trace my ancestors across the Atlantic to Europe, with little success. Only recently have I learned about the French connection—not only to my family, but also to Floyd County. This has made me interested in learning more about the French Huguenots and the resources available for research. One of the best sources of information is the Huguenot Society at Midlothian, Virginia. The Society's phone number is (804) 794-5702 and the address is 981 Huguenot Trail, Midlothian, Virginia 23113. The Society's web site is www.huguenot-manakin.org.

Based on Jean's article published in the Floyd Press *on April 27, 2006*

Chapter 21

Three Men Named John Floyd

Years ago, local history was part of our fourth grade curriculum in Floyd County and we had a Virginia history textbook that we studied all year. I don't remember many details from my history lessons back then, but a few facts, such as Jamestown 1607, have stuck with me. I also remember our teacher telling us that Floyd County and the town of Floyd were named for John Floyd, a Virginia governor. Who was this man, I wondered.

Until recently, I had no idea that there were actually *three* John Floyds (father, son, and grandson—numbers 1, 2, and 3). I would learn that later and be able to pick out the second John Floyd as the one who was Floyd County's namesake.

It was through a project of the Floyd County Historical Society that the second John Floyd's name surfaced again. To help commemorate Floyd County's 175th anniversary year (in 2006), John Floyd's photograph served as a cachet on specially prepared envelopes that were made available to the public.

The first John Floyd was born in 1751 in Amherst County, Virginia, to William Floyd and Abidiah Davis Floyd. William had emigrated from Wales to the eastern shore of Virginia in the early 1700s and had married Abidiah Davis, whose father was Welsh and mother was Native American.

Although the first John Floyd lived only to age thirty-two, he accomplished more than most people ever do. Among other things, he taught school and worked in Colonel William Preston's surveying office in Botetourt County. When Colonel Preston became owner of Smithfield Plantation (near Blacksburg) and moved his family there, John Floyd was brought along, too—as was Jane Buchanan, who had recently lost her family.

In time, the first John Floyd became engaged to Jane Buchanan, but soon after Colonel Preston sent him on two missions. The first was to the Kentucky frontier to do surveying. After that, John Floyd was put in command of a schooner as a privateer during the Revolutionary War. While sailing home, the British captured his ship, and he ended up in Dartmouth Prison in England.

He later escaped from prison and returned home to find he had been given up for dead. His fiancée, Jane Buchanan, had become engaged to another man. She quickly broke off the engagement and married John Floyd. They ended up living in Kentucky on land he had surveyed. John and Jane Buchanan Floyd had two young children and another on the way when Indians killed him. The unborn child would be the second John Floyd, the man for whom Floyd County and the town of Floyd would later be named.

The second John Floyd was born on April 23, 1783, ten days after his father died. A year later, Jane Buchanan Floyd married Alexander Breckenridge. According to sources I've read, that union was not happy, and it must have been a hard childhood for John Floyd, especially since his guardian and step uncle (General Robert Breckenridge) made life very hard for him.

After some precarious beginnings that left the second John Floyd destitute and sick, he ended up studying medicine under a Louisville doctor. He also married Latitia Preston, daughter of William Preston, owner of Smithfield Plantation.

In April 1806, the second John Floyd graduated from the University of Pennsylvania as a Doctor of Medicine. He practiced medicine in Lexington and Newbern, Virginia, and later in Pulaski, where he and his family lived at "Thorn Hill Farm," land his wife had inherited from the Preston family. From all accounts, Dr. Floyd was beloved by his patients.

During the War of 1812, Dr. Floyd volunteered his services and became a Major. After that, he became involved in politics and served one term in the Virginia General Assembly. In 1817, he was elected to the U.S. Congress, representing the Abingdon district, and served for twelve years. After a brief retirement, he went on to be elected for two terms as governor of Virginia (1830–1834).

Dr. Floyd was greatly admired by people in Floyd County. He had strong beliefs and was not willing to compromise them for political gain. As a congressman, his principles caused conflict between him and President Andrew Jackson. Also as a congressman, Dr. Floyd pushed hard for Manifest Destiny. He realized the great value of the Northwest and wanted the U.S. to annex the Oregon territory.

In many ways, Dr. Floyd's beliefs and thinking were ahead of the times. His ideas were innovative, and his strong convictions about slavery led him to attempt to get it gradually abolished in Virginia. His efforts were stymied, though, for lawmakers in the eastern part of the state refused to discuss the matter.

On April 16, 1833, while he was governor, he made the following prophetic statement: "I do believe these United States will be shaken to pieces in a few years and deluged with blood purely because the southern states tolerate slavery and the north wishes to destroy this property that they may govern by a majority in Congress and make the entire south subservient to their views."

Dr. Floyd died on August 16, 1837, at age fifty-four and is buried in Monroe County, West Virginia. He and his wife had twelve children during their happy marriage. They named one of them John Buchanan Floyd, who became the third John Floyd.

This third John Floyd spent much of his life in the Pulaski area and practiced law. He served two terms in the Virginia State Legislature and, in 1849, became Governor of Virginia. Later he was Secretary of War under President Buchanan. During the Civil War, he reached the rank of brigadier general.

All three of the John Floyds were impressive men, both in appearance and in deed, and I am pleased Floyd County takes its name from one of them. Years ago, our town was called Jacksonville, but on January 23, 1896, its name was changed to Floyd—in honor of the second John Floyd, who was a governor, physician, and U.S. congressman. Most of all, I admire this John Floyd for his unwillingness to compromise beliefs for political gain.

(Information for this chapter was obtained from several sources, including an article written by Lloyd Mathews in 2000 titled "The Three John Floyds." That article by Lloyd Mathews appeared in the *Journal of the New River Historical Society*, volume 13, number 1.)

Based on Jean's article published in the Floyd Press *on October 20, 2005*

The Floyd County Historical Society Museum opened for the first time in the Ridgemont building on May 29, 2010. It is on North Locust Street, across from Schoolhouse Fabrics. Exhibits are on the first floor of the building and the office and archives are on the second floor. The Ridgemont, built in 1913 for Dr. Martin Luther Dalton, was the first hospital in Floyd County. In later years, the building was the home of educator Marie Williams. Marie was a charter member of the Historical Society, which was organized in 1976. The Society is incorporated and has a 501 (3) (c) designation.

Chapter 22

Floyd County: Description and History

The county of Floyd officially began in 1831, but there is much history of the Floyd plateau prior to that time. In fact, this part of the Blue Ridge has some of the oldest history on earth, geologically, and much about the past may be learned from studying the rock formations and minerals. Many varieties of minerals are found in the county and, at one time, companies here mined copper, iron, nickel, and arsenic.

The elevation of Floyd County is approximately 2,500 feet above sea level, and the highest point is Buffalo Knob at 3,971 feet. All water within the county originates within the county, and no water from other places flows into the county. A watershed divide goes through the county, wherein part of the county's rainfall and streams eventually ends up at the Atlantic Ocean, and the rest of the water ends up at the Gulf of Mexico.

Historically, we know that many Native Americans were once in this area, traveling through to hunt and gather food. Archaeologists tell us they also raised crops and lived here at times, especially during the Woodland period (1200 BC to AD 1600).

The Cherokee owned a tract of land in western Virginia that included the southern part of Floyd County. On October 14, 1768, it was ceded to England by a treaty signed by John Stuart, British Superintendent of Indian Affairs. (Additional information about Native American history of the Floyd County area is in Chapter 25 of this book.)

During the 18th and 19th centuries and earlier, people in the Blue Ridge depended on the land for sustenance and healing. Wild animals were plentiful, as were medicinal plants that could be used to treat most ailments except for smallpox. Smallpox wasn't common in this area, but it was greatly feared since people knew of no herb to cure it. Boneset was an important herb in the 1800s and was especially helpful in treating symptoms of pneumonia, the most frequent killer in the mountains.

This part of the state was settled predominantly by the Scots-Irish, Germans, English, Welsh, and French—or by their descendants. Many of those immigrants had left Europe because of religious persecution. Those early explorers and settlers came to this area on foot or on horseback, and some came part of the way in flat boats called bateaux. Later on, settlers came in wagons pulled by horses or oxen.

The settlers traveled from Jamestown and other points east. They also came from the north from such places as Pennsylvania, Maryland, and northern Virginia. Those from the north usually came down the "Great Wagon Road" (now Route 11) through the Valley of Virginia. Once they were at Big Lick (now Roanoke), some veered southeast on the Carolina Road and followed it to what is now Franklin County and beyond.

Others coming down the Wagon Road from the north to Big Lick veered southwest of the mountain ahead and traveled toward what are now Shawsville and Christiansburg. Whether in current Franklin County or current Shawsville, some of those travelers climbed the mountain to what is now the Floyd County plateau.

We refer to the Wagon Road and Carolina Road as "roads," but most of those routes must have been quite primitive by today's standards, and it must have been difficult to cross creeks and rivers.

Since many of those early settlers, and their ancestors, came from a history of persecution in Europe, it is no wonder that many were willing to take up arms during the Revolutionary War or support the war in other ways. Some colonists, though, sympathized with England. A number of people living in Floyd County today have ancestors who fought in the Revolutionary War. Some are buried at Pine Creek Cemetery in Floyd County.

Land grants were awarded to early explorers and settlers—first to settlers by the king of England and later to some soldiers for serving in the Revolutionary War. After the war, Buffalo Mountain was part of a much larger tract of land known as Lee's Order. It is believed that this tract was a grant made to an ancestor of Charles Carter Lee. We do know that Charles Carter Lee lived on that property at one time.

As the highest point in Floyd County, Buffalo Knob has weather conditions specific unto itself. According to the Buffalo's caretaker (the Department of Conservation and Recreation), "the combination of high elevation, wind-exposed openings at the summit, and magnesium-rich soils, make [sic] Buffalo Mountain unlike any other place in the Commonwealth." Sub-alpine, prairie, and other significant natural communities are part of the 1,000-acre preserve, and rare plant and animal species can be found in the area.

A Presbyterian preacher named Robert (Bob) Childress came to Buffalo Mountain in 1926. He had grown up in nearby Patrick County, and the story of him and the six rock churches that he and the church congregations built is well known. The rock churches are still standing today in the Floyd–Patrick–Carroll County area, not far from the Blue Ridge Parkway.

Floyd County once had many thriving villages and communities. Among them were Check, Locust Grove, Copper Hill, Copper Valley, Willis, Indian Valley, Alum Ridge, Pizarro, Terrys Fork, Lilac, Turtle Rock, Smart, Huffville, Quartz Hill, and Burks Fork. Some (like Indian Valley, Check, and Willis) still have their own school, post office, and stores. Others, like Lilac and Turtle Rock, are barely remembered. Villages during the 1800s and early 1900s were fairly self-sufficient. Most had a post office, school, church, store, and mill. The village focus continued as long as roads were bad and cars were not readily owned.

The Floyd plateau was once part of Orange County (1734–1745) and then part of Augusta County (1745–1770). Then the Floyd plateau was part of Botetourt County (1770–1772) and, after that, it was part of Fincastle County (1772–1777). From 1777 to 1831, the Floyd area was part of Montgomery County.

On January 15, 1831, Floyd became its own county through an Act of the General Assembly of Virginia. Later on (in 1873, according to historian and researcher Gertrude Mann), a strip of land from Franklin County was annexed to Floyd County.

When Floyd became its own county, it was among the most populated counties in the area. After disagreement and indecision on where to build the courthouse, the justices finally decided on a compromise. The courthouse would be built in the center of the county, halfway between the two disputed sites. Donating land for the county seat were three men already living there in town: John Kitterman, Abraham Phlegar, and Manasseh Tise. All were of German descent.

The county seat was called Jacksonville (after President Andrew Jackson), but later, in 1896, the name of the county seat was changed to Floyd. The post office in those days was referred to as Floyd Court House. Both the county and the town were named for John Floyd, Virginia's governor from 1830 to 1834.

The first Floyd County courthouse was completed in 1834. It was not built very well, so the well-known builder, Henry Dillon, built a second courthouse on the site in 1851. That second courthouse served county residents for 100 years and then was replaced in 1951 by the current building.

When the county was organized in 1831, ten justices were appointed. Besides court duties, they also had responsibilities similar to today's board of supervisors. One big difference was that for almost twenty years, they continued re-appointing themselves.

With a population of about 6,000, Floyd County was a busy farm community during the 1850s, and chestnuts were an important part of the local economy. Historian Marguerite Tise used to talk about the town of Jacksonville. She said it was a thriving town during the mid-1800s, a crossroads with much coming and going. She said people often stopped in town for food, lodging, and other services that served both local people and travelers. A good number of ministers and teachers worked in the town. All went reasonably well in the county until the Civil War and the Reconstruction period that followed.

Many from Floyd County and the surrounding areas fought and died for the Confederate side in the Civil War. Still, some others were Union sympathizers. Dr. Amos Wood's book (*Floyd County: A History of Its People and Places*, 1981) devotes many pages to listing local Civil War soldiers. Dr. C. M. Stigleman was captain of Company A of the 24th infantry. His company, also known as the "Floyd Rifles," was the first company to be formed in the county, and he took his men into service in May of 1861. From what I've read and been told, people in the mountains here generally wanted the Union preserved, but they felt they had to protect their land. A few landowners had slaves, but most people in the county did not.

According to an article written by Marguerite Tise (*Journal of New River Historical Society*, 1995, volume 8), $10,000 was appropriated by the local Court at the beginning of the Civil War to outfit and equip seven volunteer companies in Floyd County. Money was also raised to purchase corn and wheat for families at home, and provision was made for distribution of salt. Fabric was purchased from Bonsacks Woolen Mill (on Beaver Creek), and uniforms were made locally. Soldiers had to furnish their own shoes and firearms. Still, the uniforms were not always adequate, or furnished. And, by the end of the war, shoes were worn out and clothing was often in tatters.

Under General George Stoneman's command, Union troops invaded Floyd County near the end of the war on April 3, 1865. They camped overnight in town and demanded or stole food, horses, and other supplies. The next day, they headed toward Christiansburg on what is now Old Christiansburg Pike/Route 615. Floyd County is a member of the "Virginia Civil War Trails."

No Civil War battles were fought in Floyd County, but many soldiers from here fought and died elsewhere during the Civil War. Their families back home often faced dangers or sickness, too. Besides caring for the home and family, those at home had to keep the farm going. Soldiers sometimes came home to help with the crops and then went back to the front. Some deserted their battalions entirely.

According to Marguerite Tise, Floyd County was growing again by the early 1900s. Every community had a school, church, post office, store, and mill. The county was a crossroads, and the town of Floyd was a bustling place with an assortment of stores, craftsmen, hotels, and places to eat. The town even had a hospital, ice-cream parlor, furniture store, and telephone service. Since 1896, the town had steam-powered electricity, but by 1922, town electricity was tied into a grid, with electric power coming from elsewhere. However, some outlying areas of Floyd County did not receive electricity until the late 1940s. Generally, people in remote areas had telephone service before they had electricity. Since 1854, Floyd County has had a newspaper for much of that time.

The quality of schools varied during the 1800s, but many communities had one- and two-room schools at that time. Some of those small schools, depending on the teacher, provided a good education. There was also a very fine school in the town of Floyd called the Oxford Academy. It was a private preparatory school started in 1875 by Rev. John Kellogg Harris and his wife Cloe Bigelow Harris. The school, serving both elementary and secondary students, closed in 1904. Years later, the Oxford Academy's two classrooms were used for a short time by the Floyd County Public Schools.

Mission schools were organized in the Floyd County area during the early 1900s by workers in the Presbyterian and Methodist churches. Dr. R. Gamble See was very involved in getting the Presbyterian mission schools started. Known as the Harris Mountain Schools (named in memory of John Kellogg Harris), two of those mission schools were located at Buffalo Mountain and at Cannaday School. In addition to serving as pastor and a leader of the Harris Mountain mission schools, Dr. See also organized the county's first chapter of the American Red Cross and the county's first Boy Scout troop. Dr. See served the Floyd community for over fifty years.

Eventually, a law was passed in Virginia that required *public* schools to be operational in each county of the state by 1876. Dr. C. M. Stigleman, Floyd County's first superintendent of schools, and other forward-looking persons made sure Floyd County met that 1876 deadline. By 1900, there were over 100 small public schools in Floyd County. Some of those one- and two-room schools are still standing. By 1911, there was a four-year high school in the town of Floyd—the first Floyd High School. That structure, built by Irishman Henry Dillon, still stands in Floyd and is now the home of Schoolhouse Fabrics.

So Floyd County, a thriving place in the later 1800s, was also doing pretty well in 1900. That gradually changed. In the 1920s and later, growth slowed down and the population started declining. Some men went to West Virginia to work in the mines or to other places. People in Floyd County were disappointed that the anticipated railroad was never built in the county. The closest railroad stations were at Cambria, Shawsville, and Ferrum.

Another big blow to the economy and the spirit of the people was the blight of the American chestnut in the first decades of the twentieth century. At one time, the American chestnut made up half of the hardwood forests in the Blue Ridge, and the wood was almost ideal for its many uses. The people here sold chestnuts at local stores and in nearby towns. They also shipped chestnuts by rail to Richmond, Baltimore, Philadelphia, New York City, and other places. It was a wonderful tree with many uses, and the local economy depended on it.

An Asian fungus caused the chestnut blight, which was first detected in the United States in 1904 at the Bronx Zoo in New York. Not long after that, it started making its way through the Appalachian forests. The last crop of chestnuts in the Floyd area was in 1922, according to historian Max Thomas. Ultimately, in the United States, the blight caused the death of about 3.5 billion chestnut trees in the first forty years of the 20th century.

Along with people going out of county for jobs and shopping, there had been an ongoing trend within the county for consolidation — consolidation of schools, churches, post offices, and stores. This trend took away from each community. Many community stores, post offices, schools, and churches closed. Children started riding the school bus to distant, larger schools. Some children had to get on the bus before daybreak (as they still do) and ride for over an hour. People in outlying areas especially disliked consolidation and mourned the loss and convenience of the community unit. Still, people tried to stay close to their neighbors and, even today, neighbors can be counted on to help one another in time of need.

The decline in population had started years before, but out-migration was especially high during the 1960s and 1970s. This change occurred partly because roads were better and most people had cars. But local jobs were hard to come by, and many people, by necessity, commuted out of county to work. They worked at such places as the Radford Arsenal, the elastic plant in Woolwine, Bassett Furniture, General Electric (GE) in Salem, a paint factory in Henry, Hubble Oil in Christiansburg, Rowe Furniture in Roanoke, a hosiery factory in Hillsville, and Clark Oil and a lumber factory, both in Stuart. People from Floyd County also commuted to jobs at colleges and universities and to jobs in stores and hospitals.

Back in the 1960s and 1970s, employers often spoke about the strong work ethic of Floyd County commuters, according to Max Thomas. Employers said workers from Floyd could always be counted on to be at work on time, even in bad weather.

Others during the 1960s and 1970s left the county entirely—heading off to distant places. They wrote letters to their families back home and were often homesick. They called home on the phone and returned for visits as often as they could. Regardless of the weather, they tried to get home for Christmas.

After the 1970s, the population and economy of Floyd County gradually improved, and by 2006, census reports showed that Floyd County was the fastest growing county in the New River Valley.

One thing that brought jobs to the Floyd County area during the 1930s and 1940s was the building of the Blue Ridge Parkway—beginning September 11, 1935. The state was given the task of acquiring right-of-ways for the Parkway or purchasing the land outright. The federal government was responsible for building the road.

At first, local people thought it was wonderful that the government was building them such a good road. Soon, though, they began to recognize the realities of this new road. (See Chapter 16 for more detail.) Years later, some of those same farmers, by then in their eighties and nineties, came to appreciate the beautiful road—thirty-one miles of which are in Floyd County.

Originally, the Appalachian Trail went through Floyd County—along the same route the Parkway later followed. In 1954, some 160 miles of the Trail were moved west to the Giles County area. Today, at The Saddle Overlook on the Blue Ridge Parkway, there is a short walking trail that goes up to one of the original Appalachian Trail log shelters.

A brief written history could never include all of the relevant names, facts, stories, or events relating to a description of Floyd County, its people, and its history. It would take volumes to begin to accomplish that. But even a short summary can provide motivation for wanting to learn more. To help with that learning, stop by the Floyd County Historical Society's Museum, across from Schoolhouse Fabrics on Locust Street.

Also, read Robley Evans's autobiography *A Sailor's Log* to see how a little boy from Floyd went on to world fame in the 1800s. Seek out information on the J.E.B. Stuart family and their connection to Floyd. And find out about Nathaniel Henry, Patrick Henry's son who worked and died in Floyd County. Also find out about local teacher

Annie Smith and the 1800s legend that connects her romantically to Edgar Allen Poe. Seek out information on Curtis Turner, a Floyd native who first learned to drive on Floyd County roads and went on to win eighteen Grand National NASCAR races. Or ask about Randall Hylton, the famous singer, songwriter, and guitar player from Floyd, who received the Bluegrass Music Songwriter of the Year award.

Based on Jean's article published in the Floyd Press *on January 12, 2006*

This drum, believed to have been used by Floyd County drummer Caleb Sowers in the Civil War, is owned by the Floyd County Historical Society and is on display at the Society's Museum. Prior to the Civil War, the drum was used by the 130th regiment of the 26th brigade, 5th Division, Virginia Militia.

Chapter 23

Pilgrimage to Woods Gap

It is April 29, 2006, and I am on my way to Woods Gap Cemetery in the Haycock Mountain area, just across the Floyd County line in Patrick. I am hoping to find the grave of Richard "Dickey" Wood, who is buried there beside his four wives. I want to see the place where he lived and died and the tombstone marking five graves. He was my great great great great grandpa on my mother's side, and I have heard of him and this place all of my life.

It is a beautiful spring day in the woods, and wild strawberries are blooming along the edges, as are trillium, white and purple violets, and fire pinks. Although I am making this pilgrimage with a group of people, I am alone with my thoughts as I think back to the 1800s when Dickey Wood lived here.

We make our way through the woods along an up-and-down path, crossing a small creek before our last climb to the cemetery clearing. Like many old-time graveyards, this one is on a hill. I am impressed with its tidy appearance and am surprised at its rather large size for such a remote place. Tombstones bear such surnames as McAlexander, Haynes, Griffith, Boyd, Cannaday, DeHart, and Cockram—and of course Wood. Some graves are marked with crude stones and have no inscriptions.

Some descendants of Richard "Dickey" Wood made a trip to the Woods Gap Cemetery near Haycock Mountain on April 29, 2006. In this picture, they are gathered around Dickey Wood's tombstone where he is buried beside each of his four wives: Rachel Cockram, Fannie Brammer, Elizabeth DeHart, and Lucy Via.

The Dickey Wood monument is about five feet tall and has a solid, heavy look. It is wide at the bottom and tapered toward the top. It has a smooth light gray cement base with dark cemented rocks carefully placed above. Still higher is another light cement section and each side of that part contains an inscription about one of his four wives and a listing of children. Small quartzite rocks are included on the monument sides—one rock for each child from that specific marriage. Besides a total of 18 children, I understand Dickey Wood had 108 grandchildren.

The etched inscription on the monument table reads, "Pioneer of Wood's Gap (1772–1856) Richard Wood (Father Dickey)."

The above dates are different from the ones most researchers give for Dickey Wood. Most use 1769 for his date of birth and 1859 for his date of death—giving him a life span of ninety years. Regardless, he was born before the Revolutionary War and died just before the Civil War started.

I understand Dickey Wood arranged his burial site so that a wife is buried on either side of him, as well as one at his head and one at his feet.

His first wife was Rachel Cockram Wood, who died December 13, 1823. Eight quartzite stones represent their eight children: Henry, German, Alexander, Peter, John Richard, Jeremiah, Edward, and Ann. I descend from John Richard Wood of the Rachel Cockram line.

Dickey Wood's second wife was Fannie Brammer Wood, who died on August 30, 1830. They had no children.

His third wife was Elizabeth DeHart Wood, who died on October 26, 1838. They had four children: Preston, Jackson, Dollie, and Lucinda.

His fourth wife was Lucy Via Wood, who died about 1851. They had six children: Fred, Byrdine, George, Nancy, Ruth, and Matilda. Although Dickey Wood would have been almost eighty, I understand he traveled about twenty miles to Stuart (once called Taylorsville) to record her death.

On May 30, 1935, the monument was dedicated and many descendants came for a reunion, picnic, and program. As a symbolic gesture, each brought soil from where he or she lived to spread on the graves. Barbara Thomas Spangler, granddaughter of Jefferson Pinkard Wood, remembers carrying a vase of dirt to the grave that day. Several reunions followed the first, and Betty Wood Getgood, granddaughter of Greenville Wood, said her father attended one of those reunions. His name was Greenville Darius Wood, Jr.

As we leave the cemetery, we walk down the hill to spend time at

Dickey Wood's homeplace—now a falling down two-story building with two soapstone chimneys and a stone foundation still in place. It is a most tranquil setting in a valley near a creek. It must have been a very sheltered place out of the wind, where spring would have come early. Although not blooming, yucca, day lilies, and daffodils are growing near the house. I have no idea if some of them are from Dickey Wood's time; other people have lived here since. For sure, the flora would have been different back then because the American chestnut would have made up much of the forest. Today, various other hardwood species fill in the space, and the setting belongs to pheasants and other wildlife.

During the 1930s, WPA (Works Progress Administration) workers documented buildings, cemeteries, and other places of interest. WPA worker Mae Weeks Harris recorded information about the Dickey Wood home and cemetery. She said the very narrow rough road to Dickey Wood's homeplace wound up the mountain through what is called "Low Gap" and that it was about one-half mile from Woods Gap. She dated the original family home as 1836 and described it as being built in a hollow between ridges of the Haycock Mountain. She said the house had two large rooms on the first floor and two loft rooms above. She said that one of the chimneys and a fireplace were the only original parts of the Dickey Wood house.

Mae Weeks Harris said that, in time, the original house was torn down and a duplicate with the same features was built on the original foundation. The original rock chimney on the east end of the house is quite massive—wide at the bottom and less wide near the top. The original fireplace that is part of that chimney structure is unusually wide, too. Down below the house by the creek are the remnants of an old springhouse. The WPA worker wrote about the stone wall of the springhouse that was still standing when she saw it over seventy years ago. Only part of the springhouse foundation remains today.

I doubt if I could find this place again but will always remember this day. As we leave the old house, I try to imagine what it was like here in the mid-1800s and want to know more. With all those children, how self-sufficient were they? The WPA worker saw apple trees growing on the hillside when she was here. I wonder if any of them are still growing and, if so, when they were planted.

Certainly, the Wood family must have had a vegetable garden, but what about farming on this mountainside? Did they clear trees in order to grow crops and raise farm animals? Or were they able to get most of their sustenance from the chestnuts, wild game, fruit trees, berries, fox grapes, and other wild bounty? Did they have oxen to help with work at home and to pull a wagon? I also wonder about accidents and disease and how the family coped. Was it as isolated as I imagine, or were there other families close by?

Early records show that John Wood, Dickey's father, had once owned property where Dickey and his family lived. John Wood continued to live nearby at the foot of the mountain and is supposed to be buried there. While John Wood was still living, I imagine he and Dickey and their families visited back and forth and helped one another.

And what of the old Woods Gap Road that used to make its way up the mountain by way of Dickey Wood's land and on to Floyd Court House? Was there much coming and going on that road, or was it rare to see a traveler? No doubt, an unpaved, steep mountain road like Woods Gap would have, at times, been filled with deep ruts, mud, and snow.

Theirs had to have been a hard life, but some men and women here still lived to be ninety or older at that time. In some ways, they were probably healthier than we are today—maybe happier, too.

Based on Jean's article published in the Floyd Press *on October 26, 2006*

Chapter 24

Jefferson Pinkard Wood and His Kin

My great grandpa on my mother's side was the oldest person I knew back then. His name was Jefferson Pinkard Wood, but he signed his name "J. P. Wood." Some people called him "Pink." He had a heavy mustache, and I can still picture him at his home on Route 682 (Paradise Lane) near the Blue Ridge Parkway.

Jefferson Pinkard Wood (J. P.) in his later years at his home

Seen here are J. P. and Sarah Belinda Brammer Wood, on right, and daughter Gertrude and son-in-law, Allen Vest in buggy. J. P. and Sarah Brammer Wood were the parents of Stanton, Dora, Ed, Fred, Gertrude, and Ethel.

J. P. Wood was six feet tall and pictures from the 1930s show him dressed in a three-piece suit with a pocket watch. He outlived my great grandma, Sarah Belinda Brammer, by twenty-four years. He died on December 10, 1955, at age ninety-seven. He and Sarah are buried at Harvestwood Cemetery. They had six children: Stanton Hillsman Wood, Dora Alice Wood Turner (my maternal grandma), John Edgar Wood, Benjamin Frederick Wood, Laura Gertrude Wood Vest, and Judith Ethel Wood Thomas.

This photo, made on July 22, 1928, is of J. P. and Sarah Wood's grandchildren.
On ground in front, from left: Mildred Turner, and Evelyn Wood
Row two: Lera Lois Wood, Bobby Wood, and David Vest
Row three: Margaret Wood, Frederick Wood, Vera Alta Wood, Vernon Wood, Mary Wood, Elbert Turner, and Jimmy Wood
Row four: Clara Turner, Ralph Turner, Thelma Turner, and Bernice Vest
Missing from the photo are Ethel Wood Thomas's children (Barbara, Rodney, and Richard) who were not yet born.

J. P. Wood was a justice of the peace in Floyd County and tried cases for over forty years, often in his front yard. His granddaughter, Clara Turner Thomas (my mother), who lived just down the road with her family, sometimes listened in on his court cases. She said people came "from far and near to have their disputes settled." She said he was mostly self-educated and read the Bible, newspaper, and law books. He also studied the dictionary. She remembered his big law books lined up on the mantle above the fireplace in his house.

Besides farming and serving as a justice of the peace, he was a good carpenter and rebuilt the family home after it burned down about 1937. My mother said he "made wooden caskets and kept extras on hand. He lined them with white cloth padded with cotton. . . . He covered adult caskets with black cloth and children's with white cloth."

J. P. Wood was born in Patrick County but lived most of his life across the line in Floyd County. He was the oldest of seven brothers, and their parents were Richard Johnson Wood and Judith Anne

Shortt. Richard Johnson Wood was a militia captain in Patrick County before the Civil War and volunteered as a private once the war started—serving in Company D of the 51st Regiment of the Virginia Infantry. He and his wife, Judith, are buried at the cemetery at County Line Church. Judith had previously donated land for that church and cemetery.

Judith Shortt (Feb. 17, 1834–Aug. 30, 1899) and Richard Johnson Wood (Oct. 27, 1828–Dec. 20, 1917) were the parents of seven sons and two daughters.

Richard Johnson Wood was born in 1828 and died in 1917. His wife Judith Anne Shortt was born in 1834 and died in 1899. Their first-born children were two daughters, Susan Emeline Wood (1853–1858) and Rachel Elvira Wood (1855–1858). Jefferson Pinkard Wood (1858–1955) was the oldest of the seven brothers. Other sons, in order of birth, were Daniel Hillsman Wood (1860–1954), George Bunyan Wood (1863–1930), Greenville Darius Wood (1866–1943), Amos DeRussia Wood (1869–1942), Sparrel Asa Wood (1873–1959), and Doc Robertson Wood (1877–1952).

To take the lineage back further, Richard Johnson Wood was the son of John Richard Wood (1799–1886) and Lucinda DeHart (1797–1853). John Richard Wood was the son of Richard "Dickey" Wood (1769–1859) and Rachel Cockram (died December 13, 1823). Richard "Dickey" Wood was the son of John Wood (born about 1745) and Nellie _____ (surname unknown). And John Wood was the son of Stephen Wood (believed to have been born between 1700 and

1720 and died after 1781, the date of his will) and Ann Johnson of Lunenburg.

Based on Jean's article published in the Floyd Press *on October 26, 2006*

Pictured are six of the sons of Richard Johnson and Judith Anne Shortt Wood:
From left, Jefferson Pinkard Wood, Daniel Hillsman Wood, Greenville Darius Wood, Amos DeRussia Wood, Sparrel Asa Wood, and Doc Robertson Wood. Another son, George Bunyan Wood, may have already died when the photo was taken.

This is George Wood and his wife, Betty Brammer Wood. George was one of the sons of Richard and Judith Shortt Wood. George and J. P. Wood (brothers) married sisters, Betty and Sarah Belinda Brammer, respectively.

Chapter 25

Floyd County and Native Americans

As a kid on the farm, I usually left my shoes in the house and went barefooted in the summer. Other farm kids in this area did, too. Going without shoes had its challenges, though, and I was always careful to watch my step, lest I stump my toe, step on a cow paddy, or run into briars or poison ivy. I watched for snakes, too. Looking down at the ground the way I did, I would always be on the lookout for something interesting: a quartz crystal, a jack-in-the-pulpit, a butterfly chrysalis, a newt, or something else.

One of my biggest finds would be an occasional Native American arrowhead, grinding stone, or other sculpted rock. "The old-timers never said much about those early people," said my dad, "but we know a little about them. We know about them from the stone artifacts they left on these high ridges that we always assumed were their hunting grounds."

Old people talked about peach trees planted by Native Americans, and they talked about the lack of tree stumps on these high ridges. I wonder if native people here burned parts of the forest to plant corn and other vegetables and to create meadows to attract game. The Tutelo and some other native people were known for that practice.

My dad said early settlers planted corn in an unusual way that was thought to be copied from Native American methods. By necessity in steep places, they merely dug holes on the side of the mountain and put several grains of corn in each hole.

Besides these stories, he always heard that in the late 1700s or early 1800s, there was a tribe of about fifty Indians that fled to the Otter Creek area in Patrick County, where they lived and got along with local settlers. My dad assumed they traded such things as animal skins with the settlers in exchange for such things as cloth and steel tools. And the settlers would have learned about herbs and healing from them.

My dad said his grandma, Delilah Ann Moran Vest, knew about medicinal plants used by Native Americans. When she was a girl living at the foot of the mountain near the Franklin–Patrick County line, she and her mother learned about native healing from an Indian woman. I wonder if that woman was a descendant of the Otter Creek Indians.

In time, Delilah married Samuel Anderson Vest and they lived in the Check area of Floyd County. Besides raising a large family, she worked without pay as a mountain nurse, providing good nursing care and herbal remedies she had learned about years before. She often gave her patients hot boneset tea. She used other plants, as well, and always reserved part of her garden for growing medicinal herbs.

Native Americans and European Settlers

As a child, I would follow my dad around our mountain farm, and sometimes we'd look down the mountain toward Franklin and Patrick Counties—a shear drop-off and total wilderness, even today—and imagine native people coming here. Surely they would have been drawn to our remote area and its variety and abundance of plant and animal life. It would have been a perfect arrangement: camp or live on fertile river bottom land at the foot of the mountain and come to our high plateau for hunting, gathering, and raising corn.

The natives could have come to this area from any direction, but some routes are especially worth considering. From our studies of history, we know about an early north–south route beginning in what is now Philadelphia. Originally known as the Great Warrior Path, it was later called the Great Wagon Road and was used by early settlers. We now know it as Route 11—a road I use today to avoid driving on Interstate 81.

In early times, the Iroquois controlled the northern part of the Warrior Path and the Cherokee controlled the southern part. Native Americans used it when they traveled through the Shenandoah Valley to hunting and trading sites as well as when they waged war on other tribes. "Shenandoah" is a Native American word that means deer. Wildlife would have been plentiful in the deer valley back then.

Once the European settlers started traveling that road, conflicts became a problem for all. In time, though, the English gained control of the road and valley. That occurred officially in 1744 when the Treaty of Lancaster was signed between the English and Six Nations (Iroquois). After that, even more settlers traveled the Great Wagon Road.

As people came to this part of Virginia from the north and east, they built log cabins in Big Lick (now Roanoke), in the current Rocky Mount–Ferrum area, and in the current Shawsville–Blacksburg–Radford area. Some, of course, continued on south or west toward current North Carolina and places beyond.

From the north, people could have made it to current Floyd County by ascending Bent Mountain from Big Lick. Others coming from the north would have veered to the southeast at Big Lick and made their way along the Carolina Road (once known as the Tutelo

Saura Trail and the Iroquois Warrior Trail) to what is now the Rocky Mount–Ferrum area. Still others coming from the north would have veered to the southwest at Big Lick and continued to what is now the Shawsville–Radford–Blacksburg area. In any case, some of those travelers made their way up the mountain to current Floyd County.

We know about some settler–Native American conflicts and raids in what are now the Shawsville and Radford–Blacksburg areas. We also know of such conflicts down the mountain in what is now the Franklin County area. And we know about some forts constructed in those locations by the settlers for protection from raids. Native American raids increased in those areas during the French and Indian War (1754–1763).

But what about Native American–settler conflicts in what is now Floyd County? I haven't found out much about trouble here. I've heard of a few incidents, but not like in adjoining areas.

My thinking is that people of European ancestry settled our area later than they did surrounding areas. Our remoteness, elevation, steep wilderness terrain, and shorter growing season were probably factors, resulting in only an occasional backwoods cabin dotting our part of the Blue Ridge at that time. And, too, early settlers did not record much. One other thing worth noting: the New River Indian Trail went through this area. Since that trail was used by tribal warriors on raiding missions, the settlers would have been discouraged from living near that, too.

Archaeological Findings and Studies

Native Americans were here early—10,000 or more years ago, say archaeologists. Although I am only a novice, I have compared two of my family's arrowheads to ones on a point chart by Joffre Coe, an archaeologist at the University of North Carolina at Chapel Hill.

Both arrowheads appear to be from the Archaic period (8000 to 1200 BC). One appears to be from the Guilford listing (Middle Archaic period). The other appears to be from the Kirk listing (Early Archaic period). We rarely find artifacts on our property today, but, if I am correct with my projectile point identification, people were here a very long time ago.

Some important archaeological studies have been done in places near Floyd County. The Philpott site in current Henry County (near the Franklin County line) is the location of one such study. That site is on the Smith River about three miles from Philpott Dam, where we used to fish when I was growing up. The site was first recorded by Richard Gravely in 1965. That investigation and subsequent studies

The above artifacts were found near the Floyd–Franklin County line. (Clockwise from bottom left): (1) crude celt/hatchet (2) round water-eroded black stone, probably used as a hammer stone (3) round water-eroded black stone, probably used as a hammer stone (4) pitted hammer stone, probably used as an anvil (5) chopper hoe. Arrowheads in center: white quartzite Gilford point; white quartzite broken Kirk point; and small black flint point. The small black point could have been used with a bow and may date from 1000 BC to AD 500. The white quartzite points are probably older than the black point.

by him and others are archived at the Research Laboratories of Archaeology (RLA) at the University of North Carolina.

A 1998 report on those studies concludes that the Philpott site was occupied intermittently from the Archaic period (8000 to 1200 BC) until the "contact period," when the first Europeans were in the area. From about AD 1200 to 1400, there is evidence that a substantial late prehistoric town was located at Philpott. Over 90,000 artifacts and 22 burials have been found there, as well as pottery from the Dan River phase.

Later, in the early 1600s, the Philpott site appears to have been settled again—at the time of the first contact with European settlers and Piedmont Indians. For this time period, it is unclear whether a village or just isolated households were at the Philpott site. Artifacts found for this later period include pieces of Saura pottery, European-made glass beads, and rolled copper-alloy beads.

The RLA report goes on to say that, by late prehistoric times (after about AD 1000), most Indians living in that area "were active agriculturalists." They prepared fields where they planted squash, gourds, beans, and maize (corn). Historically, maize was the last of these crops to be added to their diets. Besides farming, the report said native people "continued an earlier tradition of using indigenous cultigens such as sunflower, goosefoot, sumpweed, and maygrass."

During the 1960s, the Smithsonian Institute sponsored archaeological studies in eighteen counties in Southwest Virginia. A report by C. G. Holland on those studies is titled "An Archaeological Survey of Southwest Virginia." Those studies included seven site investigations done in Floyd County. Various artifacts from the Archaic period (8000 to 1200 BC) and Woodland period (1200 BC to AD 1600) were found at sites in current Floyd County. The report said one of those sites "may have been of village proportions."

From his own studies and from site and artifact information from people here in Floyd County, Tom Klatka, archaeologist with the Virginia Department of Historic Resources (DHR), believes there once were several native towns or hamlets in our Floyd County area. Tom said the early people in our region were of Siouan ancestry and pottery found here is from the Dan River phase. Pottery from the Dan River phase is considered late prehistoric and dates from about AD 1000 to 1450. Pottery designs, as well as remains found at archaeological sites, are used by archaeologists to date the pottery and to learn about the culture of the people who made the pottery.

Some important studies have been done in the New River Valley. The Shannon archaeological site is located in northeastern Montgomery County and the Trigg archaeological site is located in the Radford area. Members of the Archaeological Society of America, under the leadership of archaeologists Joseph Benthall and Howard MacCord, did those studies. The Shannon site is older, although both sites are considered Tutelo or pre-Tutelo.

Tom Klatka said that radiocarbon studies date the Shannon site at AD 1200 to 1300. He said Dan River pottery was found at that site, but no trade items, such as beads, were found.

He further explained that the later Trigg site dates from the 1500s to the beginning of the 1600s. Dan River pottery was also found at the Trigg site. Besides pottery, many trade artifacts were found there, as well as a large number of burials. Tom wonders if the many burials may have been from native people who died from diseases brought to them by the Europeans.

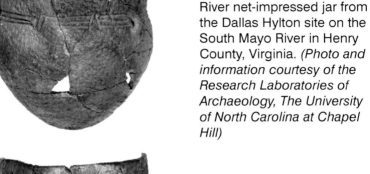

This reconstructed ceramic vessel is a decorated Dan River net-impressed jar from the Dallas Hylton site on the South Mayo River in Henry County, Virginia. *(Photo and information courtesy of the Research Laboratories of Archaeology, The University of North Carolina at Chapel Hill)*

Shown here are European trade artifacts (glass beads and rolled copper tubular beads) from the Philpott site below Philpott Dam in Henry County. The beads were probably made in Dutch or Italian glass houses and traded to the Native Americans by the English out of Jamestown. Much of that trade took place at Fort Henry, present-day Petersburg. *(Photo and information courtesy of the Research Laboratories of Archaeology, The University of North Carolina at Chapel Hill)*

This deer antler knife is from the Trigg archaeological site in the Radford area. The Trigg site, radiocarbon dated from AD 1500 to the early 1600s, is thought to have been inhabited by the Tutelo (Totero). *(Photo and information courtesy of Virginia Department of Historic Resources)*

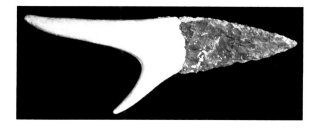

This deer antler knife is from the Shannon archaeological site in Montgomery County. The Shannon site, radiocarbon dated from AD 1200 to 1300, is thought to have been inhabited by the Tutelo or pre-Tutelo (Totero). *(Photo and information courtesy of Virginia Department of Historic Resources)*

More than a Hunting Ground

As I think about native people down the mountain from here and in the New River Valley, it seems the area that is now Floyd County could have provided some good sites for Indian villages, especially in sheltered areas by creeks and rivers. Still, I always thought of this area as a *transient* place where early people only hunted, fished, and foraged. Not so, said archaeologist Tom Klatka. They did all that, he said, but, contrary to popular opinion, "the evidence suggests they also *lived* here and in other parts of Southwest Virginia, too." I assume that would especially have been so during the Middle and Late Woodland Period (500 BC to AD 1600). In addition to growing crops, foraging, hunting, and fishing, it seems native people in our area also tapped maple trees for sap, a practice later followed in the early 1800s by some settlers.

By the early 1700s, most Native Americans had left this area, but Tom Klatka said there is evidence that some may have come back here later. He showed me a National Park Service document telling about the possible use of Floyd County by the Cherokee during the nineteenth century. As the story goes, a man living in Botetourt County was granted a tract of land in this section (Floyd County) by the government. Quoting from the 1941 Park Service document, it reads as follows:

> The man made an inspection trip of his newly acquired property in 1850 in company with a band of about one hundred riders and found a Cherokee encampment on this site. The village consisted of about ten dwellings and apparently was more or less of a permanent encampment. The man informed the Indians that they were on his property and told them that they would have to leave. These orders must have been forcibly given, because early the next morning, when he returned, the Indians were gone. . . . They had destroyed all equipment that they could not take with them, particularly cooking utensils and dishes made of soapstone taken from the quarry nearby.

The 1941 Park Service document is the only Park Service information I have seen about Native Americans in our area. I don't know if Park Service and Civilian Conservation Corp workers documented other archaeological findings during the 1930s when the Blue Ridge Parkway was built.

Tom Klatka has spent a lot of time in Floyd County doing archaeological research. During the 1990s, he studied about mining here, especially soapstone mining. Both Native Americans and the settlers used soapstone, and Tom is aware of more than thirty soapstone quarries in Floyd County. He said that around 2000 BC, soapstone was one of the most sought after materials by Native Americans and, by 1200 BC, the making of soapstone pottery was widespread. Soapstone carved easily and had many uses; for example, it made excellent cooking pots. Still later in Floyd County, especially in the 19th century and early 20th century, I know that people here used soapstone for chimneys, hearths, and tombstones, among other purposes.

Tom said there is plenty of native history in our area and he knows about some of it. Besides his findings, he is aware of the findings of others, including artifacts and artifact sites found by local people. Such relics were especially visible years ago in plowed fields. But "a lot of it [native history] has not been uncovered," Tom explained. "Unlike adjoining areas, there haven't been many projects here." (A *Floyd Press* article dated August 8, 2013, tells about a recent archaeological dig in Floyd County led by state archaeologist Tom Klatka.

This soapstone vessel was found in Floyd County and was broken when manufactured. Over thirty soapstone quarries have been located in Floyd County. *(Photo and information courtesy of Virginia Department of Historic Resources)*

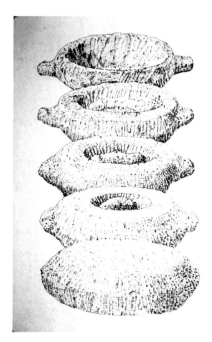

This photograph shows the manufacturing sequence that Native Americans followed in making bowls out of soapstone. The Smithsonian published this classic illustration in the late 1800s. *(Photo and information courtesy of Virginia Department of Historic Resources)*

That small dig by Little River provides further evidence of native people living in the area, rather than just passing through.)

Our maps, though, tell us about native history. A place called "Indian Ridge," south of Willis, is an area located by the historic New River Indian Trail. And then there is Indian Valley. I don't know the origin of that place name but always assumed it must have been from the many artifacts found in that area. Also on the map are Indian Creek, Little Indian Creek, and Oldfield Creek. Early county surveys refer to Old Field and Old Town sites that were thought to be of Native American origin. And then, there is Rock Castle Gorge, named for the quartz crystals there. The Cherokee, and probably other native people, revered those crystals.

Finally, I wonder about Buffalo Mountain. Almost 4,000 feet above sea level and visible for miles in all directions, it would have served as a landmark for native people and a site for judging distance in their travels. In addition, the buffalo shape of the knob must have caught their attention, especially since they hunted the woodland buffalo (bison) in this area, a buffalo smaller than the Great Plains buffalo.

Buffalo Knob, at 3,971 feet, is the highest point in Floyd County. After the Revolutionary War, the Buffalo Knob area was part of a large tract of land known as Lee's Order. The knob's caretaker today is the Department of Conservation and Recreation.

New River Indian Trail

I have learned a lot about local native history from Doug Belcher, a Native American historian from Martinsville. Besides working in education and for DuPont, he has been a lifelong student of archaeology. Back in the 1950s and 60s, he started doing local research because of his interest, he said, and "because no one else was doing it at that time." As a descendant of the Catawba and Cherokee, he also has a family interest. Doug is grateful to have worked with the late Richard Gravely, Jr., who led archaeological excavations in the Henry–Franklin–Patrick County area. Doug said Richard Gravely "was ahead of his time and scientific in his record keeping."

Doug also praises the late Oscar Hylton, who lived in the Martinsville area and died recently. "It was a joy to have met and worked with him on programs," Doug said. "He was one of the few people in our region who continued to practice herb or Indian medicine." I once heard Oscar Hylton speak about Native American medicinal plant formulas and was truly inspired.

Doug told me about the New River Indian Trail and helped me to locate it on the 1751 Joshua Fry–Peter Jefferson map that included the most inhabited part of Virginia at that time. Doug said the New River Trail began in modern Ohio, came through West Virginia (Kanawha), passed through the Narrows of the New River in Giles County, came into Floyd County at Pilot Mountain, crossed Little River, followed the present Route 221, passed by Indian Ridge, came into Carroll County, passed Pilot Knob, and turned down the mountain, Route 89, at Low Gap by Warrior Mountain. It followed the Blue Ridge Mountains into what is now Surry County, North Carolina, and crossed the Yadkin River.

Doug said the Shawnee, Cherokee, and Catawba used that trail to raid each other. During the French and Indian War, the Shawnee and their Indian allies also used the trail to raid the English at Draper's Meadow (current Blacksburg area), Fort Vause (current Shawsville area), and the Goblintown settlements (current Patrick County near the Franklin County line). He said the New River Trail was an important Native American trail and is well documented. The New River Trail was also called the Southern Trail or the Road to Carolina. After it entered North Carolina, it was known as the Catawba Trail.

Historic Tribes Here

Researchers tell us the tribes living or owning land in what is now the Floyd County area included the Tutelo (Totero), Monacan, and Cherokee. The Cherokee were from the southern Iroquois language group, and the Tutelo and Monacan were from the Siouan language group. All three tribes relied on agriculture and were probably matriarchal, taking their ancestral lineage from the mother's clan.

Besides Tutelo, Monacan, and Cherokee, people from other tribes in this region would have been here at times or at least would have traveled through this area on the New River Indian Trail. Besides their location at Fairy Stone, Siouan towns were located in what are now Franklin, Patrick, and Henry Counties—not far from Floyd County.

Doug told me some things about the Tutelo. Historically known as Totero and by several other names, those people lived in what is now the Montgomery, Floyd, and Roanoke area during the time of the first contacts with the Europeans (1600s). The Trigg and Shannon archaeological sites in the New River Valley are thought to have been Tutelo towns.

Doug said that when the Tutelo left Virginia in the 18th century, they eventually settled with the Iroquois at Six Nations Reserve in Ontario, Canada, west of Buffalo, New York. They have preserved a bean dance and grow a bean on the reserve called the Tutelo bean. The seed was said to have been brought by them to Canada from Virginia. Their language has been recorded and their food, culture, and dances have been preserved. They took ceremonial beads with them when they left Virginia, and those beads are now preserved at the Smithsonian Institute. The few hundred Tutelo people at Six Nations Reserve today are part of the Cayuga Nation.

In his book *Floyd County: A History of its People and Places*, Dr. Amos Wood said that old people remembered hearing about some members of a "Cannawhay (Kanawha)" tribe being here years ago. I haven't been able to find out much additional information on such a tribe. Still, the New River Indian Trail came through an area known as Kanawha, West Virginia. Modern Kanawha, West Virginia, with a river by the same name, supposedly is named for a Native American tribe in that area—a tribe that later became part of the Iroquois community. Is it possible that the tribe of native people mentioned in Dr. Wood's book is from that same area—current Kanawha, West Virginia? And is it possible that Kanawha on the New River Trail; Kanawha, West Virginia; and Cannawhay (Kanawha) mentioned in Dr. Wood's book relate to the same place and same Native American tribe?

Floyd—Once Part of Cherokee Nation

The Cherokee was the largest tribe in Southwest Virginia, and some of their people may have lived, at times, in what is now Floyd County. For certain, they owned land here. Their land included what are now Carroll and Grayson Counties, western Patrick, and about one-third of what is now Floyd County. During the Colonial period, the Cherokee also owned millions of acres of land in current North Carolina, South Carolina, West Virginia, Tennessee, and Kentucky.

An 1884 map by C. C. Royce shows the "FORMER TERRITORIAL LIMITS OF THE CHEROKEE 'NATION OF' INDIANS" that included part of modern Floyd County. As stated also on the Royce map, it shows the "BOUNDARIES OF THE VARIOUS CESSIONS OF LAND MADE BY THEM TO THE COLONIES AND TO THE UNITED STATES BY TREATY STIPULATIONS, FROM THE BEGINNING OF THEIR RELATIONS WITH THE WHITES TO THE DATE OF THEIR REMOVAL WEST OF THE MISSISSIPPI RIVER."

Starting in 1721, through a series of treaties with England, the Cherokee borders changed. The treaty that included part of current Floyd County and other parts of Southwest Virginia was drawn up at Hard Labor, South Carolina, on October 14, 1768. For that treaty, all 554,000 acres of Cherokee land in this part of Virginia were ceded to John Stuart, British superintendant of Indian Affairs, for the Colony of Virginia.

In that treaty, the Cherokee gave up land from the top of the Blue Ridge (Blew Ledge) to the Holston River. I understand that "Blew Ledge" came about from wording used for Blue Ridge in 1700s Halifax County records. The Cherokee word for Blue Ridge is "Sha-kon-o-hey," meaning "Blue Place" or "Smoky Place." Thanks to Dolly Parton, we have those words (Sha-kon-o-hey) in a song she sings about the Cherokee.

During the Colonial period, the Cherokee lost more than 42,000,000 acres of land to England for the Colonies. And in the later Federal period, the Cherokee lost millions more acres, all through treaties and broken treaties. First England, and then many in our United States government, pushed for those treaties. Many of the early settlers wanted Native American land, as well.

By 1738, about half the people in the Cherokee Nation had died from smallpox. Having no natural immunity, they were totally vulnerable to smallpox and other diseases brought to the Virginia colonies by the Europeans.

Besides disease, the tragic history of the Cherokee people and their forced removal from their homes in the southeastern United

States is well documented. This is part of President Andrew Jackson's legacy—his and that of others who supported and carried out the Indian Removal Act of 1830. Known as the "Trail of Tears," it is estimated that 4,000 or more died during that five-month relocation to Oklahoma. That forced walk took place from October 1938 to March 1939. Besides the Cherokee, other eastern tribes—including the Choctaw, Chickasaw, Creek, and Seminole—were forced to leave, too, but the Cherokee removal was especially cruel. In his book *This Pleasant Land: A Blue Ridge History*, Max Thomas refers to this as "an act of infamy" and "ethnic cleansing."

Native Americans Today

Today, eleven tribes have now been recognized by the Commonwealth of Virginia. They are the Cheroenhaka (Nottoway) Indian Tribe, the Chickahominy Tribe, the Eastern Chickahominy Indian Tribe, the Mattaponi Tribe, the Monacan Indian Nation, the Nansemond Indian Tribal Association, the Nottoway Indian Tribe, the Pamunkey Nation, the Patawomeck Indians of Virginia, the Rappahannock Indian Tribe, and the Upper Mattaponi Indian Tribe.

The Monacan, whose tribal home is at Bear Mountain in Amherst County, is the most western of the state-recognized tribes. The Monacan also have a living history village at Natural Bridge.

Doug Belcher, Native American historian, told me that today, there are over 5,000,000 Native American descendants in the United States (2010 census). This figure is under-counted, he said, for Virginia alone has over 80,000 people of Native American heritage. The United States census now allows for choosing two races, a change that has added to the number.

None of Virginia's tribes have federal recognition at this time. The federally recognized tribes in this part of the United States are the Eastern Band of the Cherokee Indians in North Carolina and the Catawba Nation in South Carolina. The Lumbee Tribe has half federal recognition in North Carolina but no Bureau of Native American Affairs services.

The Melungeon people of southwestern Virginia, who have had DNA studies done, have both Mediterranean and Native American ancestry, said Doug. He told me they have about one-fourth Native American blood, and each family's DNA is different. The Spanish word for mixed ancestry is mestizo and the French word is métis. Brent Kennedy, who has written about his people in East Tennessee, Southwest Virginia, and East Kentucky, estimates there are about 250,000 Melungeon people in those areas. They are not recognized in any of the states. "The sad thing," Doug said, "is that the Melungeon have been left out of Virginia history books. Even the chapters on Virginia Indian descendants fail to include them."

So what is ahead for tribal recognition in Virginia and at the national level? Besides the eleven tribes recognized by our state, other tribes existed here and people today descend from some of them. That is especially true of Southwest Virginia, where no tribes are yet recognized.

Important to Remember

As I think about our Native American history, I remember the fourth grade history book we used in the 1950s to study Virginia history. It began with Jamestown and said a little about Powhatan and Pocahontas. "Virginia history has been called a myth," Doug Belcher said, "for so much is left out."

Although the written record is incomplete or missing entirely, archaeological sites and artifacts can tell archaeologists much about early people and their way of life. If a person has artifacts on his property or knows of some elsewhere, it is important to protect them. If artifacts are to be removed, they first need to be photographed in place and documented, describing exactly where they were found. If an artifact is not documented or a site is destroyed, then that part of history is lost forever. Various laws protect archaeological sites, including sites on public (federal) lands. Native American burial sites are protected by law, as are all burial sites.

In Virginia, the Department of Historic Resources (DHR) is a good contact for questions about archaeological sites. DHR personnel document sites and can provide information to a landowner about sites on his property. The DHR phone number for our area is 540.387.5396. A very readable book on Virginia archaeology is *First People: The Early Indians of Virginia* by Keith Egloff and Deborah Woodward. That book was reprinted in 2006 and was published in association with the Virginia Department of Historic Resources.

A Big Question

Finally, I'd like to bring up an entirely different topic—a question, actually. How did the first natives get to North America? If asked today, Native Americans might say, "We've always been here."

For many years, archaeologists thought those first people came to North America from Asia during the last part of the Ice Age—that they came across the Bering Strait land bridge that existed at that time.

Well, some excavations at the Cactus Hill site in Virginia during the mid–1990s have posed some big questions. Located by the Nottoway River in southeastern Virginia, radiocarbon dates for the Cactus Hill site (and some other sites) are much too early for the Bering Strait theory. So that leaves us with questions—questions about what we think we know and questions of other possibilities. Regarding Native American history, "We are still learning," said Doug Belcher.

Based on Jean's article published in the Floyd Press
as a three-part series on May 16, 23, and 30, 2013

Chapter 26

Christmas Memories

The prettiest room in our house was unheated except at Christmas. The curtained French doors to that room, then open, revealed rarely used furniture, including a brown mohair sofa and chairs, a small table with spool-like legs, a piano, an antique love seat, my great grandma's spinning wheel, and our Christmas tree.

The upright, brown enamel-coated heating stove in that room looked better than the black cast-iron ones elsewhere in the house. Since that enamel stove was rarely used, our living room walls were pristine and free of smoke and creosote stains. It took forever for that parlor stove to heat up but, once it did, the heat flowed up the stairs to my bedroom.

Evergreens were readily available on the farm and we always cut a tree for Christmas. We sometimes had mistletoe, too, for it was a parasite and grew up high in some trees. One of our neighbors used to shoot it out of the trees with his gun. Getting the Christmas tree was Daddy's job, but my sister and I always went along to help find just the right one. He valued the white pines and would always try to steer us away from them and toward Virginia pines, which we called "bull pines" — scrub mountain trees not useful for much else. Nevertheless, we usually headed home with the tree we girls wanted, listening to Daddy's diatribe about Christmas trees being a pagan custom.

Mama first took the tree to school for her first-grade classroom. Then, when school closed for the holiday, she brought the tree home for us.

We never decorated with Christmas lights—nor did we make popcorn or cranberry chains. Our decorations were beautiful, though, and we gave each delicate glass ornament a place of honor on our tree. Depending on the year, either an angel or a star graced the top. I remember little else on the tree except for icicles and a red accordion-like, store-bought paper chain. The tree stayed up until New Year's Eve. At that time, we also took down the Christmas cards taped around interior doorways and removed the front door wreath made from "ground ivy" growing in our woods.

As a child, I never had an allowance, but my parents gave me a quarter each day for school lunch and ice cream. The ice cream cost a nickel and, in the weeks leading up to Christmas, I would save my nickels to buy Christmas presents. One Christmas, I bought Mama a box of small Christmas tree ornaments at Kress's (S. H. Kress) five-and-ten-cent store on Campbell Avenue in Roanoke. That box of ornaments cost a quarter and was probably the most special gift I ever gave anyone.

Our annual Christmas shopping trip to Roanoke was especially enjoyable and I looked forward to it every year. In those days, downtown shopping was excellent, and department stores like Heironimus, Miller and Rhoads, Pugh's, and Leggett's were beautifully decorated. It was like a wonderland as we and other shoppers passed one another, looking at store windows and listening to recorded Christmas music from the Salvation Army. Those outings always included a visit with a department store Santa.

My sister Janet and I usually ate lunch with Mama at the S. H. Kress store and ordered the turkey "blue plate special." Janet remembers that the turkey plate cost about 50 cents in the mid-1950s. She also recalls the delicious bread pudding that she and Mama loved—a bargain for 15 cents. Daddy bought himself two hotdogs for 15 cents each at the Roanoke Weiner Stand, although we just called it the Hot Dog Stand. Then he'd take us girls to see a cowboy movie at one of several downtown movie theaters, while Mama did secret Christmas shopping. As I recall, it cost about 50 cents for a matinee movie ticket back then.

Besides a trip to Roanoke, we did our Christmas shopping at stores in Floyd, and through the Montgomery Ward and Sears and Roebuck catalogs. Each of those catalog companies published a special Christmas edition each year that included pages and pages of toys. The arrival in the mail of those "wish books" was as exciting as Christmas morning. Those catalogs also got me started making my Christmas list, which I mailed to Santa. Closer to Christmas, I'd listen to the radio, hoping to hear him read my letter.

I always remember the holiday pageants my sister and I put on at home for our parents. We came up with our own programs, including skits, poems, music, and relevant Scripture. We spent a lot of time planning our programs and practiced for days. Finally, on Christmas day, Easter, or Thanksgiving, we'd perform in costume, using whatever talents we thought we had. Being seven years older than my sister, I probably took the lead in those pageants, but I remember them being an enjoyable joint effort.

The year I was six, I still believed in Santa Claus—or wanted to. But I kept watch, just in case someone else had a hand in gift-giving at our house. It was with mixed feelings that I kept watch, for I secretly hoped I was wrong and that the jolly old elf would be coming down our chimney again that year. I had questions, though, and doubted if anyone, even a magical Santa, could get down a chimney with a woodstove at the bottom. My curiosity got the best of me that year and I looked behind, under, and on top of everything I thought might harbor some treasure. I listened carefully to whispers between my parents and observed my mother's shopping habits.

A week before Christmas, my mother was helping my father outside and I was alone in the house. This was my chance to do some snooping. After checking out an assortment of nooks and crannies, I came to the kitchen, where I checked everything at eye level and below.

Finally, I climbed up a step stool to check the top shelves of the kitchen cupboards. And there on a top shelf, tucked behind some cups, was a small box. My heart quickened as I reached for the box, lifted the lid, and peaked inside. My Christmas sleuthing was over and there in the little box was the Christmas wristwatch I had hoped for.

Wiser and a little sad, I carefully closed the lid and tucked the box back where it had been hidden, vowing to keep believing in Santa. Once my little sister was born, I did all I could to perpetuate the idea of Santa Claus for her and, to this day, I think we both still believe in Santa and the spirit of Christmas.

Clara Turner Thomas (Mama)
(3/25/1910–7/30/1997)

Chapter 27

Mama

Farm living had always been a way of life for Mama, but after marrying Daddy, she was involved in every aspect of farm life, indoors and out. Besides that, she taught school for thirty-nine years. Her career as a teacher was a huge part of her life, but I'll begin with her life beyond the classroom.

In 1939, Mama and Daddy lived in what would later become the granary while he helped build their house. Money was hard to come by during that time and later, after I was born, too. "We were real poor then," Mama said, "and I made all your clothes, many of them out of colorful feed sacks. I made you a little coat out of mine."

Mama had a knack for sewing and didn't always use a pattern. On a lazy summer afternoon, I would sometimes see her sitting on the hardwood floor in the living room with a dress pattern and cloth spread out. Using flat table knives to weigh the pattern down, she worked quickly. She made me pretty dresses trimmed in rickrack or lace, with crisp white collars.

Mama always liked dolls and sometimes, if she had time and a piece of cloth left over, she'd make a new dress and hat for one of my dolls. As a child, she had especially treasured the twin boy and girl dolls her Uncle Ed had given her. She said, "Those dolls were the prettiest I ever had."

Sewing and mending continued year round, and during winter when "cabin fever" set in, she would haul out her fabric scraps and piece a quilt. She liked to embroider and crochet, and she also knew how to make split-oak baskets. Her hands were rarely idle.

The aprons Mama wore remind me of the good cooking she did. Upon first waking in the morning, I'd hear the coffee pot perking and the sound of Mama working the biscuit dough. Soon, I'd smell hot biscuits, eggs, and bacon, sausage, or country ham. We usually had white or redeye gravy, too. In winter, we often had hot cereal or pancakes. Even the laziest person would have a hard time sleeping through those tempting aromas.

Regular meals at home were good, simple food—including cornbread, soup, pinto beans, and other vegetables. I especially remember the scrambled egg sandwiches Mama made for me when I was sick in bed. Sunday and company dinners, though, were feasts. Fried chicken, ham, creamed peas and onions, mashed potatoes, green beans cooked with fatback (originally, and later with cooking oil), fried or baked apples, homemade rolls, cheesecake, pies, cakes, and fresh-made lemonade or iced tea made the table look like Thanksgiving. For those dinners, we'd sometimes have up to eight people at our table. Mama would keep busy passing food, encouraging Uncle Monroe to "be a sport" and try this, or have a second helping of that.

Whenever we were shut in because of bad weather or sickness, Mama would be out in the kitchen making soup, cookies, chocolate fudge, or some other tempting dish. Even during power outages, she cooked good meals on our wood stove. All of that cooking made the house smell heavenly and brought cheer to the drabbest of days.

Mama enjoyed holidays and eagerly joined in with my sister and me to color eggs, decorate a tree, or carve a jack-o'-lantern. Just so she'd have pretty autumn centerpieces, she grew gourds in the corner of the garden, always pleading with Daddy not to accidentally mow them down.

She took delight in the changing seasons, the arrival of a baby calf or new kittens, and the first ripe wild strawberries. I'll always remember her reciting poems and singing songs—not in public, but just to us kids at home. I remember her reciting parts of Joyce Kilmer's "Trees," Longfellow's "Evangeline," William Cullen Bryant's "Thanatopsis," Alfred Noye's "The Highwayman," John McCrae's "In Flanders Fields," and others. I also remember the fun side of Mama and how much she liked playing cards, Scrabble, croquet, and other games.

The only animal I ever saw Mama not like, besides bulls, was the billy goat that once came to our house. Enraged by Mama's shooing it away from the front porch with her broom, that goat started to butt the front screen door. She and I pushed the stovewood box against the door for protection and then I ran for help. Daddy was working in the hayfield. By the time he and I returned, the goat's owner had come for the goat and had taken it home before major damage was done.

We were hardy farm people and grew much of what we ate. Besides fruit trees, berries, and farm animals, Mama and Daddy grew a half-acre garden every summer. With all the other farm and home chores, it was a struggle to keep up with garden weeding, vegetable harvesting, and preserving. When I was quite small, Mama used to pay me a penny per cup to shell peas. That was her way of keeping me occupied and out of trouble.

Mama's summer days began at sun-up or earlier and continued until nearly midnight as she worked over a hot stove (a wood cook stove at first) to fill the last canning jars for winter. For most of her married life, she preserved food for our family and had plenty of leftovers to share with relatives and friends. At crunch times during the summer, all of us (including Mama) helped with farm work—especially when getting up hay and hoeing corn.

In addition to homegrown foods, Mama and Daddy sometimes went over in the mountains to gather watercress and wild berries. The berries could be used for jellies, jams, and wonderful pies. I usually went along on those berry-picking trips and sometimes came home with an empty bucket and a stomachache. Worst of all, having refused to sprinkle my pants with sulfur, I'd often get a bad case of chiggers that itched for days.

Besides the necessary food we grew, Mama was especially interested in growing flowers and indoor plants. Her green thumb seemed to bring life to all the plants she touched. Outside in our yard, she grew purple lilac, rose of Sharon, weigela, a snowball bush, irises, bleeding heart, peonies, phlox, and a rambling rose that climbed up the side of our old springhouse. Even in coldest January, our enclosed sun porch would be alive with jade plant, philodendron, spider plants, blooming begonias, and African violets.

One had only to walk through our house to see that antiques were another of her interests—especially ones handed down from her family. She treasured old things.

Clara is pictured here in her yard around 1960. She had a "green thumb" and her yard and indoor plants reaped the benefits of her care.

Although Mama rarely complained, her health was not always the best. When growing up, she said she had "every disease in the book," including whooping cough, measles, scarlet fever, typhoid, and diphtheria. As a result, she was thin and didn't have good health during her high school years. Her health improved in later years, although a bout with viral pneumonia left her with a deaf ear.

Mama always said she and "Old Maude," her faithful horse, went through high school together. Pizarro High School was two miles from home and she rode sidesaddle every day to school.

She was a good, conscientious student and won a prize in the seventh grade for going through the spelling book without missing a word. She was also on the Floyd County debate team in high school. She made good grades and ended up being valedictorian of her graduating class. "However, I must tell you," she added, anticipating her own punch line, "there were only three students in my class."

Clara is pictured at the homeplace where she grew up along Paradise Lane. This photo was taken in 1928 when she graduated from Pizarro High School.

Photo of Clara taken in 1931

Pizarro High School was unaccredited, so she had to pass a state exam in order to go to college. She went two years to Stonewall Jackson College, a Presbyterian school in Abingdon, Virginia. During that time, she gained needed weight and her health improved. And for the first time, she was able to play basketball.

She had wanted to go to Duke University and major in math, her best subject, but didn't have the money to go. Instead, she started teaching in the winter and going to Radford College in the summers. She received her BS degree from Radford in 1938.

Clara, wearing cap and gown, graduated in 1930 from Stonewall Jackson Jr. College in Abingdon. After that, she finished her studies at Radford College by going summers and teaching school the rest of the year. She is pictured in 1938 on the Radford campus when she graduated with a BS degree in education.

She taught children of all ages for thirty-nine years and, during the early part of her career, she taught at two- and three-room schools at Huffville, Mount Ruffner, Terrys Fork, Pizarro, Harmony, and Alum Ridge. She taught me in first grade at Harmony School.

Having taught all grades in a variety of schools, her favorite age must have been six and seven year olds. She taught first grade, exclusively, from 1953 until 1975, when she retired. Her patience seemed endless and her students loved her as she did them.

Both of my parents were teachers, and my sister, two cousins, and

Clara taught school for thirty-nine years. She began teaching in small country schools and concluded her career by teaching first grade at Floyd Elementary School. She is pictured here at Check School, where she taught second graders in 1939-40.

I often rode to school with them, rather than take the long school bus ride. Those car rides would often be filled with Mama and Daddy's talk about school. Mama, who liked to drive, would often be behind the wheel of our car. Sometimes we kids would wait after school for Mama and Daddy while they stayed for teachers' meetings. And they'd wait on us while we were at 4-H meetings or band practice.

Mama was a good-looking tall, slender woman with high cheek-bones and large blue eyes. She often wore jewelry and usually wore her light brown hair in a medium or short length with a permanent. I never saw her wear shorts. She once told me that her father felt shorts and slacks were not proper for women. She started wearing slacks when she was about fifty years old. Before that, when she would go to work in the garden, to milk cows, or to gather eggs, she would wear one of her "everyday" dresses and an apron.

About four times a year, our family got up early and drove forty miles to Roanoke for an all-day shopping trip. Now that doesn't sound like a very big trip, but that's as far as we ever went from home, except for an occasional two-hour trip to see Daddy's Aunt Sadie in North Carolina. Being a farm family, we needed to be home each morning and evening to care for animals.

On Roanoke shopping trips, my sister Janet and I would go with Mama as she shopped for dresses to wear in the classroom. Then she'd take us to Lerner's, Kiddie Corner, Leggett's, or Pugh's, where we'd try on clothes. She said she bought us the prettiest dresses she could find. And sometimes she'd talk our renegade father into buying a new suit of clothes. She liked him to look stylish—a difficult goal for a man who liked his bib overalls best.

Mama seemed to have endless energy during those times and, even after age sixty, she continued at a pace hard to match. Perhaps waiting until age forty to give birth to my sister gave her a new lease on life and kept her young. In later years, she was more willing to take a break in the afternoon to do a crossword puzzle, watch a soap opera, work on a quilt, or talk on the phone. After a break, though, she was ready to go again.

Church was always important to Mama, and she said her father (Cam Turner) thought everybody ought to go to church. She devoted a block of time each week to Bible study and had read the Bible through. Although she never talked about it much, I know she depended on her faith and prayer to see her through difficult times.

She was baptized at Sinking Springs Presbyterian Church in Abingdon during the two-year period when she attended Stonewall Jackson College there. Mostly, though, she attended— and was

Max & Clara Thomas are pictured here in their kitchen during the 1993 Christmas season with their three grandchildren, from left: Ann Schaeffer, Jennifer Schaeffer, and Rob Coiner. Clara's handmade baskets are visible overhead. Today, Ann is a certified nurse mid-wife and professor, Jennifer is a veterinarian, and Rob is a mental health counselor

devoted to—a one-room country church called Harvestwood in the Pizarro community of Floyd County. After Harvestwood Church was closed due to consolidation, she attended the Presbyterian Church in town. She was active in the church Circle and in other community organizations, such as the Retired Teachers, the Pizarro Home Demonstration (HD) Club, and the Pizarro Ladies Club.

Although she was very busy and active, Mama never shirked her responsibilities as a mother to my sister and me. Her love for us was obvious, and she was openly affectionate to us. We always knew we could count on her. But I had to grow up and become a mother myself before I understood the extent of her feelings for us.

Max and Clara celebrated their 50th wedding anniversary with family at Hotel Roanoke on September 15, 1987.

She showed that same caring for my daughters, Ann and Jennifer, and for my sister's son, Rob—and took delight in them. Whether playing cards, reading to them, or playing croquet or some other game, it was always obvious that she enjoyed life—and she shared that joy with all of us.

158

Max and Clara pose with their family in 1987. Pictured, from left, are Ann Schaeffer (granddaughter), Jennifer Schaeffer (granddaughter), Richard Schaeffer (son-in-law), Jean Thomas Schaeffer (daughter), Janet Thomas Coiner (daughter), John Robson Coiner, Jr. (son-in-law), and Rob Coiner (grandson).

Photo of Dora Wood and Cameron Lee (C. L.) Turner—Clara Turner Thomas's parents. C. L. and Dora had been married one year when this photo was taken in 1908. They were married by Elder Asa Shortt at the bride's home. They had five children: Thelma, Clara, Ralph, Elbert, and Mildred.

159

Children of C. L. and Dora Turner, from left: Mildred (married Paul Sowers), Thelma (married C. D. Houchins), Ralph (married Martha Lacey), Clara (married Max Thomas), and Elbert. Elbert died at age twelve from rheumatic fever—not long after this photo was taken.

Ralph Turner grew up in Floyd County and served for four years in the Army in the European Theatre during World War II. He took part in the Normandy Invasion and returned home in 1945. He was a brother of Clara Turner Thomas. Clara's brother-in-law, Paul Sowers, also served in World War II—in the Navy

Sparrell Tyler Turner (9/19/1846–2/24/1927) and Flora Alice Thomas Turner (6/2/1857–4/9/1923) were the paternal grandparents of Clara Turner Thomas and the parents of C. L. Turner.

Walter H. and Judith Harbour Thomas were the great grandparents of Clara Turner Thomas. They were the parents of Flora Thomas (Mrs. Sparrel Tyler Turner). Walter Thomas (4/29/1829–5/8/1919) and Judith Harbour Thomas (9/13/1839–5/28/1937) were the maternal grandparents of C. L. Turner.

Additional family photos are in chapter 24 of this book.

Max S. Thomas (Daddy)
(11/7/1908–6/1/2001)

Chapter 28

Daddy

When I was little, I used to sit on Daddy's lap and try to undo his bib overall galluses. He'd give me a half-disapproving look and say, "Ah, Jean!" Then, he'd "beard" me as I struggled to be free from his reach. He'd continue sitting in the rocking chair, reading and chewing tobacco. He'd be tired from working in the fields and would be waiting for Mama to finish cooking cornbread and pinto beans to go with the strong coffee he loved. "Plain grub," he called it.

He raised me like a boy, he always said. Maybe that's why I preferred outdoor work to housework. Or perhaps his taking for granted that I would help him outside caused me to know no other way.

Anyway, I followed him about the farm, looking up livestock, checking newly planted crops, or fixing fences. Often barefooted, I sometimes lagged behind because briars or rocks hurt my feet. When I complained, he chided, "Come on—rocks make 'em tough" and continued his pace. Rather than let him think I was a weakling, my determined spirit made me forge on. I would do anything to gain his respect.

Whether he was checking on a new calf, repairing storm-damaged fences, or doing some other work, we went up and down mountainsides, along streams, through the woods, and over grassy fields. Still, no matter what the task, he always took time to notice his natural surroundings. Perhaps his training as a science teacher made him especially aware. "Looka-here," he'd say, "this rock has streaks of iron all through it." Or he might point out some other geologic formation and explain how it came to be.

He was interested in plants, too, and told me about boneset. "The old-timers brewed this up into a medicinal tea," he said. "Here, taste the leaves." As we walked along, Daddy would sometimes cut off a young stem of birch bark for us to chew and when we were thirsty, we'd drink from a cold mountain spring.

Daddy taught me about rock formations and the geology of the mountains, and he helped me identify a wide variety of rocks and minerals on our farm. I still have my rock collection from back then.

The work Daddy did on the farm was varied and often hard; sometimes our entire family helped out—especially during crunch times when we got up hay or hoed corn. I didn't mind hay so much, but I always dreaded getting off rocks from fields and shoveling manure from barn stalls. The rocks were backbreaking, and the manure was dirty and took forever. I never liked hoeing corn, either, for it was a hot, tiring job. It took several of us a week to hoe a large field of corn, and it had to be hoed at least twice in a summer.

But I did look forward to some jobs, such as corn harvesting, which we did in the fall when Daddy was sometimes in a reflective mood. While we were shucking corn or hauling it to the corncrib, we'd talk. Sometimes he'd tell me about farm plans. "What do you think of my putting that field over there in hay next year?" he'd ask. I didn't know much about big-picture farm planning, but it pleased me that he wanted to talk with me about it. Sometimes we'd talk about a family concern, the world situation, politics, or what I might be when I grew up. It was a good time for dreaming.

Winter was a rough time in the Blue Ridge, and gale-force winds with low temperatures made farm work especially hard for Daddy. Feeding cattle, cleaning out frozen water holes, and caring for sick animals at such times was drudgery. Big snows and power outages sometimes meant we were isolated for days at a time. Yet, Mama's home-cooked meals—sometimes on the woodstove when electricity was off—made hardships more bearable. In fact, as a kid, I loved those times and felt like a pioneer. And most of all, I liked our family togetherness—us against the elements.

After daytime work was done, winter evenings were usually warm and peaceful inside. Mama would bring in homegrown apples, and the four of us would sit around the woodstove eating, talking, watching TV, or reading—sometimes reading by oil lamp, if the electricity was off.

∿∿

As a boy, Daddy had helped his family farm, and he went with his father in a horse-drawn wagon down the mountain thirty-five miles away to Martinsville to sell cabbage, apples, chickens, butter, and eggs. They made that trip several times a year. Later on, they went to Roanoke to sell butter, chickens, and eggs at the market there. After his father died at the young age of forty-three, my dad helped his mother, brother Herbert, and sister Avis keep the farm going. Those were especially hard times.

After Daddy and Mama were married in 1937, they taught school and built a house on the land where Daddy had grown up. Daddy helped Eli Board build the house in 1939 and we still have the house plans drawn on a small scrap of paper. Mama and Daddy lived and farmed there for the rest of their lives. Money was scarce during those early years, during the Great Depression, but they managed by being fairly self-sufficient and growing most of their food.

During the 1940s and afterwards, they raised my sister Janet and me, and I don't think either of us felt deprived in any way. In addition to love, we had everything else we needed, too.

Self-reliance was a way of life for us. When something broke, Daddy tried to repair it or patch it up. If he couldn't fix it, he would make do or do without.

He was never one for new-fangled ways. We heated our house by burning wood, and then coal. But around 1974, Daddy had an oil furnace installed in the house—just prior to the country's energy crisis. Then he longed for the old way and fired up a woodstove to supplement the furnace heat.

Daddy's farming methods didn't change much over the years except for exchanging horses for a Ford tractor in the early 1950s. Most of his farming techniques continued to be simple and required little except hard work and sweat. He always hoped to at least break even from his farm work, but some years he didn't. Each year, though, from the sale of cattle, he was able to purchase a savings bond for my sister and one for me. By the time we went to college, there was enough money to cover the cost.

Max Thomas was a farmer all of his life. He and his brother Herbert helped each other with farming their adjoining farms and they shared farm equipment. Max, on Ford tractor, is pictured here in 1960 in front of his and Clara's house.

Daddy continued to farm in his late 70s, but as he got older, he was frustrated that he could work for only about six hours a day before he was "plumb tired out."

Daddy was a good-looking, shy man, and was most comfortable wearing his bib overalls, work shirt, and heavy shoes. He wore overalls on the farm and a suit and tie when he dressed up or taught school. He didn't have in-between, casual clothes. My sister remembers the fedora he wore for dress up. Once it was worn out, he'd retire it to "farm hat."

In later years, he wore a Scottish tweed hat when he went into town. For farm work in cold weather, though, he wore a warm trapper-style cap with earflaps. He had plenty of outdoor farm clothing over the years, but the item my sister remembers best was a red plaid mackinaw jacket.

Daddy's appearance, in many ways, reflected his life and surroundings. Like the rugged mountain terrain, his leathery, tanned face and hands showed the weathering of time and hard work. He was happiest when he could avoid dealing with social graces and travel. "I'm better off staying home," he always said, "and besides, I can travel anywhere I want with a good book."

A straightforward, honest man, sometimes lacking in tact, he could have a quick temper, and sometimes he enjoyed poking fun. Then, he'd realize he'd carried his teasing too far and tried to mend hurt feelings.

Not a demonstrative man, he showed he loved us by his concern. Just let my mother, sister, or me get sick or have a problem, and he was ready to comfort, advise, or doctor. "Now, don't you worry,"

Max always had a heart for animals, including both domestic and farm animals. He is pictured here at home with kittens in the early 1940s.

he'd console, "I've got a feeling things will get better for you soon." Somehow, when he said it, I believed it. And they did.

When I was sick with croup and whooping cough, he gave me a whiskey-laced toddy. It tasted vile and, to this day, I dislike the taste of alcoholic drinks.

His concern for others was evident in the way he cared about his animals. I've known him to be up most of the night nursing a snake-bitten dog or a sick cow. And neighbors sometimes called on him to help when a family member or farm animal was in trouble. Neighbors helped us in return.

Daddy had lifelong health problems—asthma, emphysema, chronic bronchitis, and several bouts of pneumonia. In later years, he also suffered greatly from rheumatoid arthritis. He was pretty good at treating his breathing and pain symptoms and was always trying to figure out how to cope with chronic medical problems. He had wanted to be a country doctor and I think he would have been a good one.

He spoke in a dialect characteristic of the old-time mountain people of this area, leaving off the "g" at the end of an -ing word, slurring certain words or phrases, and adding some words an outsider might not understand. "Hillbilly," he called it. He knew correct grammar, though, and had taught it. He was a historian and author and could write a first draft of an essay that needed no editing. These capabilities and his love of history led him in 1977 to write his *Walnut Knob* book—a collection of local mountain stories and songs. Later, his book *This Pleasant Land: A Blue Ridge History* was published posthumously, in 2010.

Daddy always had a hunger for learning and was interested in almost everything. Although a self-taught man, his education must have been fine-tuned while he was a pre-med student at the College of William & Mary. By the end of his sophomore year there, he was rated 28th academically out of a class of 500. After his father died at age forty-three, Daddy moved back home and later finished his schooling in 1934 at Roanoke College with a major in chemistry.

The world situation, politics, farming methods, cattle prices, the weather, probing the mysteries of nature—all of this, and more, kept his mind alert as he continued to read and quiz others for information and opinions. Also, he read and studied his Bible most nights. He knew about Bible history and was especially interested in Bible prophecy.

Max, pictured here in 1928, was a pre-med student for two years at the College of William and Mary. He helped pay his way by working in the dining hall. After his father died at a young age, Max finished his BS degree in chemistry close to home at Roanoke College.

My sister says that, periodically, Daddy would give her "private lessons" on an assortment of topics. I had already left home by then, but she says those random lessons were on such topics as ancient history, the geology of the area, current events (such as the Cuban Missile Crisis), firsthand stories about the Great Depression, and how to do the math when solving a square root problem.

Max is pictured here in 1962 with Floyd High School science student Kenneth Epperly.

Daddy shared his love of learning with his students, too. He began his teaching career in a one-room school and concluded it by teaching high school science—biology, anatomy, chemistry, and physics. The Virginia Academy of Science named him Science Teacher of the Year twice, in 1962 and in 1972. Besides academics, he took a special interest in his students and helped them solve problems and plan for the future.

He always voted and thought others should vote, too. He had strong opinions but studied up on campaign issues and learned about the candidates. He believed in the younger generation and encouraged them to keep up with current events. He thought young people were the hope for the future. Besides national government, Daddy was interested in local and state government. He wrote letters and attended hearings—especially regarding local people's rights and eminent domain issues relating to the Blue Ridge Parkway.

In later years, Daddy continued to read and write. He also continued to grow a half-acre garden. And, as in the past, he took a great interest in my daughters, Ann and Jennifer, and my sister's son, Rob. After Mama died, he surprised us all by teaching himself how to keep house and cook cornbread and other foods for himself. As in years past, he'd finish off an evening meal with cornbread crumbled up in milk.

And finally, I remember Daddy and his love of music. Years ago, he went to singing schools and maybe that's where he first learned to sight-read shape notes. In church, he preferred congregational singing, rather than leaving the singing up to a choir. In his *Walnut Knob* book, he included the lyrics and music to twenty-three old-time songs that were handed down in his family. "I hardly hear of anybody knowing them now," he said. "As far as I know, they have never been recorded."

In 1997, the state of Virginia needed a new state song. Well, Daddy wanted a song titled "Old Virginia" to be selected. That song begins, "Tell me of a land that's fair . . ." and was sung widely during the 1920s, 1930s, and 1940s—especially in the public schools. The song's lyrics were written by John W. Wayland and the music was written by William H. Reubush.

That song had been the runner-up when the previous state song was chosen. Daddy thought "Old Virginia" was the perfect choice and wrote letters of support.

As a family, some of our happiest times had to do with music. We sang in the car, we sang in our house, and we sang on the front porch—sometimes in two- or three-part harmony. We weren't accomplished singers or musicians, but we sang and played anyway. We sang hymns and we sang old-time songs by Stephen Foster and others. All of our family played musical instruments, but I always

Max loved singing and playing music and is pictured here playing his dulcimer.

remember Daddy playing his banjo, guitar, fiddle, dulcimer, and Autoharp. He played by ear and could usually pick out a tune on most any musical instrument.

I also remember Daddy sitting on the porch on warm summer evenings—sometimes playing his fiddle, but mostly just sitting there "studying about things." He would be tired from the day's work as he sat there while peep frogs down by the creek provided a background chorus. Like his surroundings, on a night like this, he would be at peace.

Five of the eight sons of Samuel L. and Sarah Iddings Vest are pictured here—seated from left: John E. Vest and Berry M. Vest. Standing from left: Isaac H. Vest, Samuel Anderson Vest, and William F. Vest. Samuel was the maternal grandfather of Max Thomas.

Emmett Everett Thomas and Lila Ann Vest on their wedding day, April 25, 1906. They were the parents of Max, Avis, and Herbert Thomas.

Max Thomas and his sister Avis with their little brother Herbert around 1919. Their parents were Emmett and Lila Vest Thomas.

The boy on the right is believed to be Max Thomas and the oxen may have been "Pat" and "Mike," owned by Max's family. The man in the photo is unknown.

Additional family photos are in the book
This Pleasant Land: A Blue Ridge History, by Max S. Thomas.

Janet Thomas Coiner was a high school English teacher for thirty years. She is pictured here in her classroom at E. C. Glass High School.

Chapter 29

My sister Janet spent her career as a high school English teacher — mostly at E. C. Glass High School in Lynchburg, Virginia. Based on her extensive background as an educator, I have asked her to write some thoughts for this book.

Thoughts From a High School English Teacher

By Janet Thomas Coiner

For thirty years, I was a high school English teacher. Both of my parents were teachers, as were both of my grandmothers. You could say that education was the family business. My family lived in the country, close to Daddy's cows and hayfields and Mama's chickens and garden, but far from most other children. The summer before I started first grade, my cousin, who had completed fifth grade and lived ten minutes away by foot, organized formal classes for me and several others of the unschooled — namely, a few teddy bears and our two very bright collies.

As a daughter of teachers, I knew it was important to do well in school. So when my cousin named me the best student in her class, of course I was proud, already having made a good start in the "family business" at age six. Besides the basics, my cousin gave me extra assignments that the others were excused from, such as learning to tie my shoes.

I always loved going to school — what else was there to do, and where else could I see kids my own age? One elementary teacher let us do wonderful art projects, another taught us how to play "Swinging on a Star" on the harmonica, and yet another taught me most of what I know about grammar. I never had my mother as a teacher, which was too bad, since her first graders seemed to love her. In high school, I learned how to do noun declensions in Latin from my aunt, the Latin teacher. I learned how to ignore, for three years straight, the fact that the science teacher was my father. Besides chemistry, physics, and anatomy, he also taught me the skill of note-taking. Home economics and gym class could be tough, probably because they weren't "book learning." But I liked all of my classes, especially English, foreign languages, and math.

As the time for college approached, though, I told anyone who'd listen that I didn't want to be a teacher. Teachers brought home papers at night and dealt with all kinds of problems at work. They were responsible for a room of kids who could be unpredictable and who,

I knew, must be goaded with a great deal of finesse into learning and behaving. I always knew that both of my parents loved their work—one needed only to hear them talk about school to see that. But no, thank you. Not for me.

So it was strange to find myself at age 21, newly married and wearing my good blue suit, standing in front of a room of teenagers—and talking about participial phrases and Shakespeare and vocabulary words. My first year, frankly, was awful. Today I feel sorry for both the kids and myself. I was brand new to the job, and the school saddled me with four different literature preparations, 152 students, and one 500-sheet package of duplication paper that was supposed to last all year. Thankfully, chalk was plentiful. I tried to look confident, but the kids could tell I was young and green. I cried once a week on my way home from work, whether I needed to or not. Prayer was sometimes involved.

Luckily, we needed the money, so I signed up to teach another year, which turned out completely different. My husband had finished graduate school and by then we moved to Lynchburg, Virginia, where we've lived ever since. My new school assigned me only two literature preparations, a journalism class that I loved, and just over 100 students. Finally there was time to think carefully about how to present a lesson and how to help kids who needed it. Teaching is hard work—mentally, emotionally, even physically. (Most of the effective teachers I worked with were drained by the end of the day.) For the most part, though, I loved teaching. There were plenty of bright, creative, engaging kids over the years. My most rewarding experiences, though, were with kids who didn't have an easy time of it and for whom the pathway through life was uncertain. A teacher's kind words might be the only uplifting words a kid had heard that day. I remember one ninth grader who began the semester with a shy apology: "I'm not very good in English." I took great pleasure in letting her know, four months later, that she had aced her semester exam.

When people spend whole careers in education, they start to recognize fads that come and go. In the late 1960s, the "open classroom" was a popular experiment: knock down the walls, and throw all the kids together! I know little about that system, only that it didn't last long, and I am so thankful I never had to teach in an open classroom or send my son to one. It's hard to imagine how any learning took place.

That was followed by the idea that students should not be grouped by ability in academic classes. I can teach Shakespeare, for example, to all sorts of students of varying reading levels, but not to all in the same classroom. While it might hurt a child's feelings not to be in the most demanding class, it would hurt his chance to learn anything at all if taught a curriculum far over his head. Thrown together in a demanding academic class, the well prepared and capable students become bored and resentful, and the unprepared and less able students become just lost. Public education can provide only so much individualized instruction.

In the mid-1970s, my school system decided that English classes should teach students how to write expository papers. Wait, you may think—haven't schools always done that? As a student in high school and college, I was assigned papers to write but, except for formal research papers, was not taught the specifics of how to write. Either a person "knew" how to write well, or did not. For the first five years I taught, I made writing assignments but did not really give much writing instruction. In time, though, my school system offered a semester-long course that I and many other teachers took. We learned about different expository forms—argument, comparison and contrast, definition, classification, for example—and how to write a coherent five-paragraph essay with a clearly stated topic sentence.

The importance of teaching the "how" of writing, which seems so obvious now, was a new thing in my school system in 1976.

In the early 1980s, the "whole language" approach to teaching English was implemented in my school. The idea was that, for any piece of literature, we would teach grammar and writing at the same time. That sounded good in theory, but the grammar part always seemed to get shortchanged. Foreign language teachers told me they were suddenly having to teach their students English grammar before they could teach them French or Latin. If I marked a comma error on a student's paper, often he would not have the grammar background to understand what I meant by "you need a comma after an introductory adverb clause." In a class of twenty-five students, there would be at least twenty-five different grammar lessons needing to be taught after any writing assignment. There was never time for everything.

My ninth graders used to ask me, "Why does everything we read this year have death and sad stuff?" It was hard to refute their presumption. We had *Great Expectations*, in which the main character is abused, and his rich benefactor dies—colorfully at least—by means of spontaneous human combustion. Then there was *The Good Earth*, in which female babies are quietly sacrificed in times of famine. *Lord of the Flies* ends in savagery and murder. In *Ethan Frome*, after a suicide attempt, the young lovers end up crippled and bitter. And we all remember how *Romeo and Juliet* turns out. I had to admit that my ninth graders had a point about the whole death theme.

When my sister asked me to write something about teaching for her book, I procrastinated, telling myself that I was just allowing everything to percolate in my mind first. But the real problem, as I've always joked, is that English majors can never say anything without writing multiple paragraphs. So perhaps I will just make a list and call it . . .

Teaching Principles that I Believe to Be True

- As a minimum, every kid needs at least one good friend at school and one teacher who believes in him. Not everyone is motivated by a love of literature or the pleasure of dissecting a sentence. Sometimes a kid will work and learn merely because the teacher is nice to him.

- If I haven't matched every face to a name by the end of the first week, I'm in big trouble.

- If I'm allotted three personal leave days per year, I should use one to grade papers and the other two to catch up on sleep.

- If I discipline a kid with after-school detention, that time is best spent by getting to know him better. (Laughter should also be involved.)

- It's always a golden opportunity when a class witnesses the teacher doing something awkward or dumb. Examples: (a) Once I slipped and landed, unhurt but bottom down, smack-dab in the trash can. I laughed loudest of all. (b) For a time, I was the 30-year-old pregnant lady at school with braces on my teeth; who could be more sympathetic? (c) Another time I routinely asked the class to "take out your worksheets"—but I didn't pronounce the "sheets" part exactly right. What could I do but laugh right along with the kids? A perfect way to bond!

- You never know when you've made a real difference in a kid's life. For example, a couple of years ago, a huge middle-aged man ran across the Kroger parking lot to give me a hug. At fourteen, what he'd given me was all kinds of problems, and he had barely passed. But he didn't remember any of that—he seemed delighted to see me and tell me about his children.

- Most of all, to borrow my son's phrasing, evaluate people for who they are, not for who they aren't. Everybody has potential. Everybody has a future.

Chapter 30

Early Schools Remembered – Part 1

When I was a little girl, I used to look at the remnants of nearby Barton Spur School and wonder about the one-room building that once served the Walnut Knob community when my dad was a boy. Graded schools were common in the 1930s, but Barton Spur was an older, ungraded school. Originally called Mountain View, the name was changed to avoid confusion with another school by the same name. Like other country schools of that time, Barton Spur was close enough for most students to walk. It was near my dad's boyhood home, next to the Floyd–Franklin County line.

I never saw the old Barton Spur School standing, but I was privileged to attend two other country schools. The first was a two-room school called Harmony. I always thought that was the perfect name for a school. Near the Blue Ridge Parkway and Rakes Mill Pond, Harmony was in a lovely wooded setting where some of us made playhouses or swung on grapevines during recess.

The other was a one-room school called County Line, near a church by the same name. That little school by Thomas Farm Road was on a hill overlooking Alvie Thomas's strawberry patch. Neither Harmony nor County Line School is standing today.

My formal education changed after that, and I went to a modern school in town—leaving an 1800s experience behind. A one-hour bus ride made that possible. Not long after that, one- and two-room schools closed forever in this part of Virginia.

My memories of those early schools are now filed away as impressionistic snapshots in my mind, no doubt colored by nostalgia. I close my eyes and enter Harmony School. I don't remember a "cloakroom" being there, but I hang my coat along the wall. I place my lunch box on a shelf beside the other lunches and observe the water bucket on a wooden table. The bucket is full, having just been brought back from the spring by older boys. They've also brought in a supply of firewood.

I carry my "book sack" to my desk. The double, two-piece wooden desks are in rows facing the blackboard, and I share one of them with another student. A picture on the wall of George Washington stares back at us. The teacher's desk is in the front corner. I'm learning to read, using the Scott Foresman *Dick and Jane* reading series. The older students have just finished reciting the sixth line of the multiplication table and are now preparing for a spelling bee. Music is part of each day, too, and our teacher seems to have an unlimited repertoire of songs to sing with us.

We enjoy a midday break and admire each other's lunches—sometimes exchanging a ham biscuit for a can of Vienna sausages, or a fried pie for a Moon Pie. Recess is also a favorite time, and I like some of the games we play: "London Bridge," "Ante Over," "Fox in the Morning," "Pretty Girl Station," "Drop the Handkerchief," and "Hide and Seek." Yes, I can picture the way it was at Harmony School, and I can see boys and girls in bib overalls and feed sack dresses playing and learning together.

County Line School was an amazing place, too, with seven grades in one room. Just two of us were in my grade. The start of the school day was referred to as "taking up books." Before we took out our books, though, we all sat around the potbellied stove and sang songs from *The Golden Song Book*—songs by Stephen Foster and others. I had the feeling our teacher enjoyed singing as much as we did.

In our studies, we worked at our own pace, and we helped each other. We also listened in on lessons of the upper grades. Although I was young, I remember the sixth and seventh grade students "parsing sentences." They might spend an hour talking about just one sentence, for they would tell everything they could about each word. They would give the part of speech and then elaborate. For example, for a pronoun, they would give the person, number, class, case, and then tell how the word was used in the sentence. Grammar was a game, and sentence syntax was an enjoyable puzzle to be solved.

There was no such thing as boredom in a one-room school, although I do remember that some of us would finish our lessons early and be allowed to go in the back room to put on plays. We also memorized poems.

I loved the field trips we took at County Line School. They consisted of going on walks in the woods and fields as we looked for animals and plants and tried to identify them. I especially remember looking for the wildflowers of spring: lady slipper, jack-in-the-pulpit, and others. It was on one of those trips down by the creek that I saw my first pileated woodpecker.

I realize that some early schools and teachers were better than others. Yet, from my own experiences at Harmony and County Line, I can truly say they were some of the best school years I ever had. They offered all I needed for learning.

Much more could be said about country schools in this area. My first-hand knowledge is limited, but typically, those early schools were built by people in the community who also helped with school upkeep, firewood, and teachers' salaries. In their spare time, teachers were expected to visit in pupils' homes, and during census years, teachers went from house to house during the summer, taking the census.

At one time, more than 100 small schools dotted the countryside of Floyd County. Some, like Stamping Birches and Mud Hole School, had unusual names. Others, like Reedsville School, were named for families in the area. I have personally seen some of the old school buildings that are still standing: Paynes Creek, Silver Leaf, Falling Branch, Double Springs, Alum Ridge, Kelley, Kemper, Toncray, and Terrys Fork. Years ago, I remember seeing the Pizarro, Mt. Ruffner, and Huffville Schools.

Mount Ruffner School was in the Haycock Mountain area. Nancy Harman and Clara Turner taught there in 1931–32.

Huffville School was a two-room school in the Locust Grove area. Pictured here with students in 1930, is teacher Bessie Wimmer. Clara Turner also taught at Huffville School that year.

This photo of Reedsville School students was taken about 1918. That school was located in the Alum Ridge area on Reedsville Road—up the hill on the left from the intersection of Weeks Road. Martha Reed attended Reedsville School and is on the far right in the first row (number 13). Beside Martha is her brother, Opel Clifford Reed (number 12). Some other students who attended Reedsville School at various times included Amanda Reed, Rosie Reed, Daniel Webster Reed, Sr., Daniel Webster Reed, Jr., and Lizienia Reed. Some of the teachers at Reedsville School were Lean E. Cannady (1917–1918), Myrtle Harmon (1919–1920), and Ballie Simmons Reed (date unknown). (Photo from the estate of Martha Reed Miles and courtesy of Phyllis M. Sumner, daughter of Martha Reed Miles)

Country schools were more than just places of education back then. They served as community gathering places. Cakewalks, pie suppers, and dances were held there in the evenings, and sometimes string bands played.

Yes, country schools—like country churches, stores, mills, and post offices—provided a community focus and a sense of pride for people years ago. Today people in some communities are close, but consolidation has changed the focus; much of the local identity has been lost. Other places, like Lilac, Smart, and Turtle Rock—once hubs of community activity—are barely remembered today.

I'm not suggesting that we should go back to one- and two-room schools. Still, I have such respect as I think about the simplicity of schooling back then and how a teacher and community with few resources could accomplish so much.

Based on Jean's article published in the Floyd Press *on December 26, 2002*

Early Schools Remembered – Part II

I grew up in a family of schoolteachers. Mostly, the focus was on modern schools—whichever one or ones we were currently attending. But there was also talk of earlier schools my parents and grandparents had gone to as students or teachers. I was fascinated to hear their stories and have each one closeted away in my memory.

I also treasure a few keepsakes from those times: the slate my dad used at Barton Spur School, Elson-Gray readers, and a school bell my mother saved.

Mostly though I remember hearing about those schools—bits and pieces of information that I try to put together to imagine what schools were like before my time. I look at a tiny photograph and pick out my mother at age six when she attended the Wood School taught by her Aunt Ethel Wood. And I try to imagine my mother as a teenager, riding "Old Maude" through the fields to Pizarro High School.

Ethel Wood taught at the Wood School on Paradise Lane. Ethel is pictured here in 1916-17 with her students in front of the home where Ethel grew up. That house is no longer standing.
Front row, from left: Lina Turner Dickerson, Lucy Turner Houchins, Donnie Bowling, Ora Turner Nichols, Myrtle Hatcher Hall, and Clara Turner Thomas
Second row: Thelma Turner Houchins, Chester Bowling, Buel Bowling, Minnie Turner Link, and Elsie Boyd
Back row: Ethel Wood (teacher), Myrtle Fralin Akers, and Annie Hale Thompson

Teaching in those early schools must have been difficult at times, and it was not unusual to hear of a teacher being "run off" by ornery pupils. Still, many teachers back then were excellent and very dedicated. It was possible to get a good education in those days, though schools were very basic.

To add to my information, I decided to talk with some of the other teachers and students who had firsthand knowledge of those one- and two-room schools.

First, I visited **Daisy DeWitt Thomas** and asked her to tell me about the thirteen years she spent teaching at small country schools. She said she "really enjoyed teaching there, and the students were very loving." She said she was "always on the run, and only had time to teach the basics." She had little teaching equipment and no library of the type we think of today. Students purchased their books. Daisy said she was grateful to have a blackboard, and her father made flash cards that she used with her students.

Daisy told me about an embryology project she did with students at Kelley School. Most families no longer raised chicks, so Daisy arranged to have a resident hen help teach the science lesson. The incubation, hatching, and chick raising took several weeks. The project lasted until the 1½ pound chickens were sold to help pay for paper window shades for the school windows.

Daisy said students brought their lunches from home, and sometimes they brought vegetables or meat to contribute to a big pot of stew cooking on the wood stove. The stew would simmer all morning and be done in time for lunch.

Firewood and water were outside, and older students looked forward to getting out of class so they could bring in wood from the woodpile and buckets of water from the spring. Each child had a drinking cup. Daisy said the desks were homemade, and it was hard to write on their uneven tops. Some of the country schools had outdoor facilities, and Daisy remembers that a favorite Halloween prank at one school was to turn over the outhouse.

According to Daisy, normal school hours were 9 a.m. until 4 p.m., but she'd have to be there earlier to get ready for class and to build a fire in cold weather. She commuted on horseback to some of the schools, and she remembered being frightened in the wintertime when her horse would occasionally slide on ice. Sometimes she rode her horse home after dark, especially if a student had requested help with math after school.

Daisy taught at the following country schools: Iddings, Shady Fork, Washington, Kelley, Paynes Creek, and Pizarro. The Kelley and Paynes Creek school buildings are still standing. Later on, she taught at Check School, and she finished off her teaching career at Floyd Elementary School—across the hall from my mother's classroom.

Next I visited **Maude and Henry B. Shelor** to see their house on the east side of Route 221, between Floyd and Willis. At one time their house had been a two-room school known as Falling Branch.

It was interesting to sit in the Shelor house and have them tell me how it used to look when the old school was there. "The school building had two chimneys and each schoolroom was heated by a wood stove," Henry B. explained. "At the front of the building was a cloakroom, with a bell tower above the cloakroom entrance." The cloakroom façade had been moved to the back of the house, but the original tin roof is still on the building.

As Henry and Maude talked about renovations they made to their house, I could picture school children sitting there years ago at their desks. And when we went outside, I imagined them playing games and snacking on fruit from the apple trees. Out back, we could see Haycock Mountain in the distance.

After Falling Branch School closed, it went through many changes, and Henry and Maude listed them. First, it was used for Sunday school and sometimes church. Then it was used as a grange hall, and later it was used for square dances. During the war, mattresses were made in the building. After that, workers from Illinois managed a rock-crushing operation on the premises.

Henry was able to purchase the old school in 1945, and he spent about three years renovating the place and cleaning away the fine dust from the rock-crushing operation. It became home to Henry and Maude soon after they were married in 1949, and they raised their two sons there.

After I visited the Shelor home, Henry wanted to show me some other schools nearby. As we left their home, we saw an earlier Falling Branch School, now in ruins, on the west side of Route 221. Then, we turned onto Black Ridge Road and headed toward Kemper School on the left. Henry had grown up near Kemper and had walked to the two-room school until he was twelve years old. The tin-roof building is located beside Dillon's Chapel.

Henry and Maude showed me one other school along Black Ridge Road—a one-room school on the right called Toncray. As I walked up the hill to look at that old school, now used to store hay, I surveyed a 360 degree panoramic view, and I thought it couldn't get much better for teacher or students than to spend their days in a setting like that.

Henry speculated about the ages of the schools and estimated that Kemper was started in the early 1920s—before Toncray.

For years, I have been interested in fixing up an old one-room school to make it look the way I remember when I was a young student at County Line School. **Dorothy Vest** did just that. She transformed Double Springs School, making it the way it was when she was a young teacher there.

Today, as in years past, Double Springs School sits quietly on a hill overlooking two springs. Native vegetation complements the setting, and the school looks the way I picture all one-room schools — simple, with a bell tower over the entrance.

The Double Springs School was located in the Locust Grove community. Dorothy Vest taught at that one-room school years ago and restored it after she retired.

Dorothy showed me photographs of how the school looked before she started fixing it up in 1996. The roof was rusted, the windows were missing, and the building had been used for storing hay. The schoolyard, too, needed work. She really did a beautiful job with restoration.

I loved being in the old schoolhouse, and several familiar things caught my eye: green window shades, the old-time desks, a long green recitation bench, lunch buckets (once used for lard or syrup) on the shelf, a water bucket with dipper and cups, switches in the corner, George Washington's picture on the back wall, a small teacher's desk, and the U.S. flag. I saw a rope inside, and Dorothy invited me to pull it and ring the bell.

Blackboards were often just walls painted black, but some were made of real slate. It was a treat to see the real thing at Dorothy's school—a slate blackboard with Zaner-Bloser type ABC letters standing sentinel duty across the top.

It was a sunny afternoon while we were there at Double Springs School, and Dorothy and I were in no hurry. What a joy it was to absorb that long-ago atmosphere. The science table at the back of the room caught my eye, as did the "library." It was just a bookcase, but Dorothy said it would have been called a library in those early schools.

On close scrutiny, I noticed one of the desks had the initials "HRV" carved on it. Turns out that they were carved with a knife by Dorothy's future husband, Hugh Vest, when he had been a student at Double Springs School.

The restored Double Springs classroom included a single bookcase, known as a "library." That was the kind of library small schools had in the late 1800s and early 1900s. The first public library in Floyd County was started about 1970 in a four-room building near the firehouse in Floyd. That library was started and run entirely by volunteers from the Floyd County Woman's Club during the time when Betty Lineberry was president. Ersley Robinette and others from the Woman's Club worked tirelessly to set up and keep that first library going. Books for that first library were from the estate of Roberta Hewitt, a local teacher and Woman's Club member. About 1975, the library was moved to a room in the basement of the courthouse, and Pam Cadmus was the librarian there. Finally, in 1985, the Jessie Peterman Memorial Library was built in Floyd at its current location on West Main Street.

Like some of the other schools, there had been an earlier one on this site, too. According to Dorothy, the first Double Springs School had been made of logs and was built in the early 1800s. Instead of a wood stove, the earlier school is supposed to have had a fireplace.

Some of the families with students at Double Springs School included Cole, Martin, Vest, Conner, Gearhart, Lawrence, Whitenack, Hall, McNeil, and Shank. Double Springs School was near Check, at the intersection of Double Springs Road (Route 870) and Stonewall Road (Route 612).

From Double Springs School, I headed off to see two other early school buildings—Terrys Fork and Huffville, where my mother first taught school so many years ago. Dorothy went with me to show me the way.

Terrys Fork and Huffville were two-room schools back then, and the Terrys Fork School building is now used as a community center. One other school, Pleasant View, is nearby, and we saw it as we drove toward Huffville.

❧❧

Except in our memories and from information passed on, not a lot remains of the early schools of the nineteenth and early twentieth centuries. At the beginning of the twentieth century, more than 100 small schools existed in Floyd County, but few photographs are available to document their presence.

I am grateful to have attended two of those small schools, and I am glad to have learned about some of the others firsthand from my family. As a part of her thirty-nine years of teaching, which included Check and Floyd Elementary, my mother, **Clara Turner Thomas**, taught at the following small schools: Huffville, Mount Ruffner, Terrys Fork, Pizarro, Alum Ridge, and Harmony.

In addition to teaching high school science, my father, **Max Thomas**, taught at Paynes Creek, Alum Ridge, Pizarro, and Check School. He also taught at Barton Spur in Franklin County and was a teacher and principal at Endicott School—also in Franklin County.

My maternal grandmother, **Dora Wood Turner**, taught at Pizarro School, and my paternal grandmother, **Lila Vest Thomas**, taught at the Silver Leaf, Paynes Creek, Kelley, Iddings, and County Line School. Of course, my parents and grandparents also attended one- and two-room schools as students. My Aunt Thelma Turner Houchins taught school and my Aunt Avis Thomas taught at Silver Leaf School. Avis lacked only one course in getting her teaching degree from Radford College when she died at age 24.

186

I consider this school history, and I am proud to pass it on to others, especially to my children and grandchildren. For those who share this heritage, I hope they will do the same. And for all our children and grandchildren, this is part of our country's history—whether we, ourselves, experienced it firsthand, or not.

Based on Jean's article published in the Floyd Press *on January 2, 2003*

List of Early Schools in Floyd County

Today elementary schools in Floyd County are located at Floyd, Check, Willis, and Indian Valley. At one time or another, each of those schools served as a consolidation hub for smaller schools. For example, the first school consolidation in Floyd County began in the 1920s when students from the Stonewall/Locust Grove area were transferred to Check School. As roads and transportation improved, additional school consolidation took place throughout the county.

By the 1930s, over thirty small schools in Floyd County had closed, and by the early 1940s, sixty had closed. By the 1950s, only eight remained open. One- and two-room schools in the Indian Valley area closed in 1952, and students started attending Indian Valley Elementary School. When the county high schools consolidated in 1962, one public high school and four elementary schools were in operation—just as today.

To reiterate, there were over 100 small country schools in Floyd County at the beginning of the 20th century. Several lists of those schools exist, but there are some discrepancies. No doubt, information will continue to be updated. Some of the old schools are still standing and should be photographed for posterity. Persons who have photographs of schools no longer standing should preserve those visual records and attempt to identify schools, students, and teachers. Floyd County Historical Society personnel can help with identification, too. The Historical Society has scanning equipment and can make digitized copies of photographs for the Historical Society's archives.

Listed below is a best effort at co-mingling the various lists of early schools. For this master list, I have relied on information from Ruby Bishop West, Effie King Brown, Dr. Sarah J. Simmons, and my parents—Max and Clara Thomas. An asterisk (*) indicates an African American school.

"A" Colored*, Africa*, Akers, Alderman, Alleghany, Alley, Altizer, Alum Ridge, Armstrong* (originally called Squealum), "B" Colored*, Barton, Beaver Creek, Bell, Broad Shoals, Brush Creek, Buffalo

Mountain, Burnette, Cabell, Camp Creek, Caldwells, Center, Central, Chapel Hill, Chestnut Level*, Church Hill, Ciceronian, Cleveland, Conners Grove, Copper Valley, County Line, DeHart, Deskins, Dickerson, Double Springs (also called Flint), Dry Hill, Dulaney, Duncan or Duncans, East View, Ethiopia* (replaced by Huckeberry in 1905), Falling Branch, Flat Run, Flint (also called Double Springs), Forest Hill, Franklin, Gannaway's or Gannaway, Girards, Graded Road, Graham Mount or Graham's Mount, Greasey Creek, Grey Bluff, Haycock, Halls (also called Halls Graded and Locust Grove), Harman, Harmony, Harpers Ferry, Harris, Harris Hart*, Hewitts, Hobson, Howery (also called Mud Hole), Huckeberry* (previously called Ethiopia), Huckleback (also called Union), Huffville, Hylton, Iddings, Jacksonville Graded, Jacksonville Public (also called Jacksonville Public School House), Jenkins, Keith, Kelleys or Kelley, Kemper, Laurel Branch, Laurel Creek, Laurel Fork, Laurel Ridge, Lawson, Lee, Liberia*, Lick Log, Lick Ridge, Little Flock, Little River, Locust Grove (also called Halls or Halls Graded), Mangus, Meadow Creek, Meadow Run, Moors, Mossy Dell, Mount Jackson, Mount Pleasant, Mount Ruffner, Mount Sterling, Mountain Cove, Mountain View, Mud Hole (also called Howery), New Haven, North Shady Grove, Oak Hill, Oxford Academy (had been a private school but was used for awhile by public schools during the 1930s), Palmer, Paynes Creek, Peabody, Phillips, Phlegar, Pine Creek, Pine Forest, Pine Glen, Pine Grove, Pine Swamp, Pizarro, Pleasant Grove, Pleasant Valley, Pleasant View, Pluck Valley, Possum Hollow, Quartz Hill, Red Oak Grove, Reeds, Reedsville, Rifton, River View, Rocky Hollow, Rosenwald*, Rush Fork, Sears, Shady Fork, Shady Grove, Shooting Creek, Silver Leaf, Silver Pine, Simmons, Siner, Sissons, Slusher, Sowder, Spangler, Squealum* (later called Armstrong), Stamping Birches, Stonewall, Stoney Battery or Batery, Strickler, Strongs, Stuart, Sumner, Sumpter, Sunnyside, Terrys Fork, Thomas Grove, Thompson, Tice, Toncray, Union (also called Huckleback), Vanderbilt, Vaughn, Vest, Wade, Wahoo, Washington, Weldon, White Oak Grove, White Rock, Wills Ridge, Wood School. (private/public?)

Based on Jean's article published in the Floyd Press *on July 8, 2004*

Chapter 31
Secondary Schools in Floyd County

The First Public High School

Schoolhouse Fabrics is a Floyd landmark for locals and tourists alike—a reminder of Floyd County's textile heritage and the site of the county's first public high school.

That high school, located on North Locust Street, was built on a knoll of land donated by Manassa Tice, one of the town's founding fathers. According to the research and writings of educator Ruby Bishop West, the cornerstone for the first of two school buildings on the site was laid in 1847. The school was known over the years by various names: Jacksonville Male Academy, the Academy, Old Brick Academy, Floyd Academy, Jacksonville Academy, Floyd Institute, Floyd High School, and Floyd Elementary School.

Regardless of the name, the school appears to have been a private institution between the 1840s and early 1870s. Toward the end of that time, this private school was coed. Although records don't always agree, it is fairly certain that the building was used by the public schools by the early 1880s—as early as 1871, some say.

Meanwhile, in 1871, statewide changes in education were taking place that would affect Floyd County and its schools. A new law was passed that required counties to provide free public schools and have them in operation by 1876. In cooperation with the new law, preparation began in Floyd County and the first school board meeting was held. Although some counties did not meet the 1876 deadline, Floyd County did and was in compliance with the new law. That year, according to the research and writings of Dr. Sarah Simmons, fifty-two public schools opened in Floyd County and another thirteen were under construction. The student enrollment that year was 2,428.

It is not clear when the Jacksonville Male Academy's name was changed to Floyd High School, but the school was one of fifty-two schools in Floyd County considered public in 1876. It had four rooms, two upstairs and two down, and a winding stairway. On the lower level out back, there was also a small unheated room. A plank fence and wooden sidewalk were in front of the building, and a high plank fence, in back, separated the boys' and girls' playgrounds. Early photos and drawings show an impressive looking building with a wooden steeple/bell tower. In 1913, that first building on the site was razed and replaced, using the old bricks for the new school. That second building stands today on Locust Street.

The earlier building on the site had stood for over fifty years, but during its demolition in May 1913, a large black bottle was found in the cornerstone. Referencing an early *Floyd Press* article, Ruby Bishop West described the bottle's contents. She said it contained a copy of a New York newspaper dated April 1847, a list of trustees and contributors for the school, and a note. The note said, "The undertakers to build this building are H. Dillon, F.W. Lester, and J. Gill who do the work themselves." H. Dillon would have been master builder Henry Dillon, and he is remembered for erecting several other fine structures in the town and county.

The public high school on Locust Street provided a two-year program at first, but by 1911 a four-year program had been started. Those graduating in 1915, and after, went to school in the second building on the site. From 1916 to 1918, the school also offered a two-year teacher training course as part of high school work. That second building, the current home of Schoolhouse Fabrics, was the site of Floyd High School until 1939. After that, the building was used for Floyd Elementary School until 1962.

This building served as Floyd High School from 1913 to 1939, and was an elementary school after that. It is now the home of Schoolhouse Fabrics.

In 1926, the following were among the students who graduated from Floyd High School: Freeman Slusher, Georgiana Evans Hall, Daisy Sweeney, Dorothy Epperly, Lettie Dickerson Harmon, Curtis

Lawrence, Edna Agee Epperly, Thelma Turner Houchins, Angie Mae Morgan Snider, Vera Sumpter DeHart, and Grace Bishop Phillips.

In 1939, three new schools were built in Floyd County. Funds for that building program were made possible from a government grant applied for by school superintendent G. F. Poteet. The grant money was for elementary schools. As a result, brick schools were built at Check, Floyd, and Willis. The new school at Floyd was used for some elementary classes (as the grant required), but the new building also served as the location for Floyd High School—and remained as such until 1962, when county high schools were consolidated.

Except for athletic events, the schools built in 1939 at Check and Willis were used for elementary students. High school students in those two communities continued to attend school nearby in older buildings. Since 1962, all three of the schools built in 1939 have served as elementary schools. Indian Valley is the fourth elementary school in Floyd County.

Check Elementary School (on left) and Check High School (on right)
(Photo from the high school's 1941 Checkite *yearbook)*

Nine Public High Schools in Floyd County

There have been nine different buildings used for public high schools in Floyd County. At one time, high schools were located at Pizarro, Alum Ridge, Willis, Check, and Harris Hart. The remaining four were high schools at successive locations in the town of Floyd. Those high school buildings in Floyd were built in 1847, 1913, 1939, and 1962.

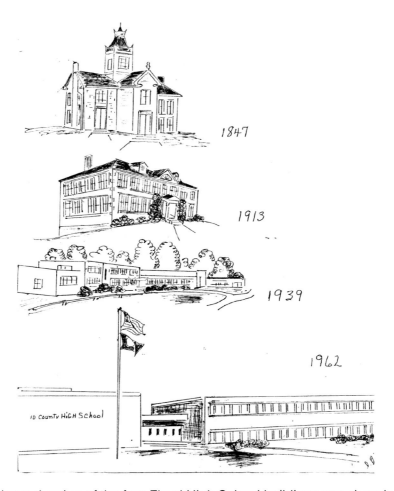

The above drawing of the four Floyd High School buildings was done by Dennette Dillon, an artist and Jean's fifth grade teacher. This drawing is from an eleven-page report prepared by Ruby Bishop West. The report is titled "Excerpts from the Records and Other Facts about Education in Floyd County: 1931–1962." Ruby was a longtime employee of the Floyd County Public Schools. In the early years of her career, she served as rural supervisor for small rural schools in the county.

In 1914, a school called **Pizarro** was established along the Franklin Pike, and for part of the time, four years of high school were offered there. For a few years (starting about 1926), **Alum Ridge** School followed a similar pattern. First, it offered two years of high school and then a four-year program.

In 1917, a four-year high school was established at **Willis**, and an organization called the "Community League" was the driving force in making the school, and successive additions, a reality. Four students

192

Pizarro School near the Franklin Pike was both an elementary and high school. Among others, students from the following families attended Pizarro School in the early 1900s: Harvey, Wood, Allen, Vest, Turner, and Thurman. During that time, around 1905, Molly Thompson was a teacher there. The school continued to serve the community during the 1920s and for a while afterwards. *(Photo courtesy of Anise Houchins)*

Pictured above, in 1926–1927 is Pizarro High School's champion basketball team.

Besides schooling for young students, Alum Ridge School, pictured here, offered two years of high school beginning about 1926—and then four years later on.

Pictured above is Willis School. According to an undated *Floyd Press* news clipping, Covy Sowers' father, Cleophus Sowers, "furnished wood for the school and also drove his horse and covered wagon to deliver children from Burks Fork to school in Willis." A new elementary school was built nearby in 1939, but the building above was used for a high school until county high schools consolidated in 1962

graduated from Willis High School in 1921. The Willis Community League continued to give sustaining support for about twenty years and was a precursor to the Parent Teacher Association there. Although a new school was built at Willis in 1939, that building was used for elementary students. High school students continued to take classes in the old building until 1962, when it was closed and countywide high school consolidation took place.

Classes in agriculture were offered at Willis High School from the start, and in 1923 Willis had the first agriculture department in Southwest Virginia. A few years later, other high schools in Floyd County added courses in agriculture, home economics, and business.

In 1916, a three-room public school was started at **Check**. At first, it was an elementary-junior high school. A fire of unknown origin destroyed the building four years later. Classes resumed in a nearby house and a new school building was constructed on the original

Check School was both an elementary and a high school in 1939–1940 when this photo was taken. Pictured are Check schoolteachers and Principal Fred Knoblock.
Row 1: Fred Knoblock
Row 2: from left, Mary Grace Hawkins, Irene Hartsock, Nelva Hale, and Maizie King
Row 3: from left, Gerene Lee, Clara Thomas, Mary Poff, Grace Hylton, and Ruby Vest
Row 4: from left, Bessie S. Totten, Kenneth Kinzie, and Max Thomas

Pictured around 1939 are Check High School students taught by
Max Thomas. He taught history and some other subjects at that time.

site. In 1922, it was decided that a four-year high school program was needed, and the Check Community League was helpful in bringing that about. Two years later, students graduated from a four-year program. An agriculture department was added in 1930 and a home economics department was added in 1931. A new school for elementary students was built at Check in 1939. High school students continued going to school in the older building until countywide high school consolidation took place in 1962.

In the early 1920s, a school for African American students was started at **Harris Hart**. The school was located by Newtown Road in Floyd, a short distance from the center of town. Harris Hart was larger than Armstrong School (also in town), and those students, among others, started attending Harris Hart. The new school, named for the state superintendent of public instruction, had two teachers. That original school building was destroyed by fire in 1946 and was rebuilt by 1948. During that building process, students were taught at the then-vacant Pizarro School building.

According to a *Floyd Press* article dated September 30, 1948, the new Harris Hart building had four classrooms, a lunchroom, combination auditorium-gym, library, principal's office, storage room, central heating plant, and two lavatories.

Harris Hart was a school for African American students from the 1920s to 1965. The school was located by Newtown Road in the town of Floyd. After a fire in 1946, a second building (pictured here) was built. Students in grades 1–7 attended Harris Hart, and later on, some students also attended high school there. Today, the Harris Hart building serves as the administration building for Floyd County Public Schools.
(Photo courtesy of Phyllis Diane Campbell Cunningham)

Walker Edward Campbell, Sr. (7/12/1914–6/11/1990)
Mr. Campbell was a teacher and principal at Harris Hart School. He started
at Harris Hart in 1937 and continued there until 1965—for 28 years. After
Harris Hart closed, he taught history at Floyd County High School. He is
pictured here in 1980 when he was 66 years old. His wife, Arlean Akers
Campbell, was a student at Harris Hart and she was a teacher there also.
(Photo courtesy of Phyllis Diane Campbell Cunningham)

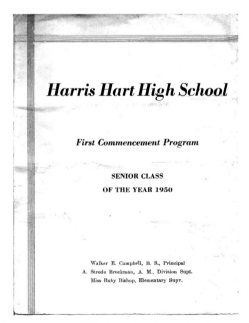

As this program shows, the first high school graduation took place at Harris
Hart in 1950.
(Photo courtesy of Phyllis Diane Campbell Cunningham)

198

Harris Hart had seven grades, but later on, for a while, Harris Hart offered two years of high school, and then four years. The first class graduated from Harris Hart in 1950. In a photo from that time, the following graduates are pictured: Jacqueline Stuart, Alease Floyd, Polly Ingram, and Katherine Vaughn. Teachers in the photo are James Baum, Dorothy Milton, Charles Campbell, Grace Beale, and Walker E. Campbell, Sr. (teacher and principal). That photo was published many years afterwards in a September 1997 edition of the *Floyd Press*. (Graduation information is from a copy of a news article supplied by Phyllis Diane Campbell Cunningham)

Later, in the 1950s, students from Harris Hart started attending Christiansburg Institute for secondary studies. Christiansburg Institute was the "First High School for Blacks in Southwest Virginia," according to a monument at the school. Also on the monument are dates for that school, 1866–1966.

On January 25, 1960, schools in Floyd County were integrated, and thirteen black students began attending white schools. Nine students registered at Floyd High School and four students registered at Check High School. Those enrolled at Floyd High School were Raymond Taylor, Daisy Penn, June McDaniel, Clark V. Helm, Edward Helm, Danny Ingram, Fred D. Pugh, Pandora Turner, and Charles Keller Akers. Those who enrolled at Check High School were Helen Stuart, Bonnie Marie Stuart, James D. Walker, and Richard Claytor. *(Enrollment information from the* Floyd Press *dated January 28, 1960)*

Early Private High Schools

Besides public high schools in Floyd County, there were also private secondary schools. One of the earliest private schools was the Oxford Academy. The Reverend John Kellogg Harris and his wife Chloe Minerva Bigelow Harris founded the Academy about 1875. The second school building remains on the Oxford Street site today. Mrs. Harris taught the lower grades there and Rev. Harris taught a college preparatory program. By all accounts, the Oxford Academy offered a high quality coed education, and it remained open until 1904. (See chapter 35 in this book for more information about the Oxford Academy.)

The Jacksonville Male Academy on Locust Street was originally private, but that building later housed the first public high school in Floyd County. Two private schools for girls were located in the town of Floyd: the Jacksonville Female Academy and the Ellen C. Staicos School.

Beginning in the 1840s, the Jacksonville Female Academy (also called "The School House") opened its doors as a private school. Later, before the building was abandoned in 1872, it appears to have been part of the public school system for a short time. It was located in back of where Gardner's Funeral Home stands today.

The Ellen C. Staicos School, also known as the Jacksonville Female Institute, was located on Main Street in town, near the current location of the Floyd Baptist Church. Records are not clear, but the school was probably started sometime between 1868 and 1870; it closed in 1885.

Many students also attended private mission schools in Floyd County. Those schools, church owned and operated, offered religious and educational programs for elementary and secondary students. The Montgomery Presbytery established the Harris Mountain Schools and they included Cannaday School (1914–1939) and Buffalo Mountain School (1921–1939) in Floyd County. The Abingdon Presbytery established the Franklin School in Indian Valley about 1922 and it closed in 1930. Also, Ferrum College founded the Ferrum Training School in the Harris Chapel community about 1917. That school continued until about 1930.

Quoting from "A Guide to the Harris Mountain Schools Collection, 1913–1961" (Virginia Tech Special Collections): "The Harris Mountain Schools, Presbyterian mission schools in Southwest Virginia, were founded in 1913 and located in Floyd, Montgomery,

This Cannaday School building was used as a dormitory for boarding students.

and Franklin Counties." The publication lists the following Harris Mountain Schools: Shooting Creek, Ferrum, Cannaday, Christiansburg, Buffalo Mountain, Sylyatus, Pippen Hill, Boone's Mill, Taylor's Mountain, Thaxton, Cave Mountain, Greenlee, Algoma, and Franklin.

While teacher training was briefly provided as a part of the Floyd High School curriculum, a more intense teacher training school was started at a private school at Hylton (Willis) about 1882. Referred to as the Mountain Normal School, Professor John B. Wrightsman

In the 1920s, students in remote parts of Floyd County had few, or no options, for obtaining secondary schooling. One option was Harris Cannaday School, a Presbyterian mission school. Pictured, in 1926 from left, is the first class to graduate from Cannaday School: Robert Lancaster, Margie Stringham, Max Thomas, Avis Thomas, Euriah Peters, and Velva Whitten.

of Bridgewater College founded the privately owned school, which remained open for about eight years. Another normal school for teachers was located at Pleasant Valley.

Based on Jean's article published in the Floyd Press *on July 1, 2004*

201

Besides academics, students years ago
occasionally went on field trips. Pictured here
are Pizarro School students on an outing at Bent
Mountain Falls.

Chapter 32
Local Impact of School Laws and Policies

Public free schools (or "common schools") were required by law to be operational in Virginia by 1876. Many Virginia counties were not in compliance with the new law that year, but Floyd County was. Where possible, previous school buildings were used. Local timber and suitable building sites were made available for the others. If there was one thing Floyd County had back then, it was plenty of trees and beautiful pastoral settings for schools. Paying for desks and other store-bought supplies—and getting them delivered to such a remote place—was another matter entirely. Yet, people in Floyd County managed. They were used to hard work and using available resources. That work ethic carried over to helping with those early, very basic schools.

At first, pencils were hard to come by. The first pencil factory in America had started production in 1860, but pencils were slow to make their way to these isolated Blue Ridge Mountains. Instead, local students used slates with slate pencils until about 1917. After that, pencils and tablet paper were available in local stores; notebook paper was available later on.

Dr. C. M. Stigleman was the first superintendent of schools in Floyd County, serving from 1870 to 1881. For the many country schools needing to be built, Dr. Stigleman drew up building specifications. Schools were to be 20 x 24 feet in overall size and 12 feet high. They were to have 4 windows with 12 panes each. The floor was to be tongue and groove, and roof shingles were to be made from American chestnut. The eaves were to project 21 inches on the sides.

Dr. R. T. Akers, school board member and an Alum Ridge doctor, talked about those early schools at the county's 100th birthday celebration. He said that in 1871, the first school census indicated there were 3,634 youth of school age in Floyd County. Moreover, those young people were spread out in all areas, many in remote places with rugged terrain—thus, the need for so many schools. By 1876, Floyd County had 52 schools open and another 13 under construction. By 1900, there were over 100 small country schools in Floyd County. Mostly, they were one- and two-room, ungraded schools. In 1914, twenty or more children were required by law in order to be considered a school. An exception could be made for 15 instead of 20 if there was "just cause." An average daily attendance also had to be maintained.

By 1915, child labor laws had been passed, meaning children couldn't be kept out of school because of factory work, mining, and other jobs. Yet children did stay home to help out in the home and on the farm. Local school funding in Floyd County would sometimes (often!) run out, causing schools to close out the school year early. A teacher might be hired under contract to teach for seven months but be paid for only five months.

In 1870, there were 36 licensed teachers in the county, and teachers were paid about $25 per month. Salaries remained low in the years ahead, and teachers were paid according to such factors as type of teaching certificate and type of teaching assignment. In 1891, a teacher had to be at least 18 years old to teach.

That same year, a resolution was passed in Virginia for uniform teacher exams. Those making 80 percent or better on the exam received a "First Grade Certificate" and were licensed to teach for three years. Those, making 70 percent or better received a "Second Grade Certificate" and were licensed for two years. Those making 60 percent or better received a "Third Grade Certificate" and were licensed for one year.

One of the duties of teachers in those early days was to visit students and their families in their homes and to enlist cooperation to improve school conditions. Sometimes teachers stayed overnight. In their monthly reports, teachers were required to document home visits.

Child school attendance laws were passed in 1915. That meant children ages 8 to 12 were required to attend school. Quoting from the 1915 *Acts of the Assembly Book for Virginia*, it states that "they [school children] had to go for at least 12 weeks of the school year, and at least six weeks needed to be consecutive . . . unless such child be weak in body or mind . . . or is attending a private school, or living more than two miles by the usual travel route from the nearest public school, or more than one mile from the line of an established public free school wagon route." Parents or guardians not complying with school attendance were fined.

References for Chapters 30–32:

Acts of the Assembly Book for Virginia (1910, 1914, 1915, 1916); *Excerpts from the Records and Other Facts about Education in Floyd County 1831–1962* by Ruby Bishop West; *The History of the Floyd County's Schools from 1831–1876* by Dr. Sarah Simmons, (1985); *The Development of Schooling in Floyd County, Virginia 1831–1900* by Dr. Sarah J. Simmons (1987); *Education in Virginia: A Bicentennial Report by Virginia Retired*

Teachers Association (1976); *Floyd County: A History of Its People and Places* by Dr. Amos Wood (1981); Various *Floyd Press* articles; oral and written information from Effie Brown, Clara Thomas, Daisy Thomas, Max Thomas, Marguerite Tise, Dorothy Vest, and others.

Based on Jean's article published in the Floyd Press *on July 8, 2004*

Toncray School was located on Black Ridge Road and that one-room building is still standing. Like many of the small schools back then, Toncray was in a lovely setting with nice views.

Kelley School, with two rooms, was located in the Lilac community near Blue Ridge Parkway milepost 149. The school was in operation, though, long before the Parkway was built. After the school closed, the building was used for a country store. The building is still standing and is now owned by the National Park Service.

By 1900, Floyd County had over 100 one- and two-room schools. Two of those are pictured above.

Chapter 33

My First Schools

County Line School

At the turn of the last century, over one hundred small schools dotted the countryside in Floyd County. One of those schools was on the Floyd–Franklin County line and it was appropriately called County Line School. Lila Vest Thomas taught there for two years, from 1948–1950, and she had seven grades in one room. She was my grandma and I was in her room for part of that time.

Barbara Thomas Spangler and her brothers, Rodney and Richard Thomas, also attended County Line School. In fact, Barbara and Rodney were students there for seven years and Richard went there for three years.

Barbara remembers some of the other teachers at County Line School: Thelma Houchins, Anise Houchins, and a Mr. Guffrie. Jacqueline Blackwell was the last teacher that Barbara remembers at County Line.

These are some students at County Line School in 1945–1946. Kneeling, from left: Maggie Midkiff and Barbara Thomas Standing, from left: Jean Radford, Tula Allen, and Christene Turner. Teacher that year was probably Jacqueline Blackwell Poff. Barbara Thomas's brothers, Rodney and Richard Thomas, also attended County Line School. *(Photo courtesy of Barbara Thomas Spangler)*

Ada Nolen, Robert Shelor's mother, attended County Line School and she, and other students there, posed for a group photo in 1915. Persons in that photo included Ernest Peters, Demoss Radford, Clarence Barton, Linkous Barton, Forest Agee, Callie Barton, Pat Barton, Noah Barton, Pearl Richardson, Earla Radford, Wilton Radford, Earla Thomas, Ruth Peters, Kate Barton, Rosa Agee, Lula Barton, Anabella Lancaster, Diamond Houchins, Ella Peters, Ella Agee, Gillie Radford, Howard Barton, Everett Agee, Moyer Agee, Fannie Cassaday, Ada Nolen, Ben Lancaster, and Lallie Lancaster.

Following are some of the students I remember from when I attended County Line School in the late 1940s: Frances Huff, Douglas Thomas, James Midkiff, Wesley Barton, Clinda Radford, Libby Radford, Maggie Midkiff, Irene Midkiff, Thomas Cole, and Bernard Huff.

County Line, on Thomas Farm Road, was up on a hill above Alvie and Avis Thomas's property. A path went up the hill to the school. There was a flat area to the left of the school for recess. It was rocky on the other side. I especially remember a rocky creek in back at the bottom of the hill—a pretty area for nature walks. The back room of the school building was used for recess in cold weather and for putting on plays. Barbara remembers using part of a desk as a sled for sliding down the snowy hill. County Line School is no longer standing.

This photo of the Harmony School building was taken sometime between 1945 and 1950. The two-room school was near the Blue Ridge Parkway and Rakes Mill Pond. Harmony was one of the last of the small schools to close and it is no longer standing. *(Photo courtesy of Betty Agee Nolen, who obtained it from the photographer, Ivadell Wade Janney)*

Harmony School students (grades 1–4) are pictured with Clara Thomas, teacher, in 1948–1949.

Row 1 (from left): Mary Trail, Betty Joyce Cockram, Joann Radford, Arnold Agee, Wade Martin, Sylvia Moran, Jack Frost Nolen, and Doris Radford

Row 2: Jean Thomas, Claude Wade, Lindal Martin, William Griffith, Jackie Agee, and Margaret Moran

Row 3: Howard Griffith, Clayton Moran, Adrian Moran, Leroy Richardson, Troy Moran, and S. W. Nolen

Row 4: Coy Wade, Junior Radford, Kenneth Duncan, Dayle and Gayle Agee, J. D. "Junior" Griffith, Harold Dean Radford, and G. W. Thomas

Row 5: Nancy Agnew, Douglas Thomas, Curtis Duncan, Harold Dean Linkous, Lula B. Moran, and Harry "Happy" Radford

Harmony School

Harmony, a two-room public school (grades 1–7), was one of the last small schools to close in this area. When it closed, many of the students went to school in Floyd, but some of the younger students went to school in Patrick County. The Harmony School building is no longer standing, but it was located on the east side of the Blue Ridge Parkway (near milepost 164), not far from Rakes Mill Pond. Teachers

From left: Hazel Moran, Mary Sue Brammer, Leonard Radford, S.W. Nolen, and Freeman Cockram

From left: ____, Arnold Duncan, Betty Jean Agee, Adrian Moran, Hazel Griffith, Shirley Agnew, Norma Peters, Harold Shelton, J. B. Goad, and William Hale

Here are some Harmony School students (grades 5–7) taught by Thelma Houchins in 1948–1949.

at Harmony during 1948–1950 were sisters. Clara Turner Thomas taught grades 1–4 and Thelma Turner Houchins taught grades 5–7.

The following is a combined list of Harmony School students for those two school terms, 1948–1949 and 1949–1950. This list is from teacher "registers" and is an amalgamation of four student rosters, alphabetized by students' last names. A few other names have been added, based on student recollections.

Arnold Agee, Betty Jean Agee, Dayle Agee, Gayle Agee, Jackie Agee, Nancy Agnew, Shirley Agnew, Tommy Agnew, Mary Sue Brammer, Betty Joyce Cockram, Corine Cockram, Freeman Cockram, Joyce Cochran, Netty Cockram, Nora Cockram, Arnold Duncan, Curtis Duncan, John Duncan, Joyce Duncan, Kenneth Duncan, Wesley Duncan, Nancy Gardner, James Goad, Harold Griffith, Hazel Griffith, Howard Griffith, Irene Griffith, J. D. "Junior" Griffith, Wayne Griffith, William Griffith, William Hale, Lee Jackson, Joyce James, Rachel Jones, Robert Jones, Rokie Jones, Harold Dean Linkous, Vivian McAdams, Edna Jane Martin, Lindal Martin, Wade Martin, Adrian Moran, Alvis Moran, Ardella Moran, Clayton Moran. Hazel Moran, Lula B. Moran, Margaret Moran, Marvin Moran, Sylvia Moran, Troy Moran, Donald Nolen, Jack Frost Nolen, Joyce Lee Nolen, Larkin Nolen, L. T. Nolen, Samuel ("S. W.") Nolen, Curtis Peters, Norma Peters, Eileen Pratt, Hattie Pratt, Palmer Pratt, Doris Radford, Harold Dean Radford, Harry "Happy" Radford, Joann Radford, Junior Radford, Leonard Radford, Leroy Richardson, Harold Shelton, Douglas Thomas, G. W. Thomas, Jean Thomas, Harlie (Harley?) Trail, Hubert Trail, Garfield Underwood, Claude Wade, Coy Wade, Joyce Wade, Thelma Wade, Nancy Faye West

Based, in part, on Jean's article published in the Floyd Press *on July 8, 2004*

Lila Ann Vest Thomas and her siblings attended Iddings School. Later on, Lila was a teacher there. She was Jean's paternal grandma.

Effie King Brown was also a student at Iddings School and, later on, she taught school there. She is pictured above in a younger pose and then, on the right, wearing her DAR ribbons. Effie was a historian and much of the information about Iddings School is from her. Among other roles, Effie was a charter member of the Floyd County Historical Society. She was also an accomplished quilter. She spent her career as a teacher and school principal

Brownlow Light (1861–1947) was a teacher at Iddings School. His brother, Scipio Light (1864–1934), was also a teacher in the Locust Grove district. Their parents were Samuel J. and Salina Link Light. *(Photo courtesy of David Shank, who received it from Christine Light)*

Chapter 34

Iddings School

Iddings School, built in 1876, was about a mile from Kings Store Road in the Locust Grove community. The school was in the middle of a large wooded area and no roads led to the school—only paths.

My grandma, Lila Vest Thomas, attended that school—along with her brothers and sisters. Effie King Brown and her siblings also attended Iddings School. My grandma Lila used to talk about Brownlow Light and thought he was a very fine teacher.

According to Effie, the following families were among those on the school rolls over the years: Vest, King, Hall, Whitenack, Aldridge, Austin, Spangler, Lawrence, and Simpson.

Effie told me that it cost $250 to build Iddings School and that cost included materials and labor. She said the school faced east and was 24 x 28 feet. Windows were on the south and west sides, and the blackboard was on the north side of the building. The spring was downhill, not far from Big Run Creek.

She said that enough land was cleared in front of the building for a playground and that it stayed muddy in wet weather. Children in the same family took a lunch in a shared basket or bucket and sat together to eat.

In 1904, the building was repainted, according to Effie, and wooden benches were replaced by desks. The last year Iddings was open was during the 1939-40 school year. After that, students attended Check School. The Iddings School building burned down in the 1960s.

Effie said the last day of school was referred to as "school breaking." During the summer, a singing school was held at Iddings, and Henry Graham was the singing master. My father said that Henry Graham was a very fine singing master.

Effie Brown shared with me the following list of teachers who taught at Iddings School from 1892 to 1940:

1892–1895 (Brownlow Light, 3 terms); 1895–1899 (Teachers and specific dates not known but believed to be Scipio Light, Charles H. King and James Clower); 1900–1903 (Brownlow Light, 3 terms); 1903–1908 (These five years were taught by Lila Vest, 2 terms; Carrie King, 1 term; other two terms unknown); 1908–1910 (Brownlow Light, 2 terms); 1910–1912 (Scipio Light, 2 terms); 1912–1914 (Mary C. Hall, 2 terms); 1914–1916 (Ida Vest, 2 terms); 1916–1917 (Carrie N. King, 1 term); 1917–1918 (Daniel S. Lucas, one-half term. He left mid-year to serve as a cashier at the State Bank of Check. His term was completed by Ruby Sisson); 1918–1919 (Maisie M. King); 1919–1920 (Grace Aldridge); 1920–1921 (Ida Vest. Miss Ida had to close school on account of poor vision. Alice Vest Thomas completed the term in late spring after her regular term had closed. Some children not ordinarily enrolled at Iddings were present. (Their regular school had closed for the term.); 1921–1922 (Lucille Bowman); 1922–1923 (Bernice Austin); 1923–1924 (Ida Vest); 1924–1925 (Green Martin); 1925–1926 (Grace Aldridge); 1926–1928 (Information not available); 1928–1929 (Sankey King); 1929–1930 (Daisy DeWitt); 1930–1933 (Goldie King, 3 terms); 1933–1934 (Grace Aldridge); 1935–1936 (Alice Vest Thomas); 1936–1939 (Effie King Brown, 3 terms); 1939–1940 (Neta DeWitt).

Effie said that some other early teachers at Iddings School were Marion Clingenpeel, Milton Link and James Clower. However, Effie was unable to determine specific years they taught. The years taught by Brownlow Light were documented by his daughter, Christine Vest.

(Information in this chapter is based on Jean's interviews with Effie King Brown, on information from Max Thomas, and on information in the following Floyd Press *articles: December 11, 1986, and November 4, 1984.)*

This photo of Iddings School students was taken in 1915 at the end of the school year.

First Row seated, from left: Bessie Vest, Harlie Vest, Berkley Vest, Valerie Aldridge, Effie King, John King, Charles King, Oakly Vest, Noel Wright, and Willard Wright

Second Row: Mamie Vest, Bertie Vest, Lura Aldridge, Annie Wright, Wilford Wright, Evelyn Vest, Anne King, Leonard Conner, Howard Vest, and teacher Ida Vest

Third Row: Sankey King, Arlie Hale, Laurel Vest, Verna Vest, Mamie Ann Vest, Goldie King, Inez Poff, and Rex Aldridge

Fourth Row: Tide Hall, Edith Vest, Erby Hall, Pearl Austin, Staunton Hall, Flora Wright, Pencye Hall, Nellie Vest, Mamie King, and Eslie Vest

(Photo courtesy of Mary Edith Hankins, who received it and identifying information from Effie King Brown)

The Oxford Academy was a private preparatory school founded in Floyd about 1875 by the Reverend John Kellogg Harris and his wife, Chloe Minerva Bigelow Harris. Pictured is the second building on the site. (The building is owned today by the Floyd County Historical Preservation Trust. Recently, the historic school building has been repaired and dressed up with a new coat of paint, new roof, and new sign.)

Chapter 35

Oxford Academy

Eight years after the American Civil War, a dedicated preacher from New York State came to Floyd Court House with his wife. He had accepted a call to pastor the old Jacksonville Presbyterian Church, which still stands on Main Street in Floyd.

Three years later, in addition to his church ministry, he pursued an additional calling and founded the Oxford Academy. The young preacher's name was John Kellogg Harris, and he had graduated from Williams College and Union Theological Seminary. His wife, Chloe Minerva Bigelow Harris, had been raised in Vermont and educated at Mount Holyoke College. Together, they offered a quality of education in Floyd County that rivaled the best precollege programs in the country.

After working with the public schools in Floyd for a brief time, the Harrises founded the Oxford Academy, a private preparatory school. Built in 1875, the school building was situated behind the Presbyterian parsonage where the Harris family lived. Both house and school were located on the north side of "Back Street" (now called Oxford Street).

According to their granddaughter, Susan Grey Akers, that original school building was a log structure with two large ground-floor rooms "opening on an unfloored porch which ran the full length of the building." Sometime between 1898 and 1900, that log building was destroyed by fire, but a replacement two-room frame structure was built and was ready for students by June 1901. That building is still standing today. (*Floyd Press*, 7/1/1976)

These days [2003], the old school sits quietly on its stone foundation, in a setting that seems worlds apart from today's hurried pace — the old oaken bucket no longer out front. Gray weathered boards cover its 52 x 24 feet expanse, and two chimneys are evenly spaced along the ridge of its tin roof. A southern exposure provides a warm entry to the building, and a backdrop of trees serves as a buffer to northwest winds. Large pine trees hug the north side of the building and a huge tree out back, like the school, must be a centenarian, too. These inviting grounds, where children once played, are now a habitat for songbirds, squirrels, and other wild beings.

Standing inside the front door of that stark tall-ceiling structure, it is easy to picture two coed classrooms, fore and aft — one with young children being taught by Mrs. Harris, and the other with high school age youth being taught by Rev. Harris.

"A common statement in Floyd during the life of the school," according to Susan Grey Akers, was that "in Mr. Harris's room anyone could get a college education if he wanted it; in Mrs. Harris's room one got a good elementary education whether he wanted it or not."

In addition to local students, the school enrollment also included students from surrounding counties. Some students boarded with the Harris family and others were day students. According to a *Floyd Press* article (11/22/62), the number of students enrolled from 1892 to 1901 varied from 35 to 86 per year. Many of the school's graduates went on to have impressive careers.

In her article about the Academy, which was cited later in the *Floyd Press* (7/1/1976), Susan Grey Akers described an old undated broadside from the Academy: "We teach much of the common College Course. . . . We give great attention to the Common School work. We offer English, Latin, French, and Greek, fitting pupils for the Universities. The Primary Department and that of Piano Music have fine patronage." According to Ms. Akers, the Oxford Academy was recognized by the University of New York state as "being equal to or above the New York schools." (*Floyd Press*, 11/22/1962)

Academics must have been rigorous at the Oxford Academy, for higher-level math and other advanced courses were taught there. Yet, it is certain that Rev. and Mrs. Harris also provided a nurturing and exciting place to study. However, the building was referred to by students as "the north pole" because it was so cold in the winter. There must have been a great warmth of spirit in that building, though.

In Dr. Amos Wood's book titled *Floyd County: A History of Its People and Places* (1981), there is a description of one of the school's extracurricular activities. It seems that each spring, the Harris couple took the entire student body to Buffalo Mountain for an outing. With plenty of food and blankets, they traveled the twenty miles in a covered wagon and spent a day and night on the knob. "The objective was to take in the extensive view and watch the sun rise on top of the knob."

Like schools today, pranks were sometimes part of life at the Oxford Academy, too. In a *Floyd Press* article (7/1/1976), Heath Dalton told the following story handed down from the early 1900s that involved a kicking mule:

> Little Joe Jett and his buddies, the instigators of the calamity, decided they were going to take advantage of the news of the San Francisco earthquake and stir up things for their Oxford

Academy schoolmates. Since a lot of boys rode mules to school back then, it was easy to obtain a kicking animal. Tying a mule to the entrance of the Academy, the boys placed a chestnut burr on its tail. Then they let nature take its course. The end result was an awful lot of kicking and the vacating of the classrooms. Those attending school that day were just sure the San Francisco earthquake had reached Floyd.

Not all was studies and fun at the school. On Monday morning, December 14, 1896, a dangerous fire broke out in the middle of town. A *Floyd Press* article three days later reported the details. Among those helping fight the fire were Rev. Harris and his Oxford Academy pupils. "Even the young ladies [students] exerted themselves to the utmost carrying water." Thankfully, no one died in that destructive fire.

An early Floyd newspaper called *The Weekly News* gave an account of "closing exercises" at the Academy on June 4, 1895. The program opened with prayer and included singing of hymns and patriotic music. Thirty-one students gave talks or recitations. Jessie Peterman's topic was "Lenten Service." A. P. DeLong delivered the salutatory speech, which was titled "The Death of Benedict Arnold."

A complete list of Oxford Academy students is included with the Harris family papers. From that list, Susan Grey Akers lists some of those students in a piece she wrote Oct. 31, 1962: Rev. Francis Phillip Price, Major B. H. Hensley, Warren Latimer, Judge John Edward Burwell, Paul Penick, Senator Wells Goodykoontz, Dr. R. T. Akers, Dr. J. T. Akers, Rev. John Smith, and Dr. S.S. Guerrant.

For almost three decades, the Oxford Academy was a paragon of education; it appears to have been one of the finest private schools anywhere. Except for seven years (1882 to 1889) when they were away doing mission work in Nebraska, the school was run continually by the Harris couple. Even in their absence, it appears the old school mostly stayed open and Rev. W. R. Coppedge, next pastor for the Presbyterian Church in town, operated the Academy during most of those seven years (according to the 1985 doctoral dissertation by Dr. Sarah James Simmons).

Even after Mrs. Harris's death in 1897, classes continued at the Oxford Academy for about seven more years. Mayday Harris followed in her mother's footsteps and was the first replacement teacher for young children at the school. The Academy closed in 1904 when Rev. Harris had to give it up due to declining health. (*Floyd Press*, 7/1/1976)

In addition to serving as pastor for the Jacksonville Presbyterian Church, Rev. Harris helped found the Turtle Rock Presbyterian Church in the Pizarro community in 1882 and was minister there for about fifteen years. The Turtle Rock Church served the Pizarro–Turtle Rock community for about thirty years before it closed in disrepair. A few years later in 1916, people in that same community paid for and built the Harvestwood Presbyterian Church, not far from where the old Turtle Rock Church had been.

A few years after Rev. Harris died, the Montgomery Presbytery began the process in 1913 of organizing and financing a mission school program for the area. As a result, mission schools were eventually started at Buffalo Mountain, Shooting Creek, Cannaday School, and other places. Although the Oxford Academy had not been a mission school, the mission school founders were greatly impressed with Rev. Harris's qualities and accomplishments and wanted to honor him by naming the new mission school program after him. They called it the "Harris Mountain Schools."

After it closed, the old Oxford Academy building must have looked lonely without its teachers and students. However, that changed for a brief time during the 1930s. During that time, the public schools of Floyd County had a shortage of classroom space, and for a couple of years, public school classes were held in that old two-room building. Margaret Smith, a retired educator, remembers being a first grade student there in 1936–1937. Her classroom was at the front of the building and her teacher was Clara Thomas. Helen Cox taught the other first grade class that year at the back of the building.

After that, the building—which had been owned by the Presbyterian Church of Floyd for many years—was used for such things as church dinners, day camps, and Boy Scout meetings. Finally, the building and property were sold in 1973 to Mr. G. M. Lovins. (Today, the Oxford Academy is owned by the Floyd County Historical Preservation Trust. Efforts have been made to preserve the building, and some repairs have been made. A sign out front has been erected and a new coat of paint dresses up the building.)

References for Oxford Academy article:

- Conversations with Max and Clara Thomas
- *Presbyterian Historical Almanac and Annual Remembrance of the Church for 1867*, by Joseph M. Wilson
- Minutes of the Montgomery Presbytery, 9/15/1910
- *Floyd County: A History of Its People and Places*, by Dr. Amos D. Wood

- *Excerpts from the Records and Other Facts about Education in Floyd County: 1831–1962*, by Ruby Bishop West
- *The Development of Schooling in Floyd County, Virginia 1831–1900*, by Dr. Sarah James Simmons, April 1987 (Virginia Tech Ph.D. dissertation)
- *The Weekly News*, 6/12/1895
- *Floyd Press* article dated 7/1/1976 that contains excerpts from an earlier article (by Susan Grey Akers) published in Chapel Hill, North Carolina, on 10/31/1962
- Additional *Floyd Press* articles

Based on Jean's article published in the Floyd Press *on April 3, 2003, and on Jean's article in the book,* The Presbyterian Church of Floyd: Celebrating 150 Years of History, *Nov 2003*

Old-Time Games

Following is information about some old-time games that my mother, Clara Thomas, remembered playing as a child—both at home and at school. Once she was a teacher, her students played some of those games, too. In her own words below, she tells how to play some of those games.

Jack in the Bush

This game may be played with marbles, pebbles, corn, chestnuts, or chinquapins. I remember playing it mostly with chestnuts. We had lots of chestnuts at our home. One person puts some chestnuts in his closed hand and says, "Jack in the bush." A second person says, "Cut him down." The first person says, "How many licks?" Then the second person guesses how many chestnuts the first person has. If he gets it right, he gets all of the chestnuts, and if he doesn't, he has to give the first person the difference. The object is to try to get all the chestnuts.

Squirrel in a Tree

Most players stand in groups of three—two with hands on each other's shoulders to make a hollow tree and one (the "squirrel") stands in the middle of the hollow tree. One "squirrel" is without a tree. The teacher or leader claps his hands and then all "squirrels" must run for other trees. The extra "squirrel" tries to secure a tree. The "squirrel" that is left without a tree has to be "it" the next time.

Stealing Sticks

The ground is divided into two equal parts. Two leaders choose up sides. Each side has a base, a prison, and twelve sticks. Sticks are 8–10 inches long. The prison is over to the left, 8–10 feet away. Each side tries to steal the other side's sticks. If a person is caught with a stick he has stolen, he is deprived of the stick and put in prison. The only way he can be freed is for a man on his side to successfully rescue him without getting caught. The object of the game is to see which side can own all the sticks first. This game for 10–30 players was played mostly at school and lasted throughout a recess period.

Chapter 36

First Do No Harm

In the fall of 1993, more than 7 million U.S. children entered kindergarten or first grade. Regardless of their backgrounds, most started school with a love for nature and a curiosity about the world around them—scientists in the purest sense.

A worthy goal in the educational process should be *primum non nocere*—first do no harm. Yet research shows that by age ten, harm *will* be done, and most of these children will find science boring. Most will be turned off to science—permanently. Little wonder that only 7 percent of them will graduate from high school prepared for college-level science.

These same children will grow up in the most scientific and technologically advanced world society has ever known. Yet, most will make non-science career choices and grow up to be scientifically illiterate voting citizens.

Upgrading U.S. science education has been a timely topic since the 1960s. Yet some of the same goals agreed to in the Sputnik era keep recurring in the literature of science reform. How do we make change happen?

I believe we must begin at the beginning—in kindergarten or first grade while children still have a curiosity and interest in science. We must nurture that interest and make sure it is not stifled in the following four or five years, when studies show it usually dies. Teaching no science to young children may be preferable to teaching it poorly.

Above all, science needs to be made relevant to young children's daily experiences, laying a foundation for more challenging, abstract learning later. Rather than a dry bookish approach, science teaching needs to be spontaneous—teachers and students exploring, investigating, and questioning together. Yes, *questioning*.

It is not a crime for a teacher to say, "I'm not sure of the answer. Let's look it up." In fact, encouraging young children to question may be the most important science lesson of all. No one knows *all* the answers in science, but it is important for teachers to serve as role models for scientific inquiry.

How exciting for students and teachers to discover something together, and for teachers to lead them to what one writer has aptly called "the threshold of their minds." Science processes, as well as trial and error lead to the wonder of science—not isolated, dull facts.

What do young children need to know about science? They need to know that science is interesting, that it's all around them and can be studied on the playground, in a snowstorm, or in the kitchen making cookies. That we can learn science while doing a reading lesson, math, or creative writing. They need to know science is an "equal opportunity" subject. That girls and minorities—the most "at risk" groups in science classes—can hold their own with the best.

Perhaps the most important science lesson any elementary teacher can teach her students—I say *her* because most elementary teachers are women—is to be a confident role model, showing them that science is interesting and not to be feared. It's a way of thinking—a "no holds barred" approach to learning.

In an already tightly programmed elementary school day, what can be done to enable teachers to teach science this way? First, school principals must make science a priority and encourage teachers. Second, every elementary teacher needs a network of school and community resources and a science mentor. And third, the majority of in-service and future teachers need more training in science subject matter and pedagogy.

Although in-depth college training in science is not essential for elementary teachers, present requirements are inadequate. It is unacceptable that, as the Project 2061 report showed, "few elementary teachers have even a rudimentary education in science and math." It is not enough for only 3½ percent to be specifically trained for math and science teaching (as estimated by the National Science Teachers Association). Obviously, such deficiencies cause subject-matter insecurity and limit teachers' creativity.

Recognizing these problems, it is important that state teacher certification boards and universities work together to set standards in science training for elementary teachers. Future and in-service teachers probably need to take at least four semesters in laboratory sciences—two semesters in the physical and earth sciences and two semesters in the life sciences.

Twenty-five years ago, two years of science was typical of elementary teacher training, but in recent times only one or two semesters may be required, or a less rigorous alternative. Sometimes, the best refresher for tenured teachers is *retaking* a freshman-level survey course in a laboratory science.

Beyond lab-science courses, future and in-service teachers need at least one college course in science pedagogy. Preferably taught by professors with backgrounds in science and precollege teaching experience, such a course should focus on the "big ideas" of science in the context of the elementary curriculum. The course should be hands-on science, modeling how to make science exciting to young children.

The answers to precollege science education are not simple, but it is critical that the early grades be carefully looked at as an important part of the problem.

Certainly, as local and national groups explore solutions, elementary teachers must be included in the thinking and decision-making process. They are the most familiar with the classroom situation, and their input and cooperation are essential for lasting success.

If the difference is to be made with this year's kindergarten and first grade students, it is going to take serious commitment at all levels and a resolve to "first do no harm."

(While still a second grade classroom teacher, Jean worked with Dr. Larry Wiseman, Biology chair at The College of William and Mary, on a research grant. The purpose of that research was to consider ways to better incorporate science into elementary school classrooms. Jean wrote this commentary as an outgrowth of that work)

Based on Jean's article published in "Education Week,"
volume XII, Number 26 on March 24, 1993

Members of the Floyd Senior 4-H Club around 1958:
1st row from left: Janet Nixon, Narleen Belcher, and Mary
    Jo Peters
2nd row: Rebecca Weeks, Loreeta Nixon, Mary Louise
    Sowers, and Anna Weeks
3rd (back) row: Jean Thomas, Lena Ruth Via, and Diane
    Hatcher
The club's 4-H leader was Cora Huddle and the 4-H
Extension Agent at that time was Peggy Moles

Chapter 37

Hands-On Learning for All Ages
4-H and the Cooperative Extension Service

This book's section on education would not be complete if I didn't tell about 4-H and the impact it made on my life. School was important, but my learn-by-doing experiences in 4-H made learning especially fun and relevant. 4-H tapped into every interest I had—including music, travel, camping, leadership, public speaking, writing, and community service. I also found it interesting to learn about such subjects as entomology, veterinary science, forestry, and nutrition. My experiences were often self-guided.

I also learned about accountability and how to document what I had done, for that was a 4-H requirement—whether completing a project book, applying for a 4-H scholarship, or something else. Years later, that kind of experience was invaluable as I applied for college and jobs.

I loved being part of our local 4-H club, and we did all kinds of interesting and worthwhile community projects. And when I was a teenager, I also organized a 4-H club of my own. It was for children nearby, and we learned about many things—how to cook and give a cooking demonstration, how to make an insect collection, how to care for animals, and how to run a meeting with elected officers.

As a farm family, we were never able to travel, but through 4-H, I had the opportunity to participate in out-of-county events and meet new people. I especially enjoyed 4-H camps and conferences. 4-H also afforded me opportunities to travel to other parts of the United States and to Ireland and Northern Ireland as an International Farm Youth Exchange (IFYE) delegate in 1964 for six months.

4-H is the youth development program of the nation's land-grant universities and the Cooperative Extension Service. 4-H got its start in the early 1900s after the Smith-Lever Act of 1914 established the Cooperative Extension Service. Originally a program for rural youth, 4-H reaches out to all young people today—including youth in inner cities. Most every county in the United States has an Extension office that serves both youth and adults.

I always remember my mother attending Extension Homemaker meetings. Originally referred to as Home Demonstration Clubs, she and other women in the Pizarro community met each month. Extension Homemaker clubs were, and still are, part of the

Cooperative Extension Service. And farmers continue to ask for advice from the County Agent (agriculture agent). Now, though, the general public looks to the Extension office for all kinds of help—lawn and garden, financial planning, health and nutrition, parenting education, and more. Such services provide opportunities for life-long learning for us all.

These Pizarro Home Demonstration (HD) Club members learned how to refinish wooden floors at this meeting, around 1948.
Kneeling, from left: Mildred Ingram Nolen, Charles Sutphin (child), Clydie Sutphin, and Goldie Gardner
Standing: ____, Lou Barnard, Myra Peters, young girl, Maggie Nichols, Annie Thompson, Minnie Cock, Mrs. Percy Lawrence, ____, and Agnes Sutphin

Pizarro HD members, around 1947, are displaying their lamps. The Home Extension Agent, Frances Graham (center front), had taught them how to convert oil lamps to electric lamps that day.

Pictured on front row, from left: Clydie Sutphin, ____, Frances Graham, Jean Thomas (child standing), Myra Peters, Agnes Sutphin, and Lula Nichols (standing)

Standing in second row, from left: Zonie Peters, Thelma Houchins (with baby Alicia), ____, Clara Thomas, Ella Turner, Sadie Wright, ____, ____, and Annie Thompson (on far right)

The Pizarro HD Club later became known as the Pizarro Ladies Club.
Pictured here, around 1985, are some of the women who were part of one or both of those groups:

Seated, from left: Verla Huff, Louise Thompson, Jacqueline Blackwell, and Effie Brown

Standing, from left: Ann Arrington, Annette Ware, Shelby Hall, Audrey Harris, Agnes Sutphin, Ingrid Hearn, Clara Thomas, Catherine Vest, Dorothy Vest, Judy Blackwell, Myra Peters, and Lucy Tanner

This is another photo of women in the Pizarro community who were members of the Pizarro HD club, Pizarro Ladies Club, or both. The photo was taken around 1985.
Bottom row from left: Susie Vest, Alice West, and Irma West Otto
Middle row: Agnes Sutphin and Lucy Tanner
Back row: Ann Arrington, Effie Brown, and Clara Thomas

Chapter 38

Early Schoolbooks

When I was a little girl, children's books were not as available as today, and Floyd County had no public library. The books that appealed to me at home were the *Little Golden Books* that cost 25 cents, comic books, and the *World Book Encyclopedia*.

I also liked the old reading textbooks at our house—ones my parents had either studied in school or used for instruction when they taught in one- and two-room schools. I thought those early 1900s textbooks were fascinating, and they are still a reminder of how I learned to read and came to love books. They were also a comfort to me when I was sick in bed and needed to entertain myself.

The ones that interested me most were the old reading books. As I look through them now, I am amazed at the variety of textbook companies represented: Allyn and Bacon, Rand McNally, Ginn and Company, Hall and McCreary, Houghton Mifflin, The University Publishing Company, The Macmillan Company, Thompson and Wilson, D. C. Heath and Company, American Book Company, and Scott Foresman and Company. We know that many textbook companies were publishing books back then, but how was it that such a variety of them ended up in small schools in Floyd County?

Public education in Virginia had been mandated since 1876, and county commissioners had been making decisions about which textbooks to use. Decisions were made, but obtaining textbooks, desks, and other school supplies was a challenge in this mountain area. Trees were available for building one-room schools, but state and local funds provided little money to pay for schoolroom supplies—including textbooks.

As a result, during the early 1900s, families were required to purchase textbooks, and those books were handed down from sibling to sibling. By the time the youngest child got a book, it was usually well worn. Teachers and pupils used what books they had or could get. I've heard old-time teachers say they never got rid of schoolbooks, for they were "so hard to come by."

Local grocery stores were sometimes able to order textbooks, and families purchased books there. During the 1920s and 1930s, some families purchased songbooks for school use, too. According to educator Effie King Brown, families in her area bought textbooks at John Gray's General Store at Check.

Even though there was a shortage of books, they were at the

very center of education in those days and served as *the* curriculum. Children brought their books to school in "book sacks" (book bags). The start of the school day was referred to as "taking up books."

Although I never saw a copy, except on the Internet, my dad talked about the "Will and May" book he first used for reading. Published in 1906, that book's official title was *Playmates: A Primer*, and it was written by M. W. Haliburton and published by the B. F. Johnson Publishing Company. That 96-page, illustrated book was about playmates named Will, May, Kate, and others. My dad used to quote from the first pages of that book: "This is Will. How do you do, Will? This is May. How do you do, May?" Interestingly, there was an American Sign Language chart at the beginning of that book, and I wonder if that book was ever used for teaching children who were deaf.

My dad also talked about the "Blue Back Speller" he used in school. Published in 1824, that book's official title was *The American Spelling Book*. That 198-page book by Noah Webster was used for a century. Besides word study, the "Blue Back Speller" included rhymes and the alphabet.

Of all the old reading textbooks at our house, the ones that interested me most were the *Elson-Gray Readers* and the *Fact and Story Readers* of the early 1930s. *Elson-Gray Readers* were written by William H. Elson and William S. Gray and were published by Scott Foresman and Company. The *Fact and Story Readers* were by Suzzallo, Freeland, McLaughlin, and Skinner, and they were published by the American Book Company.

Both reading books were ones my mother had used as a student or when teaching. What was it about those books that attracted me so? First of all, they were available for my enjoyment at home. But it wasn't just that. I loved their stories and illustrations. They tapped into my imagination in a wonderful way. I loved the folktales, fables, fairy tales, stories about animals, stories about holidays, and stories about other countries. I also loved the poetry—poems by Robert Louis Stevenson, Elizabeth Madox Roberts, Walter de la Mare, Vachel Lindsay, and others.

From those readers, I especially remember old-time tales such as "The Billy Goats Gruff," "Johnny Cake," "The Little Red Hen," "The Fairy Shoemaker," "The Three Little Pigs," "Jack and the Beanstalk," "The Princess Who Could Not Cry," "Why the Rabbit's Tail is Short," "Cinderella," "The Lion and the Mouse," "The Lambkin," "The Monkey and the Doll Hats," "The Little Blue Dishes," and "Bobby Squirrel Plays a Joke." I also liked such poems as "My Shadow" by Robert Louis Stevenson.

People years ago could recite poems from memory, and Effie Brown, local historian and educator, said she was required to memorize all the poems in one of her *Elson-Gray* readers—poems such as "The Real Santa Claus" and "Arrow and the Song." I, too, did some memory work and I still remember the words to John Greenleaf Whittier's "The Barefoot Boy." That poem comes as close as any writing to expressing how I feel about nature and my upbringing.

Besides focusing on silent reading and literature, those *Elson-Gray* readers were sight word–vocabulary based. By the late 1940s, schools were using the *Dick and Jane* basal readers. I read Dick and Jane books in primary school and thought those realistic, everyday stories were not so interesting as the old readers we had at home—the ones my parents had used. Ironically, the *Dick and Jane* stories got their start in the *Elson-Gray Readers*. Those first *Dick and Jane* stories later morphed into their own *Dick and Jane* books. The Scott Foresman Company published the *Elson-Gray Readers* and the later *Dick and Jane* books. They did not include phonics study.

In the 1800s, prior to the *Elson-Gray* type of reading books, my grandparents studied *McGuffey's Eclectic Readers*. Written and first published in 1836 by William Holmes McGuffey, the *McGuffey* books may have been the best-known school reading series in American education history.

The *McGuffey* books were a "graded series," later referred to as "basal readers," and they marked the beginning of efforts to standardize education and textbooks in this country. *McGuffey* books stressed phonics, penmanship, and word study.

McGuffey's Readers had small print and some black and white pictures that looked like engravings. The series contained seven books: a primer and a first, second, third, fourth, fifth, and sixth reader. The lower level readers included stories about nature and stories with moral lessons. The Second Reader included twenty-five poems, including "Sweet and Low" by Alfred Lord Tennyson and "Twinkle, Twinkle Little Star," written by Jane Taylor in 1806. The higher-level *McGuffey's Readers*, especially the 5th and 6th readers, focused on prose and poetry of 19th century England and America.

In 150 years of reading pedagogy, some beliefs and practices, such as the teaching of phonics, have come full circle. For example, the teaching of phonics was in vogue during the McGuffey period. Later, phonics was replaced by other teaching methods because critics believed the phonics-based program wasn't working—that reading comprehension was not good enough.

Rather than phonics, the emphasis during the 1930s was on a "look–say" approach that included reading for meaning and silent reading. Reading textbooks at that time included folk tales, fables, fairy tales, and other interesting stories. Poetry continued to be included. In the 1940s and 1950s, sight words were still taught and a period of realism brought textbooks, like the *Dick and Jane* series, to the classroom. Reading test scores were not impressive.

During the following years, the "whole language" approach became the focus for teaching reading and writing. Relying on library-type books, rather than basal readers, the "whole language" approach emphasized high-quality, culturally diverse literature. "Whole language" implied something special and comprehensive and included reading and phonics, understanding and appreciating literature, writing, spelling, vocabulary, pronunciation, and grammar. Yet, phonics and grammar often fell by the wayside.

Reading test scores did not improve, and educators began looking back at Rudolf Flesch's 1955 book titled *Why Johnny Can't Read*. Flesch blamed reading problems on a de-emphasis on phonics.

During the 1980s and after, many teachers once more began including phonics instruction as part of the reading curriculum. When I taught reading to my second grade students, I thought it worked best to use a combination of approaches, with emphasis on phonics.

I am not here to debate teaching methods for reading. It is interesting, though, to think back on textbook history and the various ideas and fad methodologies that have surfaced, and repeated themselves, over the years for teaching reading. Modern technology adds an additional variable to the learning—or not learning—process.

The main thing, it seems, is to use whatever it takes to help children learn to read and to enjoy reading—beginning with parents reading to their children while holding them on their laps. For society, reading may be more important than any part of the educational process. As Mahatma Gandhi said, "You don't have to burn books to destroy a culture. Just get people to stop reading them."

Based on Jean's article published in the Floyd Press *on August 1, 2013, and on her graduate studies research at Hollins University*

Old-time reading books and their publishers from the 1930s: *Day by Day* from Allyn and Bacon; *My Other Reading Book* from Rand McNally; *Fact and Story Readers* from the American Book Company; and *Elson-Gray Basic Readers* from Scott, Foresman and Company

Pages 48–49 of *Moore-Wilson Readers: A Peep into Fairyland*, published by D. C. Heath & Company in 1927

Pages 116–117 of the *Smedley & Olsen New First Reader*, published by the Hall & McCreary Company in 1928

Afterword in Verse

Their Majesty

Twice my age and more,
these grand old trees are all
that's left of life I knew
back then.

Eighty feet tall they stand,
their girths too big
for me to hug.

Survivors, these
enduring giants
from nature's storms
and loggers' saws
and grazing gypsy moths.

And now, downwind
from distant stacks,
invisible particulate bathes
each leaf and stem.

During growing times
and other times,
the bombardment
continues on.

And from above
the oxides come—
a noxious fallout mist.

And on the ground
developers scheme—
mighty lucre,
their main goal.

They cut and chop
without a thought—
a century's growth
now prone.

This crazy quilt
of painful change—
it leaves a tragic wake.

(Written by Jean in 2002)

Nature's Concert – a sonnet

O let me join your great, symphonic band
And play a part in your enchanted vales,
Where fluted breezes blow across the land
Through evergreens that mute those treble wails.
Where nature's brown thrush trills its happy song,
Where chirping crickets strum their pulsing wings,
Composing lively music all day long
To glorify the other living things.
And here, I find a tiny winding stream—
Its gurgling notes play on the rocks below,
A harpsichord in Mother Nature's theme
With rhythmic tones precisely full and sweet.
Where will your maestro let me take my stand
While he directs this joyful singing band?

(Written by Jean when she was in high school. Poem later published in the Radford Review, *Volume XVI, Number 2, Spring 1962.)*

Chicory

Chicory lined the roadsides—
its cornflower blue petals
reaching out in comfort
as I looked after my mother
that summer.
Years before we gathered
those flowers, she and I,
and put them in a vase—
a pretty bouquet
that soon faded to white.
We always laughed
about the color change
that greeted our guests.

(Written by Jean in 2002)

Stepstone

Years ago, old buildings sometimes had stepstones—a stone laid before a door, as a stair to rise on when entering a house. When the Floyd County Historical Society Museum (once a hospital) first opened on May 29, 2010, Jean read a poem she had written for the occasion. She was thinking of the museum as a stepstone—a stepstone from the past, and a bridge to the future. (Poem published in the Floyd Press *on June 3, 2010)*

Step lightly as you enter the door.
Come inside and linger awhile.
Be alone with your personal thoughts
And take time to learn things new.

This place was once for healing.
Some still remember that time.
Like then, we've come today.
The stepstone draws us still.

Picking Peaches

I never paid much mind
to the old peach tree out back
until last week,
when we took our buckets
and went picking.

With these thinning bones,
I thought my tree climbing
days were over,
but I was a kid again—
egged on
by a ninety year old man,
my dad.

(Written by Jean in 1999)

Country Road

Come, my friend,
and walk with me
along this country road

on an unpaved path
that weaves its way
across the years of time.

'Twas always here,
this little road,
at least since I was young.

It's a one-mile road,
a dead-end road,
a road that goes nowhere.

"But why," you ask,
"do you bid me come
on such a road as this?

"Its twists and turns
make walking hard
on a road that goes nowhere."

You're right, my friend,
to be concerned.
I cannot promise much.

But take my hand
and walk with me.
It's the steps that matter most.

(Written by Jean in 2004)

New Life

Years ago
when I was young,
a creek flowed by our house.

A bubbling sound,
I hear it still.
It takes me back in time.

Its source, a spring,
a few yards off—
its waters headed west.

No doubt this stream
had far to go.
I knew that at the time.

I loved the creek
and all it was—
a play-yard just for me.

It drew me there
'most every day—
a creek that had no name.

And then one day
its waters stopped.
It happened just like that.

The spring dried up,
the creek-bed too.
A time of rest had come.

The years went by
with little change
except that I left home.

And one by one
The others left—
the place then on its own.

With decades gone,
I'm back there now,
and change is in the air.

I see it most
in the little creek
and the boldness
of that stream.

The drought is done
and rains have come—
new life to a place that was!

(Written by Jean in 2003.)

Appendix A

Early Post Offices in Floyd County

Maurice Slusher, postal service historian, has worked diligently to research and obtain information on the postal service dating back to the time when Floyd became a county in 1832. As part of that research, Maurice contacted personnel at the National Archives in Washington, requesting historical information about Floyd County post offices. The information he received was on microfilm, dating from 1837.

Although some information on the microfilm is washed out and not usable, Maurice has been able to determine locations for most post offices, except for Fork Road and Goodsons. He used other sources for locating those post offices. The Goodsons post office was located in Montgomery County and closed in 1832. Whether it became part of Floyd County is now unknown.

Maurice said it was a challenge to locate early post offices. Still, from his own knowledge and by referring to the microfilm documents, he was able to place markers for 103 post offices on an old Floyd County map.

Maurice said it is "reasonable to assume there were post offices here prior to the time that Floyd became a county in 1832" when this area was still part of Montgomery County. A case in point, Maurice cited a 1979 *Floyd Press* article about the closing of the Simpsons Post Office. In that article, the Simpsons postmaster, Clyne Angle, stated that the Simpsons Post Office had a "history of 156 years." That means that it would have been established in 1823. "It is obvious," said Maurice, "that more research needs to be undertaken to determine what post offices existed in our area prior to 1832."

Based on his research and help from others, Maurice compiled the following list of Floyd County post offices—a list that includes name of post office, date established, date discontinued, and name of first postmaster.

ABRAHAM POST OFFICE (established 6/29/1886, discontinued 4/30/1904 – Abraham Jones, first postmaster); AKERS (6/4/1884 to 4/19/1896 – Washington Akers); ALDERMAN (1/21/1901 or 1/29/1901 to 12/31/1904 – Jacob B. Alderman); ALUM RIDGE (4/24/1877 or 4/25/1877 to 6/28/1985 – Harrison D. Reed); AMOS (9/7/1883 to 9/13/1913 or 9/30/1913 – William T. Williams); ARSENIC (5/16/1902 to 10/15/1904 – Alma F. Walters); **ARIA** (2/14/1910 to 4/30/1917 – Elizabeth L. Wertz); **BASHAM** (1/25/1882 to 1952 or 2/1953 /now in Montgomery County – Callie E. Basham); **BAY** (3/22/1900 to 1/24/1905 – Lucy R. Vest); **BEAUFORD** (6/29/1886 to 12/31/1904 – Beauford Cox); **BOOTHS MILL** or **BOOTH'S MILL** (4/25/1877 to ? – George B. Booth); **BOXWOOD** (4/2/1890 to 5/11/1893 – Samuel Hurd); **BROADSHOALS** or **BROAD SHOALS** (3/4/1878 to 11/30/1904 – Virginia A. Fulcher); **BRINTON** (7/21/1909 to 10/15/1915 – J. L. Angle); **BURKS FORK** (9/4/1874 to 6/15/1906 – Charles F. Page); **CAMP CREEK** (5/22/1871 to 12/15/1931 – Asa Booth); **CAMP MILLS** (8/19/1847 to 1851 – John Howard; post office name changed to Laurel Creek 7/30/1851 and closed 1859); **CANNADAY GAP** (11/31/1849 or 11/21/1849 to 4/14/1858 – Issac Lemon); **CARTHAGE** (7/19/1893 to 9/23/1955 – Psalters Akers); **CHECK** (7/23/1883 to present – Christopher A. Conner); **CLAYCE** (3/26/1895 to 10/31/1904 – Mandana L. Altizer); **CLIO** (9/9/1899 to 12/31/1904 – Peter Dickerson); **CONNERS MILL** or **CONNOR'S MILL** (4/14/1870 to 10/7/1872 – William D. Conner); **COPPER HILL** (9/4/1854 to present – Samuel Griggs); **COPPER VALLEY** (6/29/1857 to 11/30/1972 or 12/30/1972 – Samuel Lucas); **DULANEY** (5/22/1890 to 10/31/1913 – Jessie Booth); **DUNCANS** or **DUNCAN'S** (8/6/1878 to 6/15/1906 – Fleming H. Duncan); **EAST VIEW** or **EASTVIEW** (9/12/1881 to 7/14/1906 – Creed T. Stigleman); **EGO** (3/16/1887 to 3/27/1908 – George W. Reed); **ELMETTA** (2/11/1902 to 8/13/1904 – Elmetta Lester); **EPPERLY** (9/10/1898 to 6/15/1906 – George W. Epperly); **EURIE** (2/25/1885 to 6/5/1886 – John B. Moses); **FALCON** (4/2/1890 to 6/31/1903 – Louisa T. Lester); **FLAT HEAD** (5/26/1860 to 7/9/1866 – Jonathan Pierce); **FLINT** (10/5/1882 or 6/17/1886 to 1/15/1907 – C.M. Thurman); **FLOYD** (7/11/1892 to present – James D. Martin); **FLOYD COURT HOUSE** (1/3/1832 to 7/11/1892 or 7/20/1892); **FORK ROAD** (8/18/1837 to 1842 – James Goodson); **FRED** (1/12/1900 to 5/31/1905 – Jacob Moses); **GAGE** (8/21/1901 or 8/23/1901 to 11/30/1907 – Asa Simon Smith); **GIBEON** (3/12/1857 to 5/4/1858 – Stanton R. Aldridge); **GRAYSVILLE** (6/14/1872 to 11/30/1909 – Thomas K. DeWitt); **GREASY CREEK** (6/30/1840 to 5/3/1880 – Peter Slusher); **HAYCOCK** (3/5/1883 to 6/30/1908 – Elkaniah Hatcher); **HEMLOCK** (1/28/1904 to 5/15/1914 – Ethel Wickham); **HOWERY** or **HOWERYS** (9/20/1886 to 7/31/1906 – Franklin P. Rutrough); **HUFFVILLE** (9/21/1857 to 11/15/1919 – Dr. P. Lawrence); **HYLTON** (5/3/1880 to 2/2/1894 – Harden P. Hylton); **INDIAN VALLEY** (2/19/1851 to present – Robert W. Phillips); **QUOIT** (3/30/1890 to 1913 – Chostley H. Puckett); **JACKS MILL** (11/6/1879 to 12/2/1904 – Charles J. Pace); **LAUREL CREEK** (7/30/1851 to 1859 – Peter S. Moore (see Camp Mills info above); **LEACH** (7/21/1890 to 10/29/1892 – Lewis A. Martin);

*LEAH (9/22/1898 to 1/14/1904 – Jimmie L. Graham); **LELIA** (4/29/1895 to 4/15/1902 – Lelia Williams); **LILAC** (12/21/1901 to 1/14/1904 – John W. Gray); **LITTLE RIVER** (5/10/1842 to 1/31/1906 – Thomas Franklin); **LUCIANS** (3/26/1887 or 4/13/1887 to 10/16/1891 – Henry D. Carter); **MAME** (2/10/1885 or 2/14/1885 to ? – William T. Howery); **MIRA FORK** (3/4/1878 to 8/14/1909 – Solomon Slusher); **MONDAY** (10/26/1887 to 6/20/1904 – Samuel J. DeHart); **NARCOTT** (12/8/1884 to 10/15/1904 – William W. Lowery); **NASTURTIUM** (7/8/1897 to 2/28/1905 – James Earls); **ONEAL** or **O'NEAL** (10/10/1881 to 5/15/1905 – A. M. O'Neal); **OSCER** (12/6/1899 to 10/31/1903 – Preston G. Roberts); **OTHO** (3/11/1901 or 5/11/1901 to 1/14/1904 – Abbie E. Vest); **PARRAN** (12/11/1901 to 8/15/1906 – Elias H. Reed); **PAX** (6/12/1882 to 6/15/1906 – Austin Hilton); **PHARA** (4/18/1890 to 5/31/1893 – Statiry Boyd); **PHILLIPS** (6/18/1883 to 5/15/1905 – Tobias D. Phillips); **PIZARRO** (4/17/1886 to 1/11/1939 – Robert O. Harvey); **POFF** (6/1/1903 to 10/31/1943 – Calvin E. Spangler); **POSEY** (6/18/1885 to 12/31/1905 – William T. Lester); **QUOIT** (3/31/1890 to ? – C. Puckett, Jr.); **RAKES** (4/13/1886 to 1890 – Samuel P. Rakes); **REWALD** (5/9/1904 to 5/15/1907 – James E. Thomas); **RIFTON** (10/9/1899 to 7/31/1906 – Sherman Ridinger); **RUSH FORK** or **RUSH'S FORK** (8/12/1874 to 9/4/1874 – Charles F. Page); **SANTOS** (4/13/1886 to 5/31/1905 or 11/31/1905 – William M. Slaughter); **SHOWALTER** (6/18/1883 to 8/31/1905 – William Turpin); **SILVER LEAF** (11/3/1879 to 9/30/1895 – Gabriel Radford); **SIMPSONS** or **SIMPSON** (1823 or 6/9/1832 or 9/18/1843 to 8/10/1979 – John Gray or William Simpson); **SLATE** (3/5/1900 to 6/15/1906 – John P. Burnett); **SMART** (7/9/1900 to 11/15/1926 or 11/25/1926 – Sparrel T. Turner); **SMITH** (3/5/1900 to 7/31/1906 – John F. Smith); **SOWERS** (10/22/1900 to 7/15/1937 – Albert L. Epperly); **SPANGLER** (8/27/1885 to 1886 – Calvin E. Spangler); **SPURLOCK** (11/30/1898 to 7/6/1899 – Jane Wade); **STAMPING BIRCHES** (2/14/1871 to 12/9/1899 – Edgar M. Jett); **TARLAC** (12/9/1899 to 1/14/1904 – George Hungate); **TERRYS FORK** (10/17/1879 to 12/14/1918 – William T. Clower); **TINDALL** (12/21/1893 to 12/31/1926 – Vada Dickerson); **TONCRAY** (1/20/1904 to 5/31/1905 – Andrew F. Green); **TOPECO** (11/12/1889 to 11/30/1906 – James A. Sutphin); **TORY CREEK** (5/17/1878 or 5/27/1878 to 11/17/1879 – Wigington Dickerson); **TURMAN** (6/18/1883 to 7/31/1905 – Elijah G. Turman); **TURTLE ROCK** (4/14/1871 to 7/31/1906 – Jacob T. Helms); **VAUGHN** (9/12/1881 to 8/13/1904 – Thomas A. Vaughn); **VICK** (5/12/1900 to 12/31/1904 – Victoria B. Phillips); **VOCAL** (4/13/1886 to 8/27/1888 – Issac T. Hall); **WALCOTT** (4/4/1884 to 10/31/1908 – Maliasa R. Booth); **WEDDLE** (3/3/1890 to 1/14/1905 – Andrew Weddle); **WEST***

*FORK (1880 to 1881); **WEST FORK FURNACE** (1/16/1854 to 3/19/1860; reestablished in 1866 and closed 9/12/1881; opened at a later date and closed in 1900. At some point, Robert L. Toncary was postmaster at this post office. Location of this post office is not certain.) ; **WILLIS** (2/2/1894 to present – Silas G. Cundiff); **WILLS RIDGE** and/or **WILLIS RIDGE** (8/31/1853 or 8/9/1869 to 8/26/1872 or 10/4/1866 – Jacob Harmon or ?); **YATES** (no information)*

This list is from Jean's articles that appeared in the Floyd Press *on January 29, 2004 and August 18, 2011*

Appendix B

Harvestwood Quilt (1922)

This quilt was made by women in the Harvestwood Church community for the Reverend R. Gamble See in honor of his 44th birthday on August 15, 1922. Each quilt square has either the name or initials of the person who did the needlework. One name is repeated and some of the embroidery is so ornate, or worn from time, that it is difficult to make out the letters. Nevertheless, this is an attempt to transcribe the words and letters from the quilt. In some cases, additional information has been included in parentheses.

From left to right:
Row 1 (back row): Mrs. W. R. Turner; SJ WTLLIAMS (or A. J. Williams?); Bertie Hatcher; A. J. Williams, H. A. Cannaday; Emma Vest (Emma Thurmond Vest)
Row 2: Dove Hatcher; Ada M. Shelor; Exonie Hall; P. G. Nolen (Pearl Gay Nolen); Lillie E.
Row 3: Emma Vest (Emma Thurmond Vest); E.J.W. ; ALA Huff; Fannie West; Tonia Hatcher, Lula Hatcher
Row 4: Mary Hall; Lila Harvey; E.S.P. ; Amelia Harvey; Rachel L. Lancaster, Thelma Turner
Row 5: Myrtle Hatcher; Nan Hall; Sue Wood; S.B.W. (Sarah Belinda Wood); Virgie Nolen; Clara Turner

Row 6: Mrs. P. H. Black; D.A.T. (Dora Alice Turner); Zada Huff; Evaline Hall; Emma Hall; Aug. 15, 1922 (date of Rev. See's birthday and probably the day quilt was presented to him)

Row 7 (front row): Jan. 1922 (the date quilt probably was started); SJ WTLLIAMS (or A. J. Williams ?) ; D. L. Cannaday; Eula Hall; Bertie Underwood; (last square is blank)

Based on Jean's article published in the Floyd Press *on August 28, 2003, and on her article in the book,* The Presbyterian Church of Floyd: Celebrating 150 Years of History, *Nov 2003*

Appendix C

Early Pine Creek Church Members

Following are some names from the Pine Creek minutes of persons who joined that Primitive Baptist church over the years. If admission date is known, it is listed by the name, along with other information, such as date of death. Some persons were received into the church by letter of transfer from another church and, if known, that is noted, too. Some names were difficult to make out in the minutes, and others may have been spelled incorrectly or in an alternate way from what we see today. An asterisk (*) by a name indicates the member was black and, in 1822, "joined in full fellowship"—according to the church minutes. Note that minutes are missing for some periods of time. In some cases, a business meeting may have not been held. Other minutes may have been recorded but misplaced. For example, minutes for the period 1930 to 1957 have not yet been located.

Aldridge, Alice; Aldridge, John; Baker, Mary; Becket, Anna (or Annie) - 1806; Becket, Susanne - 1796 (died 1827); Beckett, John; Black, Emily E.; Black, Margaret E.; Booth, Daniel - 1803 (deacon, ordained 1820); Booth, George; Booth, Nancy - 1808; Booth, Rhoady (or Rhodah Bothe) - Feb 28, 1899; Boothe, Abigale - Nov 6, 1802; Boothe, Isaac - 1822; Boothe, Rachel; Bore, Fanny; Bower, Emma - admitted by letter; Bower, John; Bower, Rachel; Bower, Susanah; Bowers, Catherine; Bowers, Methias; Brame, Nancy - admitted by letter; Briant, Ambrose - May 1802; Briant, Eligia; Briant, Frances - Oct. 2, 1802; Briant, Lucinda; Clark, Deborah; Clark, Henry; Crage, Sare (or Sarah Craig); Dickerson, Barbara; Dickerson, Elvina; Dickerson, Moses - 1823; Dickison, Jamima - 1823; Dickson, Elizabeth; Duncan, Green Beryl; Duncan, John; Duncan, Lucinda; Duncan, Rodah; Epperly, Nancy; Farris, Elizabeth - 1823; Fisher, Rona; Foster, Nancy; Fuson, Owen; Graham, Elizabeth; Graham, Gay; Graham, Henrietta; Graham, Lawrence; Graham, Leah; Graham, Martha - 1822; Graham, Mary; Gray, Nancy; Grier, Eleanor; Habes, Mary; Halido, Elizabeth; Hill, Polly; Hopkins, Jemima; Hopkins, Jonathan; Howard, Caroline; Howard, Ira - 1822; Howard, John; Howard, Lettice (Letty) - 1822*; Howard, Permelia - 1822, died Jan 25, 1835; Howard, Peter - Mar 3, 1795 (licensed to preach in 1802, ordained 1804, first Pine Creek preacher; died 1827); Howard, Romelio - 1822; Howard, Sarah - Mar 3, 1795 (She and husband Peter Howard were the first Pine Creek members); Howard, Squire - 1822 *;   Howard, T. H.;   Howell,

Elkanah; Howell, Henrietta; Howery, Ealoner - 1823; Howery,
Elizabeth; Howery, Michael - Feb 2, 1822 (licensed to preach 1826,
died Aug 1873); Howery, Sarah - 1822; Howry, Virginia - (died Dec
1933); Hudson, Ruth; Huff, Oreana; Hungate, John; Hungate,
Mary; Hungate, Susannah; Laurence, S. P.; Laurence, Sallie A.;
Lawrence, Clarence; Lawrence, John; Lawrence, Nancy; Leiver,
Sarah M. (or Lewever); Martin, I. F. ; Martin, Martha A.; Martin,
Mattie Moore - baptized Sept 14, 1958 (died Jan 30, 1969, last
Pine Creek member); Martin, Melica A.; Martin, Sarah; Moore,
Isaac; Moore, Nancy; Moore, Noah (died Aug 31, 1901); Moore,
Sally; Paul, Catherine - admitted by letter; Paul, Mike; Paul, Sally;
Plumley, Sarah; Presise, Rebecca; Proffit, J. P.; Radford, Elenda;
Radford, Joshua; Radford, Robert; Ratliff, Agnes; Regency,
Mary; Roberson, Thomas L.; Roberson, T. S.; Rose, Lavica - 1888;
Semons, Crawford; Shelor, Anor; Shelor, Lott - 1822; Shelor,
Rhoady (or Rhoada) - 1822; Shelor, Thomas; Short, Lidia - 1809
(received by letter from Smith's Run Church, later known as Charity
Church); Shortt, John - admitted from Charity Church Feb 2,
1857; Shortt, Judith - admitted from Charity Church Feb 2, 1857;
Simmons, Charles - Nov 5, 1802 or 1803 (ordained 1804); Simmons,
Ealoner - 1803; Simmons, Thomas - 1822 (served as clerk, led sing-
ing); Snead, Olive; Sowers, Cuana; Sowers, Edward; Sowers,
Mary; Sowers, Nancy; Sowers, Noony; Sowers, Prissy; Spangler,
Bertie - admitted by letter; Spangler, Jacob F. - admitted by let-
ter; Sumner, Eliza; Sumner, Owen - 1823; Sumner, Sarah - 1822;
Sumter, Joseph - admitted by letter; Sumter, Matilda - admitted by
letter; Terry, Patience; Thomas, Bettie; Tice, Emily - admitted by
letter; Underwood, Jessie; Underwood, Joseph; Vier, Jessie (or
Via); Wells, Alse - 1822 * ; Wells, Jane (or Jone Wells) - 1822 (died
Aug 28,1857) * ; West, Hester; West, Sarah - 1823; Whitlock, Sealy;
Wickam, Jane; Wickam, Nathaniel; Williams, Corah - admitted by
letter; Young, Mary J.; Young, Nancy Jane.

Based on Jean's article published in the Floyd Press *on November 24, 2011*

Appendix D

Descendants of Max and Clara Turner Thomas

Max and Clara Thomas were married on 15 Sept 1937
in Floyd, Virginia.
They were the parents of
Emily Jean (born 17 Feb 1943) and Janet Lynne (born 5 Apr 1950).

Janet Thomas married John Robson Coiner, Jr., and their son,
John Robson Coiner III (Rob), was born 2 Nov 1980.

Jean Thomas married Richard Lee Schaeffer and their daughters are
Ann Meredith Schaeffer and Jennifer Lee Schaeffer. Ann Schaeffer
was born 25 Mar 1970 and is married to John Paul Ashenfelter. Their
children are Samuel Thomas Ashenfelter Schaeffer (born 10 June
2001) and Matthew Elliott Ashenfelter Schaeffer (born 3 July 2004).
Jennifer Schaeffer was born 24 Feb 1973, and is married to Walter
Megonigal III. Their children are Jack Cameron Megonigal (born 21
July 2006) and Erin Lee Megonigal (born 12 Jan 2009).

Ancestors of Max and Clara Turner Thomas

Ancestors of Max Thomas

Max Stone Thomas was born on 7 Nov 1908 in Franklin County and
died on 1 Jun 2001 in Franklin County. (Harvestwood Cemetery on
Franklin Pike in Floyd County)

Max's father, Emmett Everett Thomas, was born on 31 Jul 1885 in
Franklin County and died on 1 July 1929 in Franklin County. (Radford
Cemetery on Silver Leaf Road/Route 888 near Floyd-Franklin line)

Max's mother, Lila Ann Vest Thomas, was born on 27 Aug 1885 in
Floyd County and died on 10 Mar 1963 in Franklin County. (Radford
Cemetery on Silver Leaf Road/Route 888 near Floyd-Franklin line)

Max's paternal grandpa, Nathaniel A. Thomas, was born on 21 June
1831 in Patrick County and died on 19 Jan 1905 in Franklin County.
(Radford Cemetery on Silver Leaf Road/Route 888 near Floyd-
Franklin line)

Max's paternal grandma, Lucinda Shortt Young Thomas, was born on
1 Nov 1841 in Patrick County and died on 8 Feb 1936. (Buried near her
daughter at Walnut Grove Cemetery in Bluefield, West Virginia)

Max's maternal grandpa, Samuel Anderson Vest, was born on 11 Apr 1852 and died on 4 Dec 1923 in Floyd County. (Samuel L. Vest Cemetery near King's Store Road and then Vest Tannery Road in Floyd County)

Max's maternal grandma, Delilah Ann Moran Vest, was born on 9 Dec 1849 in Patrick County and died on 17 Nov 1914 in Floyd County. (Samuel L. Vest Cemetery near King's Store Road and then Vest Tannery Road in Floyd County)

Max's great grandpa, Peter Thomas, was born in 1807. Peter Thomas and Sarah Akers were married on 14 Dec 1826 in Patrick County.

Max's great grandma was Sarah Akers Thomas. Sarah Akers and Peter Thomas were married on 14 Dec 1826 in Patrick County.

Max's great grandpa, John Young Shortt, was born on 2 Nov 1796 and died on 20 Nov 1877. (Old County Line Church Cemetery near County Line Church Road and near the Floyd-Franklin line)

Max's great grandma, Judith Thomas Shortt, was born on 20 Jan 1803 and died on 19 Jun 1902. (Old County Line Church Cemetery near County Line Church Road and near the Floyd-Franklin line)

Max's great grandpa, Samuel L. Vest, was born on 8 Jun 1813 and died on 22 Sept 1890. (Samuel L. Vest Cemetery near King's Store Road and then Vest Tannery Road in Floyd County)

Max's great grandma, Sarah Iddings Vest, was born on 1 Nov 1817 and died on 27 Jun 1890. (Samuel L. Vest Cemetery near King's Store Road and then Vest Tannery Road in Floyd County)

Max's great grandpa, James (Jimmy) Samuel Moran, was born on 12 Oct 1812 and died on 15 Nov 1874. (Jack Martin Cemetery in Patrick County)

Max's great grandma, Delilah A. Cannaday Moran, was born on 19 Nov 1814 and died about 1900. (James–Via Cemetery in Franklin County)

Additional Information about Ancestors of Max Thomas

Peter Thomas's parents were Charles Thomas, Jr., and Deborah Jourdan (of Quaker ancestry). Peter's grandparents were Charles Thomas, Sr. (of Welsh ancestry) and Judy Patterson, and also Thomas B. Jourdan (Quaker ancestry) and ____.

Sarah Akers Thomas's parents were Nathaniel Akers and Elizabeth

Akers. Sarah's grandparents were William Akers and Dolly Blackburn, and also John Akers and ____.

John Young Shortt's parents were Reuben Shortt and Lydia Clark. John's grandparents were Young Shortt and Mary Bilbo (of French ancestry), and also John Clark and Susan Nix. John Young Shortt's great grandparents were William Shortt and Elizabeth Skipwith (Bart.), and also William and Obedience Clark. Elizabeth Skipwith's father was Sir William Skipwith.

Judith Thomas Shortt's parents were Pleasant Thomas and Mary Cannaday. Judith's grandparents were Charles Thomas, Sr., and Judy Patterson, and also James Cannaday and Elizabeth Raikes.

Samuel L. Vest's parents were Littleberry Vest and Sarah James. Samuel's grandparents were John Vest and Agnes Davidson, and also William James and ____. Samuel's great grandpa was Moses Vest (from Germany).

Sarah Iddings Vest's parents were Henry Iddings and Abigail Richardson.

Jimmy Moran's parents were Nelson Moran and Mary Owen. Jimmy and John Moran (twin brothers) were born in Patrick County and married sisters.

Delilah A. Cannaday Moran's parents were William Cannaday ("Patrick Billy") and Patsy Wright. Delilah's grandparents were James Cannaday and Elizabeth Raikes (She lived to be 105.)

Ancestors of Clara Turner Thomas

Clara Easter Turner Thomas was born on 25 Mar 1910 in Floyd County and died on 30 Jul 1997 in Franklin County. (Harvestwood Cemetery on the Franklin Pike in Floyd County)

Clara's father, Cameron Lee Turner, was born on 26 Feb 1885 in Floyd County and died on 3 Feb 1969 in Floyd County. (Harvestwood Cemetery on the Franklin Pike in Floyd County)

Clara's mother, Dora Alice Wood Turner, was born on 4 Oct 1882 in Floyd County and died on 4 Nov 1959 in Floyd County. (Harvestwood Cemetery on the Franklin Pike in Floyd County)

Clara's paternal grandpa, Sparrel Tyler Turner, was born on 19 Sep 1846 and died on 24 Feb 1927 in Floyd County. (Peter Cannaday Cemetery on Route 793 in Floyd County)

Clara's paternal grandma, Flora Alice Thomas Turner, was born on 2 Jun 1857 and died on 9 Apr 1923. (Peter Cannaday Cemetery on Route 793 in Floyd County)

Clara's maternal grandpa, Jefferson Pinkard Wood, was born on 4 Nov 1858 and died on 10 Dec 1955 in Floyd County. (Harvestwood Cemetery on the Franklin Pike in Floyd County)

Clara's maternal grandma, Sarah Belinda Brammer Wood, was born on 27 Apr 1860 and died on 1 Mar 1931 in Floyd County. (Harvestwood Cemetery on the Franklin Pike in Floyd County)

Clara's great grandpa, Charles H. Turner, was born on 25 Jun 1818 and died on the 29 May 1857. (Charles and Violet Turner Cemetery near Runnet Bag Road in Franklin County)

Clara's great grandma, Violet Ann Hall Turner, was born on 6 Nov 1817 and died on 8 Apr 1906. (Charles and Violet Turner Cemetery near Runnet Bag Road in Franklin County)

Clara's great grandpa, Walter Henry Thomas, was born on 29 Apr 1829 and died on 8 May 1919. (Walter H. Thomas Cemetery near Elamsville in Patrick County?)

Clara's great grandma, Judith Virginia Harbour Thomas, was born on 13 Sep 1838/39 and died on 28 May 1937. (Walter H. Thomas Cemetery in Patrick County?)

Clara's great grandpa, Richard Johnson Wood, was born on 27 Oct 1828 and died on 20 Dec 1917. (County Line Church Cemetery on Thomas Farm Road near the Floyd-Franklin line)

Clara's great grandma, Judy Shortt Wood, was born on 17 Feb 1834 and died on 30 Aug 1899. (County Line Church Cemetery on Thomas Farm Road near the Floyd-Franklin line))

Clara's great grandpa, Jonathan L. Brammer, was born on 7 April 1833 and died on 28 Feb 1908. (Brammer Cemetery up the hill on the south side of Paradise Lane in Floyd County)

Clara's great grandma, Juliana Burnett Brammer, was born on 27 Sept 1833 and died on 27 Jun 1923. (Brammer Cemetery up the hill on the south side of Paradise Lane in Floyd County)

Additional Information about
Ancestors of Clara Turner Thomas

Charles H. Turner's parents were Francis Turner, Jr., and Nancy Thomas. Charles' grandparents were Adam Turner and Mary Pilson. Charles' great grandparents were Francis Turner, Sr. (born in Ireland) and Elizabeth ____. Charles' great great grandparents were James Turner and Mary ____.

Violet Ann Hall Turner's parents were Thomas Rowe Hall and Sarah (Sally) Fuson. Violet's grandparents were Rev. Nathan Hall and Ann Rowe. Violet's great grandparents were John Hall and Sarah ____. Violet's great grandparents were also William Fuson and Hannah Bates. In addition, Violet's great grandparents were John Fuson (of Welsh ancestry) and ____ Wheeler.

Walter Henry Thomas's parents were Richard Thomas and Martha (Mattie) Turner. Walter's grandparents were Charles Thomas, Sr., and Judith Patterson.

Judith Virginia Harbour Thomas's parents were Richard Harbour and Judith Nolen.

Richard J. Wood's parents were John Richard Wood and Lucinda DeHart. Richard J. Wood's grandparents were Richard ("Dickey") Wood and Rachel Cockram, and also James DeHart and Ellen Dennis. Richard J. Wood's great grandparents were John Wood and Nellie ____, and also Aaron DeHart and ____. Richard J. Wood's great great grandparents were Stephen Wood and Ann Johnson.

Judy Shortt Wood's parents were John Young Shortt and Judith Thomas. Judy's grandparents were Reuben Shortt and Lydia Clark, and also Pleasant Thomas and Mary Cannaday. Judy's great grandparents were Young Shortt and Mary Bilbo (of French Huguenot ancestry). Judy's great great grandparents were William Shortt and Elizabeth Skipwith (Bart.) Elizabeth Skipwith's father was Sir William Skipwith.

Jonathan L. Brammer's parents were William Brammer and Belinda Lancaster. Jonathan's grandparents were John Brammer and Sarah Lee, and also Dr. Lewis (Washington) Lancaster and ____ Wheeler.

Juliana Burnett Brammer's parents were Jeremiah Burnett and Sarah Campbell.

Charles Thomas History

This information on Charles Thomas, Sr., is included because he was an ancestor of both Max and Clara Turner Thomas. The offspring of Charles Thomas, Sr., included Charles Thomas, Jr., Richard Thomas, and Pleasant Thomas. Max descended from both Charles Thomas, Jr., and Pleasant Thomas. Clara descended from both Richard Thomas and Pleasant Thomas. The following information, not readily available, focuses on the descendants of Charles Thomas, Sr., and Charles Thomas, Jr.

Charles Thomas, Sr., was born about 1743 and died in 1836. He was thought to be of Welsh ancestry. He probably lived in what is now the Richmond area, or north of there, but eventually he settled at Poplar Camp Creek in Patrick County, Virginia. He married Judith Patterson or Mary Ripley (the record is unclear), and their children were: John, Patsy, Richard, Pleasant, Neal or Neah, Joseph, and Charles Jr.

Charles Thomas, Jr., was born about the time of the Revolutionary War. He married Deborah Jourdan (of Quaker ancestry) and their children were: Nancy, Fleming, Peter, Mary, and others.

Peter Thomas was born about 1807 and married Sarah Akers. Their children were: Nathaniel, Evaline, Ruth, Elizabeth, Fleming, Jourdan, Sarah, David, Lucretia, and others. (about 24 children in all)

Nathaniel Thomas first married Nancy Boyd and they had three children: Claiborne (married Judy Martin), Ruth (married George Ingram), and Allie (married Jimmy Martin). In 1862, at age 32, Nathaniel was drafted into the Confederate army as a private in Company D of the 51st Regiment of the Virginia Infantry and served four years in the Civil War. His wife Nancy died while he was at war.

On July 24, 1866, Nathaniel Thomas married his second wife, Lucinda Shortt Young, in Floyd County, at the home of her parents, John Y. Shortt and Judith Thomas Shortt.

Lucinda's first husband, Joe Young, had been killed near Chattanooga during the Civil War. Joe and Lucinda had two children—Tula Young (who married Willis Peters) and Jeff Young (who married Mary Janey).

In addition to children from each of their first marriages, Nathaniel and Lucinda Thomas had the following children together: Marquis de "Dee" Thomas (married Minnie Shivley), Kemper Thomas (married Addie Hill), Ophelia Thomas (married Magrueder Rakes), Maude Thomas (married Tuggle Moran), Walter Thomas (married Nettie

Moore), Emmett Thomas (married Lila Vest), and Thaddeus (Thad) Thomas (unmarried).

This information on Charles Thomas is from:
- *Glendola Shivley, a descendant of Sam and Fleming Thomas*
- *Evaline Thomas, daughter of Peter Thomas and sister of Nathaniel Thomas*
- *Sallie Porter Banks (probably Sarah), daughter of Peter Thomas*
- *Max Thomas, son of Emmett Thomas and grandson of Nathaniel Thomas*

About the Author

Jean Thomas Schaeffer, M.Ed., is pictured on the back cover and has been an educator and writer for most of her life. She grew up on a mountain farm in Virginia on the Floyd–Franklin County line—near the Blue Ridge Parkway. In 1999, she and her husband retired from careers in Northern Virginia and moved to the family farm where Jean grew up. She has been writing about coming home and her Appalachian heritage ever since.

After returning home, Jean also edited some of her father's writings and, on his behalf, turned them into a book. That book by Max S. Thomas is titled *This Pleasant Land: A Blue Ridge History* and it was published, posthumously, in 2010.

Jean enjoys living close to nature and recording what she sees on paper and on film. A number of her pieces have appeared in the *Floyd Press* these past years. This book, *Raised on Songs and Stories: A Memoir of Place in the Blue Ridge,* is an outgrowth of fifteen years of writing about her heritage and decades of living.

Besides her writing and publishing, Jean and her husband treasure being with members of their family and spend as much time as they can with them.

BOOK ORDER FORM

Please mail a *copy* of this order form with check to
Harvestwood Press, P.O. Box 395, Floyd, VA 24091

For more information about Harvestwood Press books,
send an e-mail to info@HarvestwoodPress.com
or check out www.HarvestwoodPress.com.

Please send me the limited-edition book
RAISED ON SONGS AND STORIES:
A Memoir of Place in the Blue Ridge
By Jean Thomas Schaeffer
(ISBN 978-0-9703758-3-4)

_____ copies @ $19.95 each = $_____

5.3% Sales Tax (in Virginia only) = $_____
($1.05 per book)

*Shipping within U. S.
One book = $ 3.25
$0.50 each additional book = $_____

Total amount enclosed = $_____

Your Name _____

Street _____

City _____ State _____ Zip _____

Phone Number _____

E-mail _____

Total amount for your enclosed check is $_____

*International Shipping: $9 for 1st book
and $5 for each additional book.